DISCARDED
From Nashville Public Library

What Makes Us Think?

What Makes Us Think?

A Neuroscientist and a Philosopher Argue about Ethics, Human Nature, and the Brain

Jean-Pierre Changeux
and Paul Ricoeur

translated by M. B. DeBevoise

PRINCETON UNIVERSITY PRESS - PRINCETON AND OXFORD

PUBLISHED BY PRINCETON UNIVERSITY PRESS, 41 WILLIAM STREET,
PRINCETON, NEW JERSEY 08540
IN THE UNITED KINGDOM: PRINCETON UNIVERSITY PRESS
3 MARKET PLACE, WOODSTOCK, OXFORDSHIRE OX20 1SY

PUBLISHED WITH THE ASSISTANCE OF THE FRENCH MINISTRY
OF CULTURE—CNL

LIBRARY OF CONGRESS CATALOGING-IN-PUBLICATION DATA
CHANGEUX, JEAN-PIERRE.
[CE QUI NOUS FAIT PENSER. ENGLISH]
WHAT MAKES US THINK? : A NEUROSCIENTIST AND A PHILOSOPHER
ARGUE ABOUT ETHICS, HUMAN NATURE, AND THE BRAIN /
JEAN-PIERRE CHANGEUX AND PAUL RICOEUR ; TRANSLATED BY
M.B. DEBEVOISE.
P. CM.
INCLUDES BIBLIOGRAPHICAL REFERENCES AND INDEX.
ISBN 0-691-00940-6 (ALK. PAPER)
1. ETHICS. 2. NEUROPSYCHOLOGY. 3. CHANGEUX, JEAN-PIERRE—
INTERVIEWS. 4. NEUROSCIENTISTS—FRANCE—INTERVIEWS.
5. RICOEUR, PAUL—INTERVIEWS. 6. PHILOSOPHERS—FRANCE—
INTERVIEWS. I. RICOEUR, PAUL. II. TITLE.
BJ45 .C4313 2000 153—DC21 00-024827

THIS BOOK HAS BEEN COMPOSED IN GARAMOND

THE PAPER USED IN THIS PUBLICATION MEETS THE MINIMUM
REQUIREMENTS OF ANSI/NISO Z39.48-1992 (R 1997)
(PERMANENCE OF PAPER)

WWW.PUP.PRINCETON.EDU

PRINTED IN THE UNITED STATES OF AMERICA

1 2 3 4 5 6 7 8 9 10

Contents

Translator's Note

As with Jean-Pierre Changeux's earlier book of conversations, with Alain Connes, also published by Princeton University Press, I have taken minor liberties with the French text in the interest of making it read more smoothly in English; and, with the approval and assistance of both authors, added a certain amount of new material, particularly to the notes, in order to give a fuller picture of the current state of research on the various topics they discuss. Changes in the location and description of several of the illustrations have been made as well, and a number of errors in the original edition corrected. I owe thanks, finally, to Chris Westbury, at the University of Alberta, who looked at a draft version of the translation, and to Larry Kim and Janis Sawyer for research assistance.

M. B. DeBevoise

Prelude

Was it unreasonable for a publisher to ask a scientist and a philosopher to examine the achievements and prospects of the neurosciences, in particular the capacity of these sciences to provide a basis for discussion of morality, social norms, and peace? On the one hand, it meant having to confront the prejudices of a public that places its trust in science—indeed, shows enthusiasm for science—while at the same time fearing its influence over modern life and the threat it is imagined to pose to the future of mankind. On the other hand, it meant having to contend with the narcissism of philosophy, a discipline concerned above all to assure its own survival and, preoccupied by an immense textual heritage, one that is uninterested for the most part in recent developments in the sciences.

To overcome popular resistance to critical scientific knowledge, Odile Jacob called upon a working scientist whose research is concerned primarily with the brain and whose work has been familiar to the general public since the appearance of *Neuronal Man* (1983). To draw philosophy outside of its ivory tower, she chose a philosopher who, having summarized the main themes of his thought in *Oneself as Another* (1990), has continued to take an interest, together with judges, physicians, historians, and political scientists, in what during the medieval period were called "disputed questions."

The publisher's wish, then, was to have a dialogue in two voices. It ought to have been an exercise in contradiction. Indeed it was, with all that implies in the way of testing the composure of each participant: the philosopher found his devastating arguments undermined, the scientist his incontrovertible facts overturned. Ultimately, our encounter represents a vote of confidence in the maturity of the judgment of the reader, who is invited to enter into the debate as a partner rather than as a referee. Candid and honest discussion of ideas is seldom found in the world today. Peremptory assertion, unilateral criticism, incomprehensible digression, and facile derision stand in the way of fair debate, with no regard for the need to make arguments that, before they can be convincing, must aspire first to be thought plausible, which is to say worth defending.

In the event, the chance to engage in a wholly free and open dialogue proved to be an exceptional experience for each of us. First there was unstructured conversation, followed by recorded debate. Once transcribed and edited, the dialogue assumed a more incisive—sometimes more acerbic—aspect. The result is an example on a small scale of the difficulties that every debate encounters once it submits to a demanding standard of argumentation. Our hope is that, by sharing this dialogue with a wide audience, an exchange between two people will lead to understanding among many.

We would like to thank Juliette Blamont, who helped harmonize our voices in written form, and Odile Jacob herself, who inspired, encouraged, and closely monitored the progress of this dialogue, for their devoted efforts in bringing it before the reading public.

Paul Ricoeur

Jean-Pierre Changeux

What Makes Us Think?

1 – A Necessary Encounter

Knowledge and Wisdom

Jean-Pierre Changeux: You are a well-known and admired philosopher. I am a scientist. My professional career has been devoted to the theoretical and experimental study of the elementary mechanisms involved in the functioning of the nervous system and, particularly, the human brain. If I seek to understand the brain by approaching it through its most microscopic structures, which is to say the molecules that compose it, this hardly excludes a desire to understand its highest functions, which traditionally come within the domain of philosophy: thought, the emotions, the faculty of knowledge, and, of course, the moral sense. As a molecular biologist I find myself confronted with a formidable problem: how to discover the relationship between these elementary molecular building blocks and highly integrated functions such as the perception of beauty and scientific creativity. After Copernicus, Darwin, and Freud there remains the conquest of the mind, one of the most formidable challenges facing science in the twenty-first century.

Since the most ancient antiquity, philosophers have argued about what traditionally in France is called *l'esprit*—not *l'Esprit* with a capital E, or "Spirit," but what Anglo-American authors mean by "mind." Even though our respective positions may seem as far removed from each other as they could be, the encounter between philosophy and neurobiology seems to me not merely welcome but necessary. I have enormous admiration for your work. I have not found many authors in France—perhaps owing to the fault of my own ignorance—

who have thought as deeply about the problems of morality and ethics as you have. Why should we not work together to try to construct a common discourse on these topics? Perhaps we shall not succeed. But our attempt will at least have the value of identifying points of agreement and, still more importantly, of exposing areas of disagreement and throwing into relief the gaps that one day or another will have to be filled.

Paul Ricoeur: I wish to respond to your words of welcome with an equally warm greeting addressed to a renowned man of science and the author of *Neuronal Man,*[1] a work worthy of the closest and most respectful attention.

What we are undertaking is a discussion, in the strong sense of the word. It is motivated first by a difference in our approach to the phenomenon of human life that has to do with our training, respectively, as a scientist and a philosopher. But it is motivated also by a desire, if not to resolve the differences related to this difference in our points of view, at least to raise them to a level of argumentation permitting the reasons of one to be regarded as plausible by the other, which is to say worthy of being defended in the context of an exchange governed by an ethic of debate—what the philosopher Jürgen Habermas calls *Diskursethik*.

I want to make my position clear at the outset. I am a partisan of a current of European philosophy that contains three distinctive approaches, typically referred to as "reflective philosophy," "phenomenology," and "hermeneutics." The first approach, reflectivity, emphasizes the mind's attempt to recover its power of acting, thinking, and feeling—a power that has, so to speak, been buried or lost—in the knowledge, practices, and feelings that exteriorize it in relation to itself. Jean Nabert is the leading representative of this first branch of the tradition to which I belong.

The second, phenomenology, refers to the ambition of going back "to things themselves," which is to say to the manifestation of what presents itself to experience as the least encumbered of all the constructions inherited from cultural, philosophical, and theological history. This concern, by contrast with the reflective approach, lays stress on the *intentional* dimension of theoretical, practical, and aesthetic life and defines all consciousness as a consciousness of something. Husserl is the eponymous champion of this branch.

The third term, hermeneutics, refers to an approach that derives from the interpretive method applied first to religious texts (exegesis), classical literary texts (philology), and legal texts (jurisprudence), and stresses the plurality of interpretations associated with what may be called the reading of human experience. The masters of this third branch, which challenges the claim of any philosophy to be devoid of presuppositions, are Dilthey, Heidegger, and Gadamer.

Henceforth I will use the generic term "phenomenology" to designate the philosophical tradition that I represent in this discussion in each of its three branches—reflective, descriptive, interpretive.

Changeux: In my case the experience of belonging to the world of scientific research, and more particularly of biological research, has profoundly influenced my thinking.

While still quite young, as a student, I took part in what might be called the molecular biology movement. Its aim, in the 1960s, was to elucidate the structure and function of the molecules that are situated at the ultimate boundaries of life. This program met with success, as is well known,[2] and led to further research. Certain of these molecules, called allosteric proteins, possess a crucial and dual feature: they serve, on the one hand, to determine a particular biological function, for example a chemical synthesis; on the other hand, they obey a

signal that regulates this function. These proteins introduce flexibility into cellular life, acting as switches that help to coordinate the functions of the cell but also to promote the cell's adaptation to the conditions surrounding it.[3] To understand in strictly physico-chemical terms biological functions that are essential to the life of the cell has been, and continues to be, the objective of a tradition of research of considerable scope and vitality with which I enthusiastically align myself.

More unexpected was the demonstration that followed. The brain was shown to possess molecules that are very similar to these bacterial switches—receptors of chemical substances known as neurotransmitters that assist communication *between* nerve cells.[4] Our cerebral functions, from the most modest to the most elevated, are also rooted in physico-chemical nature by virtue of the fact that they are mediated by these molecular switches.

The extreme complexity of cerebral organization and its development became accessible to the methods of molecular biology by the end of the 1960s, opening up a second line of research. It was no longer possible to think of the brain as a computer composed of circuits prefabricated by the genes. To the contrary, connections between nerve cells are gradually established over the course of development by a process of trial and error. The selection and elimination of such connections are regulated to a substantial degree by the newborn infant's interaction with the environment and with itself. In short, the brain cannot be viewed as a strictly genetic machine; it incorporates, within a defined genetic envelope peculiar to the species, a series of nested "epigenetic" imprints that are established by variation and selection.[5] Another way of stating this hypothesis is to say that evolutionary (epigenetic) competition inside the brain takes over from the biological (genetic) evolution of species and creates, as a consequence, organic links with the physical, social, and cultural environment.

A very fruitful interface is produced in an entirely natural way, then, with the human sciences and society.

A third line of research, so far theoretical for the most part, relies on the new methods of modeling made possible by computer technology to try to further exploit our still quite partial knowledge of the functional organization of the brain. It consists, for instance, in devising the simplest plausible neural architectures that constitute a formal, or artificial, organism capable of carrying out a defined cognitive learning task. Two features distinguish this approach. On the one hand, it is "neurorealist" in the sense that it appeals only to known elementary components of the brain, for example the molecular receptors of neurotransmitters I have already mentioned; on the other, it tries to define the minimal degree of complexity that a network of nerve cells capable of carrying out specifically human tasks must possess.[6] The theoretical program consists in trying to give an account, in a rigorously formal way, of a behavior defined on the basis both of the anatomical organization of a network of nerve cells and of the activity that takes place in this network. This enterprise, known as connectionism, has illustrious antecedents: the cybernetics of Norbert Wiener, the universal computing machine conceived by Alan Turing, and the first neural network model developed by Warren McCulloch and Walter Pitts to represent the "embodiment of mind."[7]

As a member of the faculty of the Collège de France, I am required to present the current state of knowledge in my field, which is continually evolving, in a didactic form. *Neuronal Man,* to which you referred a moment ago, represented a synthesis of my first seven years of lectures. Its aim was to make the dazzling progress of the sciences of the brain more widely known. I realize today that this attempt to organize the available knowledge regarding the brain, from the molecule to mental activity, has had a powerful retroactive effect on my own conception of the brain and its functions. In this regard I share with René Thom the view that what counts in the modeling process is its *ontological import,* its impact on our conception of the origin of things and beings—in other words, its underlying philosophy. While writing *Neuronal Man* I discovered Spinoza's *Ethics* and the full rigor of his thought. "I shall consider human actions and appetites," Spinoza says, "just as if it were an investigation into lines, planes, or bodies."[8] Can anything more exciting be imagined than to try to reconstruct human life in a way that rejects teleology, that rejects anthropocentrism, that rejects all conceptions of the world that take shelter in religious superstition—what Spinoza called the "refuge of ignorance"? This reading came to complete and enrich my acquaintance with the pre-Socratic philosophers. I have always been and remain still very attached to Democritus, in particular, among the ancient atomists.

None of this suffices to explain the very marked interest I have in ethical questions, which led me to read your work *Oneself as Another.*[9] The decisive event was a talk I gave on the neurosciences shortly after *Neuronal Man* appeared to a working group of the Comité Consultatif National d'Éthique dans les Sciences de la Vie et de la Santé, the committee that advises the French government on issues in bioethics. In the very lively debate that followed I found myself driven into a corner. How can neuronal man be a moral subject? I have not ceased since to reflect upon this question, to make a serious attempt to give new meaning to an ethics of the good life—a joyful, humanist ethics compatible with the free exercise of reason. It is this attempt that sparked my interest in talking with you today.

The cleavage between scientists and philosophers is relatively recent. In antiquity, philosophers such as Democritus and Aristotle were also excellent observers of nature; mathematicians such as Thales and Euclid were philosophers as well. With the Hippocratics, a rational medicine grew up alongside the shamanistic medicine (or medicine not far removed from shamanistic traditions) that was still dominant in ancient Greece. Rationality came to be introduced into the domain of traditional medicine with the rejection of all assumptions of magical or divine intervention and the search for natural causes. The physician made a diagnosis and, on the basis of this, proposed a treatment, a course of medication. Instead of hunting demons, a pharmocological agent was now employed to attack material causes of illnesses. No longer a demiurge, the physician was now a rationalistic and scientific philosopher.[10]

The cleavage between scientists, philosophers, and artists occurred after the Renaissance, though one still finds during this period artist-scientists such as Leonardo da Vinci and later, in the nineteenth century, a certain tradition of philosophical thought among scientists—I am thinking here, for example, of Augustin Cournot and Henri Poincaré and, more recently, Jacques Monod. On the other hand, a tradition of interest in scientific knowledge has been carried on in philosophy by William James, Henri Bergson, Bertrand Russell, Rudolf Carnap, Maurice Merleau-Ponty, and, in our own time, by philosophers such as John Searle, Daniel Dennett, and Paul and Patricia Churchland.

Ricoeur: I think of Georges Canguilhem, also Gaston Bachelard. For me, Canguilhem's *La Connaissance de la vie*[11] is an important point of reference. Canguilhem was both a philosopher and physician. He showed how human beings structure their environment and project "vital values" that give *meaning* to their behavior. They thus manage to inaugurate a normativity that is distinct from the operation of physical law. As for Bachelard, he recognized in *La Formation de l'esprit scientifique*[12] a distinct form of inventiveness related to the power of "epistemological rupture" but comparable to poetic creation.

Changeux: Bachelard examined the mental activity of the scientist in a particularly original way, it is true. One might also cite the dialogue between Karl Popper and John Eccles, the one a philosopher and the other a neurobiologist, as it happens. In their joint work *The Self and Its Brain*[13] one finds an entire program worked out, in fact.

Ricoeur: They tried to construct a philosophical system that organized in a hierarchical way the levels at which the sciences of the brain and the philosophy of mind interact. No doubt we will encounter this problem quite often in our discussion as well.

Changeux: Yes. We have therefore at least one relatively recent example of dialogue between a philosopher and a neurobiologist. Eccles's approach was different from mine, however. He was interested in the electrical activity of the nerve cell and of groups of neurons. The point of departure for his thinking was therefore at a level more organized than that of the molecule, which may explain some of the differences between our points of view. Eccles was also perhaps one of the last neurobiologists to believe in the dualism of mind and brain.

Knowledge of the Brain and Self-Knowledge

Changeux: The exchange of views to which we both look forward turns on a question that seems to me essential, namely to what extent the spectacular progress that has been made in our understanding of the brain over the last twenty years or so will lead us to reexamine the fundamental problem of what is usually called the relation between body and mind or, as I would prefer to characterize it, the relation between the brain and thought. The past few decades have seen the emergence of an entirely new field, cognitive science, that draws upon work in physiology, molecular biology, psychology and the human sciences. It has given rise to highly promising interdisciplinary collaboration involving not only researchers in the natural sciences but also anthropologists and other social scientists. This new alliance holds out the prospect of achieving a unified and synthetic view of what was formerly a question reserved for philosophy (when it was not reserved for religion) by building upon our present state of knowledge about the brain and its functions. It now becomes possible, I would argue, for a neurobiologist to legitimately take an interest in the foundations of morality, for example, and, conversely, for a philosopher to find material for reflection, even edification, in the results of contemporary neuroscience.

The fundamental question—a philosophical question, on which I would like our debate to focus—is whether the progress of knowledge in the sciences of the nervous system, the brain, and, more generally, cognition calls for a reexamination of the crucial distinction made in the eighteenth century by David Hume, which many philosophers and scientists seem still to endorse today, between the factual—what is—and the normative—what ought to be; that is, between knowledge, in particular scientific knowledge, and moral rules. Does this distinction need still to be upheld or can we now inquire into the relationship between moral rules and nature by using our scientific knowledge of the brain and its higher functions to enrich ethical reflection? I am aware that this question, despite its importance, is a highly sensitive one. Many of our fellow citizens continue to regard morality as belonging to the domain of religion. In fact, I should think that most people believe that morality serves to protect us against science and technology. Well-intentioned persons wonder with what right a scientist can chair a committee on bioethics, as I did for six years, rather than a jurist, for example. Others challenge the very presence of scientific experts on such a committee. As a result, it is hard to see how any cooperative relationship can be established between scientists and ethicists.

Few members of the general public realize that the idea of a science of ethics is not new. It is found in the work of Auguste Comte,[14] who proposed a positive morality of altruism subordinating selfish desires to sympathetic instincts that would stand as the "seventh science," the science par excellence, uniting the natural with the scientific and the social to produce morality. Comte even went so far as to propose "phrenological physiology" as a scientific basis for morality, relying upon Gall's notion that the seat of each innate and irreducible faculty is localized in a particular part of the brain. Comte exploited Gall's model in order to advance the hypothesis that the more or less complex interaction of these faculties affects the emotional states that govern moral judgments.

Comte was not the only one to posit scientific laws of morality. Spencer, and after him Darwin, did so as well, though in contrary ways: Spencer emphasized the doctrine of laissez-faire and the success of the fittest at the level of society, Darwin the enlargement of sympathies and the social instinct peculiar to the human species. After them, the Russian prince Peter Kropotkin, remembered chiefly as the theoretician of anarchism, found in nature an objective moral law in the form of mutual aid. Similarly, the French politician Léon Bourgeois, a prime minister under the Third Republic and later one of the founders of the League of Nations, advocated solidarity as a secular republican morality on the model of Pasteur's theory of protection against contagious disease.

Here one must be extremely careful. The grave perversion

of biology, and particularly of genetics, on behalf of exclusionary ideologies that encouraged racism and genocide is well known. Nonetheless the question whether ethics can be reconceived as an objective science of morality remains a very lively and topical one. Habermas, for example, has argued forcefully that moral judgment comes under the head of truth. For me, this question—at bottom an ontological question—is the first one we need to address.

Ricoeur: Is this question, which you call ontological and which I would call one of philosophical anthropology, really the first question we ought to consider? Permit me to come back to the way you pose the question of the relationship between nature and moral rules. I quite agree that this fundamental difficulty, well formulated by Hume, is one that we must tackle. But we cannot, to my way of thinking, take it up without first having clarified the epistemological status of the neurosciences. For my part, I cannot avoid taking a position with regard to a problem bequeathed by the most ancient philosophical tradition, from Plato to Descartes and from Spinoza and Leibniz to Bergson, namely that of the relation between the soul and the body. This relation is located at the level of ultimate, irreducible, primitive entities that are constitutive of what analytic philosophers like to call the furniture of the world. This is the level of fundamental ontology. In Descartes's time—and that of his followers, Malebranche, Spinoza, Leibniz—it was supposed that ultimate reality could be apprehended in terms of substance, which is to say in terms of something that exists in and of itself. The question thus arose, on the assumption that things are made of substance, whether man is made of one or of two substances. This grand quarrel, sustained by a considerable argumentative apparatus, survives today only in bastard and skeletal forms such as psychosomatic parallelism, interactionism, reductionism, and so on. To oppose spiritualist dualism to materialist monism amounts to a crude oversimplification of what was at issue in the seventeenth century.

I do not propose to argue on the ontological plane, whose bases were undermined by Kant in the Transcendental Dialectic of the first *Critique*. Relying instead on the resources furnished by phenomenology, I will restrict myself, modestly but firmly, to considering the semantics of two distinct discourses—one concerning the body and the brain, the other what I will call the mental.

My initial thesis is that these discourses represent heterogeneous perspectives, which is to say that they cannot be reduced to each other or derived from each other. In the one case it is a question of neurons and their connection in a system; in the other one speaks of knowledge, action, feeling—acts or states characterized by intentions, motivations, and values. I shall therefore combat the sort of semantic amalgamation that one finds summarized in the oxymoronic formula "The brain thinks."

Changeux: I avoid using such formulas.

Ricoeur: I proceed, then, from a semantic dualism that expresses a duality of perspectives. The tendency to slip from a dualism of discourses to a dualism of substances is encouraged by the fact that each field of study tends to define itself in terms of what may be called a final referent, something to which appeal can be made as a last resort. But this referent is final only in its respective field, and comes to be defined at the same time as the field itself is defined. It is therefore necessary to refrain from transforming a dualism of referents into a dualism of substances. Prohibiting this elision of the semantic and the ontological has the consequence that, on the phenomenological plane where I take up my position, the term *men-*

tal is not equivalent to the term *immaterial* in the sense of something noncorporeal. Quite the opposite. Mental experience implies the corporeal, but in a sense that is irreducible to the objective bodies studied by the natural sciences. Semantically opposed to the body-as-object of these sciences is the experienced body, one's own body—my body (from which I speak), your body (the body that belongs to you, which I address), the body of another (his body or her body, about which I make up stories). Thus the body figures twice in the discourse I propose, both as "objective" body and as "subjective" body or, as I would rather say, one's own body. I prefer to speak of one's own body, rather than of the subjective body, because the body in question is not only mine but the body of others as well. Therefore: body as part of the world, and as that *from which* I (you, he, she) apprehend(s) the world for purposes of orientation and in order to live in it. Here I am very close to P. F. Strawson's position in *Individuals,*[15] where he shows that two series of heterogeneous predicates can be applied to the same person, considering him or her either as an object of observation and explanation or as enjoying the relationship indicated in our language by possessive pronouns such as "mine," which themselves belong to the list of expressions that linguists call "deictic," or demonstrative—here, there, now, yesterday, today, and so on. The deictic form that interests us here is the "mine" of my body. My initial hypothesis, then, which I submit for your consideration, is that I do not see a way of passing from one order of discourse to the other: either I speak of neurons and so forth, in which case I find myself in a certain language, or I speak of thoughts, actions, and feelings that I connect with my body, to which I stand in a relation of possession, of belonging. Thus, I can say that my hands, my feet, and so forth are my organs in the sense that I walk with my feet, I grasp with my hands—but this comes under the head of personal experience, and I do not have to commit myself to an ontology of the soul in order to speak in this way. By contrast, when I am told that I have a brain, no actual experience corresponds to this; I learn about it in books—

Changeux: Except when you have a headache or when a cerebral lesion, due to an accident for example, has deprived you of speech or of the capacity to read and write.

Ricoeur: We will come back later to the question of what sort of instruction clinical observation may provide for the conduct of life, that is, apart from the need for treatment, the need to adjust behavior to a "reduced" environment, to use Kurt Goldstein's phrase.[16] For the moment, let's stay on the epistemological plane. A critical point, which at first sight appears to be simply linguistic but which in fact goes far beyond this, is that there is no parallelism between the sentences "I grasp with my hands" and "I think with my brain." Everything that I know about the brain is one kind of knowledge. However, there are other kinds of knowledge as well. I suspect you and I may disagree about the answer to the following question: Does the new knowledge that we have about the cortex add to what I already know through direct bodily experience and, in particular, everything that I know about emotions, perceptions, everything that is genuinely psycho-organic and connected with my possession of my body? There is only one body that is mine, whereas all other bodies are outside me.

Changeux: I see the problem. First, I agree with you that there exist two types of discourse that refer to two distinct methods of investigation in the sciences of the nervous system. One bears upon the anatomy, the morphology of the brain, its microscopic organization, nerve cells and their synaptic connections; the other concerns conduct, behaviors, emotions, feelings, thoughts, and actions on the environment. These two modes of description have long been separated from each other, all the more so because at the beginning of the century one tradition of research on animal and human behaviors—behaviorism—deliberately omitted to take into account the anatomical and pharmacological aspects of the central nervous system. The brain was put aside as a "black box." This research nonetheless had a positive effect: it led to the objective analysis of animal behavior in experimental situations—learning, for example, or feeding habits, vocalizations, sexual behavior, and so on. These observational data, described in their own special terms, are indispensable for research in the neurosciences. In many cases where one attempts to model cognitive processes, in fact, such behavioral data constitute an obligatory point of departure.

But the description of cerebral anatomy concerns objects and uses a vocabulary that in no way coincide with the objects and vocabulary of behavior or, as you call it, personal experience. No neurobiologist would ever say that "language *is* the posterior part of the frontal lobe of the cerebral cortex." That is meaningless. One says instead that language "makes use of" or, better yet, "mobilizes" particular areas of the brain. The term *mobilize* is particularly appropriate because it involves a set of processes that is not covered by either of your two discourses: dynamic and transitory *activities* that occur throughout the neural network. These electrical and chemical activities constitute an internal link between the anatomical organization of neurons and connections, on the one hand, and behavior on the other. It becomes necessary to introduce a third discourse, anticipated by Spinoza, that draws upon this functional dynamic in order to *unify* the anatomical and the behavioral, to link the neuronal description with that which is perceived or experienced. I would say therefore that I am not guilty of semantic confusion, or amalgamation, but that I utilize instead several "discourses," or descriptions, that need to be related to each other in an adequate and operational form.

Ricoeur: It's not only the anatomical and the behavioral that have to be related to each other, for they both fall under the category of objective knowledge; but observed and scientifically described behavior, on the one hand, and, on the other, personal experience—and this in a meaningful way, in terms of what Canguilhem called "vital values." It is at this level that the duality of discourse presents a problem.

Changeux: A problem, to be sure, but not an incompatibility. With regard to your second point, once again I find myself in agreement with you. The discourse about the body-as-subject, "my body from which I speak" and "his or her body that I make up stories about"—as distinguished from the discourse about the objective body, or brain, whose anatomy *and* observable activities I describe—comes under the head of the subject's processes of conscious perception and the attribution to others of mental states, knowledge, emotions, and even intuitions. At first sight it may seem impossible to pass from the one discourse to the other, as you suggest. This is an issue of great importance, and we will certainly come back to it at length.

At this stage of our discussion I shall content myself with making two points. It is, of course, true that a person's individual history, the memories accumulated during childhood together with the course of one's affective life, give each person's experience a particular "color," "tone," or "value"; but this owes nothing to some elusive metaphysics. It has to do instead with an epigenetic signature stabilized in our patterns of cerebral organization and acquired by each person over the course of his or her life. But the simple fact that we can communicate this experience with others through narratives, may lead us to have a certain disposition toward association, toward benevolence; but given the existence of violence and war, proscriptions must be devised, against murder and incest for example, so that we find ourselves faced with both continuity and discontinuity—continuity between life and an ethics rooted in life, and discontinuity at the level of a morality that compensates for its own costs, as it were, life having abandoned us to our own devices without providing rules that would make peace prevail over war and violence. This position, at least with regard to discontinuity, links up finally with that of Kant. I am very attached in particular to Kant's essay "Idea of a Universal History from a Cosmopolitan Point of View" (1784), in which he shows that life has bequeathed us the burden of an "unsociable sociability" and entrusts us with the "task" of devising a peaceful political order.

What is the origin of this task? This is the problem. There are several possible replies. On the one hand, as I say, there is the continuity of ethics, which is very deeply rooted in life, and on the other there is the discontinuity of morality, which is born in a moment of rupture. I was recently reading Thomas Nagel, one of the best contemporary moral philosophers, on the subject of impartiality.[17] For Nagel this is the moral moment par excellence, to which he attaches almost more importance than to justice; but the two come to the same thing, to the extent that justice consists in treating equals equally. This subject will need to be reserved for another time, however. For the moment I distinguish three discourses: yours, on the objective body; a second discourse on one's own body, with its vast ethical implications; and finally a normative discourse, dealing with legal and political issues, grafted on the two preceding discourses.

Changeux: You raise two important questions: does what one knows about the brain lead to changes in ordinary experience?

poems, and works of art indicates, I believe, that despite individual variability our brains give us access as human beings to experiences that are in agreement with—if not always very similar to—our own. Moreover, despite obvious errors to which we are all liable, the capacity to attribute our own mental states to others indicates that another person has "personal experience" that is close to "mine." We will see that new technologies of brain imaging allow the experience of others to be "objectively" analyzed and reproduced from one individual to another.

Nonetheless, I grant you, this type of neuroscientific investigation has so far yielded only partial advances. Such research is concerned with highly integrated functions of the human brain, conscious processes that open onto the world. The ability to model them constitutes a crucial step forward for our discipline. There is much that is unknown, but for all that nothing that is unknowable! Just the same, we must proceed with great care and humility. Grand though our ambitions may be, we are nonetheless obliged to take small steps, proposing models that are simple, partial, and fragmentary.

Ricoeur: The particular "tone" of each person's personal experience does not depend on some "elusive metaphysics"; it depends on descriptions that have their own criteria of significance and that lend themselves to what may be called an essential analysis. As for the narratives, poems, and works of art that you rightly evoke in this connection, these are modes of discourse or expression that are on the same plane of understanding and interpretation. The way in which you present the research program of the neurosciences, incorporating conscious processes in it, makes it clear you are not a reductionist.

Changeux: Thank you very much—I am very frequently accused of being one!

Ricoeur: Reductionism is a reaction against ontological dualism. This leads on, if you will permit me to continue, to the next part of the question you regard as primary. I, too, am concerned with a dualism—a semantic dualism. If I had to claim a philosophical ancestor it would be Spinoza, whom you have mentioned already. For him the unity of substance was to be sought at a much higher level, which in Book I of the *Ethics* he calls *Deus sive natura*. Either I speak the language of the body, a finite mode of discourse, which for Spinoza was that of space; or I speak the language of thought, a distinct finite mode, which he persisted in calling the soul. I speak both languages without, however, being able to merge them. Whence my question: does any knowledge that I may have of the brain add to the knowledge that I have of myself simply through direct acquaintance with my body, without knowing anything about my brain? This initial question finds an echo in the ethical sphere to the extent that I am entirely prepared to say that ethics is rooted in life and that normative ethical behaviors find their origin in the impulses of life. Here again we find the problem of the duality of discourse. Life may mean two different things: there is life as seen by biologists, and life as it is—

Changeux: Experienced.

Ricoeur: Yes, as it is experienced. I do not much like this expression on account of its immediacy, which I think is quite influenced by language—a conversational, narrative language. In this regard I am something of an anti-intuitionist. In any case it seems to me there are three problems. The first results from the existence of two ways of talking about the body, one a discourse of appropriation and belonging, the other a discourse of distance, in which I consider a brain—the brain—that is not characterized by any property of appropriation or

by any deictic; it is neither here nor there, wher body is here in relation to other bodies that are own body may belong to me or to another perso incarnate—

Changeux: An observer.

Ricoeur: An observer who has a body, a body to which he in the same relation of possession; a corporeal, embodie server for whom there are bodies, physical bodies, and an these physical bodies the brain. My first problem is there epistemological: do the neurosciences allow us to correct linguistic dualism that I am insisting on? This would be t case if one could show that what one knows about the brai leads to changes in ordinary experience outside pathologica or—to use Goldstein's term—catastrophic situations, and that therefore I would speak differently about myself once I had acquired knowledge about the brain. I have my doubts, but at the same time I wish to keep an open mind on account of the second problem, which arises from the implications of theories of evolution and their application to moral issues. Is this doctrine, which is known as "naturalism," anything more than an attempt to shore up ethics by appeal to the biological facts uncovered by the science of the brain and observation of the behavior of living beings? Now, I am ready to grant much to the idea that human experience has a biological basis, much more than Kantian moralists would do. In this respect I am quite Aristotelian. What I call ethics—as opposed to morality, with its laws and prohibitions—seems to me to have deep roots in life, even if I cannot avoid passing over into the normative sphere at some point.

What makes this passage from ethics to morality obligatory? Well, because in the course of evolution, life has left us in the lurch, so to speak. By this I mean that biological organization

Is it necessary to create any sort of discontinuity or rupture between ethical discourse, which you regard as rooted in life, and moral, normative discourse? Later we will examine this problem in detail, drawing upon the most recent scientific results. My immediate response will be to refer to two philosophers: Lucretius, who affirmed in *De rerum natura* that "Our terrors and our darknesses of mind must be dispelled [. . .] not by sunshine's rays, not by those shining arrows of the light, but by insight into nature";[18] and Spinoza, who extended this conception of knowledge to man and the "human soul." As Robert Misrahi has pointed out, Spinoza in the *Ethics* constructs "an integral knowledge of man and of his situation in the world," a sort of "rational psychology."[19] His new ethics aimed to show that the sources of the *value* of our actions and of our passions are to be discovered in man himself.

Whatever interpretation may be given to Spinoza's philosophy, I take from it the notion that reflective knowledge of our body, our brain, and its functions (the soul) is fundamental to ethical reflection and moral judgment. I do not find grounds for assuming any moment of rupture; instead I carefully examine such new questions as may arise. To create a priori ruptures in discourse opens the way to irrationality, to the arbitrary and authoritarian normative discourse that we hear in so many parts of the world today. Is there any better way to protect ourselves against such irrationality than to lift the veil and to relentlessly seek *all* those truths to which scientific knowledge in its various forms and disciplinary expressions gives us access, without regard for the type and level of organization of the object studied? Why posit a discontinuity of discourse when objective knowledge of what determines our behavior holds out the prospect of greater wisdom, perhaps even greater freedom? As Spinoza remarked, "Experience tells us no less clearly than reason that it is on this account only that men believe themselves to be free, that they are conscious of their actions and ignorant of the causes by which they are determined."[20]

Ricoeur: Do you mind if I interrupt you in connection with Spinoza? This remark must be put in its full context, beginning with the theory of the unity of substance and the multiplicity of attributes and modes in the first book of the *Ethics* and concluding with the wisdom and bliss of the marvelous fifth book. The freedom that Spinoza criticized was that of the free Cartesian arbiter. But there is another philosophy of freedom, understood as necessity. This becomes clear only in relation to the beginning and end of the *Ethics*.

Changeux: There have, of course, been many reappropriations of Spinoza—particularly by persons belonging to the same school of thought as those who persecuted Spinoza during his lifetime. But I would like to come back, if I may, to the virtually inscrutable lines of demarcation that you draw between types of discourse. Such semantic dualism has had dramatic consequences not only for the development of ideas but also for the way in which scientific research is carried out and how research institutions function. The tendency to disciplinary isolation is very strong as it is, particularly in France, where physicists speak a language that is comprehensible only to physicists, where physiologists and sociologists alike use concepts that only they understand. These examples could be multiplied. The tendency to disciplinary partitioning undermines the work of our research institutions, although everyone is well aware of the considerable contribution made by physics to brain imaging, by chemistry to the symptomatic treatment of mental disease, by archaeology and history to the search for the origins of the major religions and to the redaction of their founding texts, and so on. The institutional gap that separates the life sciences from the humanities and social sciences has had catastrophic results. Experience has shown that it is often at the boundaries between disciplines that great discoveries take place. Why rule out, as a matter of principle, the possibility that advances in reflective knowledge may succeed in establishing a continuity between analysis of the objective body and of one's own body, between ethical discourse and normative discourse? An interdisciplinary approach is likely to be fruitful, it seems to me, so long as one is scrupulously attentive to the meaning of words and the proper use of concepts.

I am nonetheless grateful that you do not insist on directing our conversation toward questions that from my point of view are without interest or even, as in the case of reductionism, a future. If I understand you correctly, we will also be able tentatively to put to one side all reference to systems of belief in a soul distinct from the body or in the immortality of the soul that so often figure in discussions of morality. I am delighted by this.

Ricoeur: You cannot decide in advance what is without interest or without a future. The question of reductionism is at the heart of philosophical discussion in Anglo-American circles; beliefs about the soul and the body have exercised the greatest minds and deserve to be discussed "within the limits of reason alone," as Kant did in his philosophy of religion. As for research on reflective knowledge, I do not evaluate it a priori since it is on the basis of exactly such research that I seek to pose the problem of the relationship between reflective knowledge and objective knowledge. It is also the basis on which I pose the problem of normative discourse. And there I am in agreement with you. I believe in the universal character of morality.

Changeux: So do I—but do we believe in it for the same reason?

Ricoeur: There are several kinds of reason. Charles Taylor in *Sources of the Self*[21] distinguishes a first kind, on the level of ordinary discourse, that he calls "strong evaluations"; another kind consisting of philosophical or other rationalizations; and a third kind, what he calls "sources" or deep motivations for belief, that is found in the cultural heritage of the great civilizations. Our own heritage Taylor sees as deriving from three traditions: Judeo-Christianity, the Enlightenment, and also Romanticism, which in his view extends up through the ecological movement of the present day. I believe that democracy draws upon this treasure of sources, or resources, and rests upon the capacity of citizens not only to support each other but also to aid each other. This capacity has its roots in all three traditions, the first of which founds justice on love, the second on reason, and the third on our relationship, and that of the natural environment, to life.

Changeux: This is a very Western view of "sources" and cultural heritages. It seems to me just as important to take into consideration those of Confucianism and Buddhism, as well as the heritage of the philosophical atomists of Greek antiquity, in addition to the Judeo-Christian tradition. On the other hand, I think that you make quick work of democracy. We should not forget the extreme animosity of Enlightenment thinkers toward Judeo-Christianity.

The Biological and the Normative

Changeux: One of the issues we ought to tackle at the outset, it seems to me, has to do with the relationship between the language we use and the objects that matter to us and that we deal with in everyday life. It strikes me as essential, first, that together we examine whether a bridge cannot be created between the first two discourses, the one involving the body and the brain as objects of knowledge by an external observer, and the other a discourse of the self resting on a representation that we have of our body. For a neurobiologist such as myself, the notion of representation in this context constitutes a central point that may allow us to establish a real link between what might be called the objective and the subjective—I oversimplify, but these are the terms that are customarily employed. In trying to establish such a link we would be following the lead of certain philosophers today who are attempting to "naturalize" phenomenology. This is a rather rough way of putting things, I realize. The question at issue here is how far the knowledge that we have about our brain gives us a new conception of ourselves, a different representation of our ideas, our thoughts, and the dispositions that intervene when we make judgments. With regard to moral judgments, in fact, it is fundamental. The knowledge that we are now in the process of piecing together about the human brain ought to allow us to have a clearer idea—I am perhaps overly optimistic—of the direction in which we wish to see human society develop. Spinoza encourages us to construct a model of man as a social being that we can contemplate with satisfaction both now and in the future. I would like to see how far we can succeed in matching up these two discourses about the body, in achieving a synthesis that at first sight may seem to be impossible.

Ricoeur: I quite agree with this program; but before we try to put the two discourses about the body in correspondence with each other, I would like us first to assess the implications of the semantic dualism that I defend. This dualism, formulated in strictly corporeal terms, propagates itself along a line that divides personal experience from all the ways of objectifying integral human experience. It extends to mental phenomena for which a knowledge of the brain does not seem pertinent, such as high-level cognitive activities associated with language and logic. I am thinking here of all those functions in which philosophers of mind and cognitive scientists are interested—beliefs, desires, and wishes expressed in terms of what are called propositional attitudes ("I believe that . . .", "I desire that . . .", "I decide that . . .").

I would argue, however, that a still more subtle semantic dualism insinuates itself between experiences organized at a prelinguistic level and disembodied representations of mental experience that may be computationally formalized. It is not an exaggeration to say that the semantic gap is as great between the cognitive sciences and philosophy as it is between the neurosciences and philosophy. The gap between phenomenological experience and objective knowledge extends the full length of the line dividing these two approaches to the phenomenon of human existence.

But I hasten to say that this semantic dualism, expressing a genuine asceticism of reflective thought, can only be a point of departure. Owing to the multiplicity, abundance, and completeness of human experience, the two discourses continually intersect at a great many points. In a certain way—how I am not at all sure—it is the same body that is experienced and known; it is the same mind that is experienced and known; it is the same person who is "mental" *and* "corporeal." From this ontological identity arises a third discourse that goes beyond both phenomenological philosophy and science. To my mind this would be either the poetic account of creation in the biblical sense or the speculative discourse that was raised to its height by Spinoza, overcoming the division between the attributes of thought and extension in order to assert the unity of substance. Descartes had hoped to be able to compose such a discourse but, in the end, abandoned the attempt. Spinoza, however, had the daring to go forward with it. Here one must read Descartes's sixth *Meditation,* the *Passions of the Soul,* and the *Letters to Elizabeth*. In his system, which remained unfinished, it was to be the discourse of what some commentators on Descartes have called "the third substance," namely man. Well, the semantic dualism from which I proceed contains a comparable reference, if not to this possible third substance (and, beyond this, to Spinoza's doctrine of the unity of substance), then at least to man *tout court*. But I do not hesitate to say that as a philosopher I profess considerable skepticism with regard to the possibility of constituting an overarching discourse of this sort, above and beyond the profound unity of what appears to me sometimes as a neuronal system, sometimes as mental experience. In the last analysis we are dealing with two discourses of the body.

Changeux: I concur with your distinction between these various discourses, between organized experience and objective explanations of such experience, and I note your reluctance to propose an ontological identity involving a third scientific discourse. I do not join you, however, in seeing this attempt as a poetic discourse of creation in the biblical sense. You characterize your position as one of cautious agnosticism. Isn't *not believing* in the possibility of constituting such a third discourse evidence of an idealist prejudice? Doesn't this amount to weakening somewhat the *emendatio intellectus,* the discipline of thought, the asceticism of reflective thought that both of us uphold? Spinoza's speculative discourse seems to me quite distinct from poetic discourse, from the many myths of creation to which you compare it. His approach seems to me to be immensely more constructive. Spinoza himself wished to proceed with the same rigor of method as geometry. The scientist formulates hypotheses that, taken together and stated formally, constitute a theory. The researcher cannot hide from the facts. He runs the risk of being wrong. Scientific models are subject to the verdict of facts. They are judged by facts. The exactitude of models can be tested. They can be falsified—and if they prove to be false, they are abandoned. Theory assumes the intelligibility of the world in advance of experiment. Nonetheless it is constrained by natural processes, by the phenomena that are studied. It is not a matter of discovering the Truth about being, but of progressing step by step in the acquisition of truths, aware that no scientific model can pretend to exhaust reality, whether it be physical, mental, or "experienced." Why shouldn't we revive Spinoza's doctrine of the unity of substance, while acknowledging that the word *substance* no longer has the same meaning it had in the seventeenth century and that it must be redefined on the basis of present knowledge? You yourself have said that an ontology remains possible in our time, to the extent that the philosophies of the past remain open to reinterpretation and reformulation.

Ricoeur: There are several points to be made in response. I do not put the poetic discourse of the biblical myth of creation—which I mentioned a bit provocatively, I admit—on the same plane as the speculative discourse of Spinoza's *substantia actuosa,* though they speak of the same fundamental unity. The one belongs to a realm of myth that is no longer ours (which is why you will not see me challenge evolutionary theory with any form of creationist dogma) but that may still stimulate thought in a free, speculative way that draws upon an ancient fund of wisdom disguised as a narrative account of origins. The other belongs to a speculative style of thought that has perhaps become inaccessible to us since Kant, unless through Fichte, Schelling, and the great system builders. For my part, I maintain a cautious agnosticism toward this kind of unitary discourse. But why then dismiss doubts about the possibility of elaborating a third discourse as an idealist prejudice? As for your quite Popperian pleading on behalf of modeling and verification/falsification, I consider it irrefutable in your field, which is to say in the service of objective knowledge of nature and man. But this discourse does not move us an inch nearer to a renewal of Spinoza's unity of substance, which, once again, supposes that we accept the definitions of the first part of the *Ethics* and the final theorems of the fifth part. Spinoza's anthropology cannot be separated from his entire system. Nonetheless, despite my epistemological caution, I remain interested in attempts to reexamine and rework the great metaphysical doctrines of the past.

That said, I agree entirely that we should take the notion of representation as our touchstone in assessing the correlation of the two discourses, because it will force me to defend my presumption that in using this term there is a particularly great danger of confusion. The use of the term *representation* in the two languages, I fear, is ambiguous.

Changeux: Is the danger one of confusion or fusion?

Ricoeur: You notice that I referred to a "presumption" on my part. I enter into this discussion with a certain wariness: on the mental level I know what a representation is, because I have the notion of intentionality, the notion of purpose, the notions of subject and object; but I do not see how I will find representations in the brain.

I am therefore wholly in agreement about taking the notion of representation as central. Let me make it clear at the outset that it interests me not only on the epistemological plane, where the question of truth is at issue, but also in the context of our subsequent discussion of the passage from the vital, biological level to the normative level—to the moral plane. More important for me than the notion of representation, however, is the notion of capacity, which plays such a great role in Aristotle and Leibniz. For me, the able man is one who is capable of speaking, acting, talking about himself, subjecting himself to norms, and so on. Certainly the endowment with capacities is deeply rooted in the biological world, but the accession to moral competence supposes language, moral obligation, institutions—a whole normative, juridical, and political world. Here we meet again with the problem I mentioned a moment ago of continuity and discontinuity. Now this problem does not exactly coincide with that of the correlation between the neuronal and the mental with which we began. The problem in establishing such a correlation is a theoretical one, in which the scientific point of view confronts the phenomenological point of view. But with the question of human capacities we enter into the practical sphere. It is at this moment that the continuity-discontinuity problem presents itself. I propose therefore to distinguish between two problems, one associated with the idea of representation and the other with the idea of human ability or capacity to act.

Changeux: The notion of predisposition, or capacity, is essential for the neurobiologist. I unambiguously distinguish between dispositions to form representations and representations themselves.

To summarize the foregoing, then, I would say that the question we must address amounts to examining how far the normative can be rooted in the biological evolution and cultural history of humanity. Can a "new ethics" be devised according to which, following Darwin, the propagation of moral norms throughout human societies proceeds through the learning of "social instincts" of sympathy that have their origin in the evolution of species?

Ricoeur: That is precisely the question.

2 — Body and Mind: In Search of a Common Discourse

The Cartesian Ambiguity

Paul Ricoeur: How can the discourses of mind and body be unified? In reflecting upon this question I thought once more of a work that I have already mentioned, Descartes's sixth *Meditation,* where he employs the word *man* following upon a methodological section in which he speaks alternately in terms of thought and of space. This is the mixed discourse of the *Letters to Elizabeth* and the *Passions of the Soul.* The problem, at bottom, is to identify the conditions under which such a discourse is possible. I expect this will be very difficult to do. I would look for such conditions in the experience of man in the world, of being in the world, but I believe that we ought first to describe each of the two prior discourses separately.

Jean-Pierre Changeux: I think that these two discourses also involve a historical aspect since they developed independently. If we find ourselves talking to each other today it is perhaps because we have arrived at a moment in history when it has become possible to link them up. This at least is my point of view, my hope.

Let us begin by examining Descartes's use of the word *man,* with reference to a fundamental work to which he gave precisely the same name—*L'Homme*—and which, owing to his fear of the Inquisition, he never finished. It is not hard to see why. Here is how the book begins: "These men will be com-

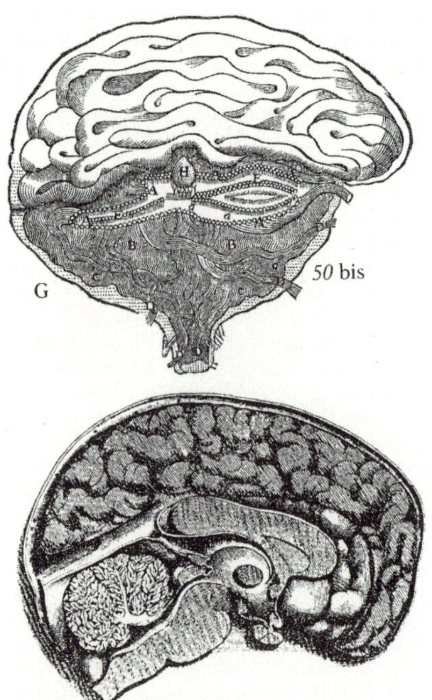

FIGURE 2.1. Comparative representations of the brain in *L'Homme* (Treatise on Man) by René Descartes (1596–1650) and the *Discours sur l'anatomie du cerveau* (Dissertation on the Anatomy of the Brain) by Nicolaus Steno (1638–86).

The top illustration, which appeared as the next-to-last figure (50 bis) of the second edition of the *Treatise on Man* (1677), is a representation of the human brain based on sketches left by Descartes, now lost. Small "nerve fibers" stand out against the wall of the "concavities" of the brain, in the center of which is located the pineal gland (H). This gland, Descartes held, serves to unite the rational soul (*l'Ame raisonable*) with the "body's machine" via the action of animal spirits. It will be noted that the cerebral cortext is left blank, being located on the side of the soul.

The illustration below comes from the *Dissertation on the Anatomy of the Brain,* published in 1669 after having been delivered orally at the home of Melchior du Thévenot, who became librarian to Louis XIV. Nicolaus Steno, as he is known to us, was born Niels Steensen in 1638 in Copenhagen. Steno owes his fame to works on anatomy

posed, as we are, of a soul and a body. First I must describe the body on its own; then the soul, again on its own; and finally I must show how these *two natures* would have to be joined and united in order to constitute men who resemble us."[1]

Two pages before the end of the text we read the words, "But before going on to describe the rational soul. . . ."[2]—but Descartes never gets around to it. The year was 1633, the same year as Galileo's condemnation. Replying to Père Mersenne, from whom he heard the news, Descartes wrote: "My desire to live in peace obliges me to keep my theories to myself."[3] He thus left the *Treatise on Man* unfinished. It was to be published in this fragmentary form only after the author's death.[4]

In the *Treatise on Man,* Descartes's argument is developed around an essential theoretical principle, the hierarchical organization of cerebral functions and architecture. What is more—and this is the key point of the demonstration found there—such hierarchical stratification is displayed by anatomical schemas (figure 2.1). At the lowest level one finds the sense organs, muscles, and nerves—the latter are described as "great tubes that contain several other small tubes" whose "marrow is composed of tiny fibers." At the highest level one finds the rational soul with "its principal seat in the brain," the attributes of which correspond, I would argue, to what is conventionally called today the higher functions of the brain. Lo-

---

and geology (the discovery of fossil shark teeth was due to him) as well as theology. The quality of observation found in this work is far superior to that of Descartes and approaches that of the English anatomist Thomas Willis (1621–75), several of whose errors he corrects in passing. Steno contested the role of the pineal gland attributed to it by Descartes. "I say nothing here against his machine, whose artifice I admire," he wrote in the *Dissertation*. "[But] the connection of the gland with the brain by means of the arteries [can] no longer [be considered] true."

cated at their juncture is the famous pineal gland, which according to Descartes is a sort of mechanical switch. Here "centripetal" signals issuing from the sense organs meet "centrifugal" signals emanating from the rational soul. The Cartesian machine is not a macroscopic mechanical model but rather a singular attempt to relate the functions of the human body to its microscopic organization.

The schema is, of course, very artificial; but it is perfectly logical. Comparing it with present-day data concerning the architecture of the brain naturally poses a problem. Nonetheless it represents the first attempt to model reciprocal regulation *between* levels of organization. The point of the Cartesian enterprise as a whole, in my view, is to establish a causal relation between neural structure and sensory-motor—ultimately, cognitive—function at each defined level of hierarchical organization. Descartes's model appeals only to anatomical organization, which it describes in terms of "small tubes" and the activity that circulates in them, the "animal spirits" that he compares to the air that "pass[es] from the wind-chests to particular pipes" of "the organs in our churches" and that "have the force to change the shape of the muscles . . . , to move the limbs" (figure 2.2).[5] In this Descartes anticipates present-day work in cognitive neuroscience that consists in modeling our knowledge acquisition apparatus (I use Desanti's term) with the ultimate aim of establishing a correspondence between what Descartes globally characterizes as the "rational soul" (cognitive functions) and the relevant cerebral architecture (in this case the cerebral cortex—the area left blank in figure 2.1). It may legitimately be maintained that Descartes elaborates here the first connectionist model of the functional organization of the nervous system. He proposes a complete schema that causally relates, in terms of the "circulation" of "animal spirits," the perception by sense organs of muscular movement and action upon the world, from the automatic movements of

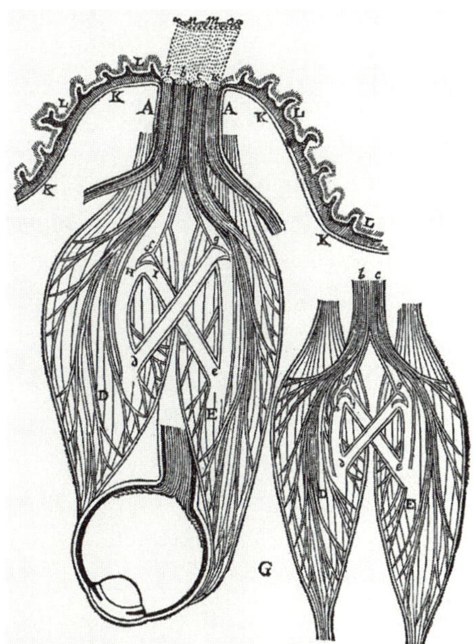

FIGURE 2.2. Innervation of the motor muscles of the eye. Wood engraving taken from the second edition of Descartes's *Treatise on Man* (1677).

Descartes unambiguously distinguishes *anatomical organization* (muscle D and the "tube[s] or small nerve[s]" *b* and *c*), the *activity* that circulates in the network ("the Animal Spirits that enter it or go out from it"), and *behavior* or action on the world, here the movement of the eye ("when the Animal Spirits enter inside, they cause the whole body of the muscle to swell up and to become shorter, and thus to draw the eye to which it is attached"). Anticipating the notion of a synapse, Descartes introduces "small membranes [*peaux*] or valves *f* and *g*" that produce a polarity in the transfer of signals from the nerve to the muscle.

the eye, breathing, and swallowing to the alternation of states of waking and sleep, indeed to the play of the imagination. In this respect his insight proved to be prophetic!

More courageously still by comparison with the thinking of the age, the *Treatise on Man* concludes with the statement that "in order to explain these functions, then, it is not necessary to conceive of this machine as having any negative or sensitive soul or other principle of movement and life, apart from its blood and its spirits, which are agitated by the heat of the fire burning continuously in its heart—a fire which has the same nature as all the other fires that occur in inanimate bodies."[6] The reference here to ancient atomism is explicit. Some years earlier Vanini had been burned at the stake for not much more than this.[7] Nor did the Church mistake Descartes's allusion. His works had the honor in 1663 of joining those of Copernicus, Galileo, and Pascal on the Index of Prohibited Books.

Ricoeur: That the *Treatise on Man* was unfinished was not only due to circumstances connected with the Inquisition. Here one has to look at the *Meditations* and Descartes's replies to the objections brought against it (published together as *Objections et les Réponses*). The paradox resides in the fact that Descartes, through his famous dualism, made it possible to develop a philosophy of bodily subjectivity, as François Azouvi has shown.[8] Whereas the scholastics, following Aristotle, got lost in difficulties connected with "hylomorphism," or the union of matter and form, Descartes in the second *Meditation* held that the soul has nothing to do with the body, that no soul belongs to a particular body and no body is the property of a particular soul. Hence the question of the sixth *Meditation:* on what does this feeling of ownership—of my body being mine—rest once the principles on which the scholastics relied had been undermined? The feeling of belonging has to be made a reason beyond reason, as it were. This reason belongs to what Descartes calls "the teachings of nature." These teachings lead us to say that a person is not housed in his body as a captain is in his ship: a wounded person will say "my leg" whereas the captain will go on seeing the hole in the hull of his ship as something external to himself. It thus becomes possible to imagine a duality of points of view corresponding to the rational criteria that govern the dualism of the soul and the body. A person's body ceases to be just any body. As Azouvi quite rightly points out, "to wonder whether individuality is conferred by the soul or by the body is to remain within an ontological perspective, whereas Descartes, in asserting the equivocacy of the body, was able to posit a phenomenology of subjective corporeal existence"—a phenomenology that would later be worked out in detail by Maine de Biran.

Changeux: Just the same there is a profound ambiguity in Descartes's mature thought that many authors have noted.[9] Whereas the theoretical demonstration in the *Treatise on Man* rests on observation and proceeds from the microscopic to the macroscopic, in the *Principles* and the *Meditations* Descartes bases his thought on the *cogito.* On the basis of simple introspection he believes he can separate "intellection or pure conception" from the brain, which is to say the soul from the body. He finds himself trapped in the untenable position, whose contradictory character he himself points out, of asserting the existence of a soul that is both "truly conjoint" and at the same time "totally distinct" from the entire body. Of course he could not possibly have foreseen the immense ontological opportunity that would later be offered by the theory of the evolution of species. Even so, it is telling that he calls God to the rescue. "Without upsetting the order [of nature]," he writes, "I could not prove only that the soul is distinct from the body, [without having proved] before the existence of God."[10] This recourse to divine guarantee signifies the abandonment of scientific reflection. Descartes is now more interested in flattering the Prince and ingratiating himself with the Church than trying to push a scientific and philosophical line of thought to its furthest limits, even if it were never to be published. "*Larvatus prodeo,*" he writes—"Masked, I go forward."[11]

Ricoeur: I do not see any need to question Descartes's intellectual honesty. The difficulty is quite real in such a system, which I interpret literally. Beyond the dualism of the first *Meditation* one finds the paradox of the sixth *Meditation,* which leads to the *Passions of the Soul* and the *Letters*. Recognition of the corporeal ambiguity that is associated with this paradox leads me to try to correct—compensate for—the sort of conceptual asceticism that I advocate in opposition to any semantic amalgamation of the plurality of discourses about man, on the one hand, and on the other a discourse about the brain, an autonomous organ that has its own internal rules. Accordingly, I recommend treating the mixed discourse uncritically employed by scientists and philosophers with great tolerance. This tolerance seems to me justified by the correlations and intersections arising from a quite remarkable situation, which I would summarize in the following way: my brain does not think, but when I am thinking something is always going on in my brain—even when I am thinking of God!

From this working hypothesis, which makes possible an exchange of information and arguments among philosophers and scientists, I draw a maxim not of convenience but of concession: the scientist, faced with well-established connections, permits himself—or rather is authorized by the tacit agreement of the scientific community—to introduce in his explanatory models certain mixed and abbreviated explanations that contradict semantic dualism. Thus the scientist permits himself to say that the brain is "concerned" or "involved" by such-and-such a mental phenomenon, that it is "responsible" for such-and-such a phenomenon. This loose way of talking is so common that I no longer notice it when I read the scientific literature.

The philosopher has a duty, then, in reading scientific texts, to combine semantic tolerance with semantic criticism—to accept in practice what he denounces as a matter of principle, namely, confusions that result from illegitimately converting correlations into identifications. The discourse of the neurosciences is littered with such shorthand expressions—semantic short-circuits, in effect. They would be innocent enough if they were recognized as such, if their compressed semantic content were recognized, and in particular if they were not improperly used to support "eliminativist" arguments made by philosophers such as Patricia and Paul Churchland[12] and related claims for a materialist ontological monism, which I find naïve.

The Contribution of the Neurosciences

Changeux: I would like to lay out a number of arguments that summarize the contribution of the neurosciences to this debate. Until recently the knowledge one had of oneself, of one's body, emotions, was uniquely accessible by means of introspection. Introspection was rejected by Auguste Comte, for example, but also by many scientists, on the ground that it did not bring objective information to bear upon the question. A very important reorientation in the behavioral sciences, and in the neurosciences in particular, subsequently made it possible to approach scientifically not only what is manifested through behavior toward the world but also what happens inside the "black box" that John Watson and the behaviorists had set aside and refused to take into consideration.

The Brain as a Projective System

Changeux: The break with the traditional conception of the mind as separate from the brain and of psychology as separate from neurology is due to five scientific advances. The first of these—not chronologically, but for purposes of exposition—

came after Watson and the behaviorists, in the 1930s, with the work of a gifted experimentalist, Edward Tolman. In *Purposive Behavior in Animals and Men* (1932) Tolman introduced the notion of anticipation—intentional behavior. He saw that something was going on in Watson's black box. Operations spontaneously develop inside it that are neither immediately nor systematically manifested in behavior but that nonetheless have an influence upon it. This entailed a change in how the relationship between the brain and the psyche was conceived. Instead of conceiving of the brain as functioning according to the standard behaviorist "input-output" model (later associated with the computer), the central nervous system was now seen by contrast as a "projective system" that continually projects its hypotheses onto the external world, putting them to the test of experience.[13] Sometimes it gives meaning to what has no meaning.

If you have the chance, visit the National Museum of Taiwan and especially the room in which ancient oracular bones are displayed (figure 2.3). In addition to cleaned and polished scapular fragments, there are ventral plates of tortoise shell, dating from about 1200 B.C. during the Bronze Age, on which are engraved the first Chinese characters. On closer examination one notices that these signs have been arranged in the vicinity of randomly distributed cracks. Deciphering these inscriptions we find that they are divinatory in nature. The soothsayer produced the cracks by applying a red-hot branding iron to the bone or shell and then, having posed a question about the success of a military campaign, or the weather, or the sickness of a family member, deduced the answer by interpreting the orientation of the cracks—a striking example of our capacity to give meaning to what has no meaning! Our brain is constantly attributing significance. For example, I see you look in my direction, I try to anticipate your response and then what

FIGURE 2.3. Oracular bone from the Shang Dynasty (twelfth century B.C.). Musée Guimet, Paris.

These fragments of tortoise shell (or bovid shoulder blade) were exposed to an incandescent branding iron that produced a fracture whose orientation predicted the response ("There will be . . ." or "There will not be . . .") to the question posed by the soothsayer. The inscriptions are the earliest known example of Chinese writing and give meaning to lines of fracture that otherwise have none.

I might say to you several seconds after that. I give meaning to your search for meaning.

Ricoeur: I would like to pause for a moment, if you don't mind, to consider what you identify as a crucial moment of rupture with the tradition that separates the mental from the neurological, namely, the conception of the brain as a projective system. This conception is itself subject to two interpretations, one neuronal and the other phenomenological. A phenomenology of action allows us to give meaning to the notions of anticipation and projection that marked a break with the reactive conception of early behaviorism, which assigned priority to stimuli emitted by the world as it was understood by the scientist, and not as living beings organize it and structure it by choosing meaningful signals. Your example of the look of another person is very interesting in this context, because it brings out both the connection and the discontinuity between the two discourses. From the optical point of view, light comes into the eye, passing from the outside to the inside. But from the mental point of view, you look out, which is to say that your look goes out from your eyes. The two points of view cross each other. You attribute this to the brain's capacity for projection. But what I call "projection" involves a mental activity that I understand reflectively. In this sense, the discourse of the mental includes the neuronal and not the other way round.

Changeux: I don't think so. What we wish to do is link up the two discourses *with each other.* Observers produce representations and perceive them.

Ricoeur: But the notion of the neuronal is itself a mental construction.

Changeux: I do not underestimate the difficulty of the task facing neurobiologists in trying to put neuronal events into correspondence with mental events. Thus it took almost a century to match up the structure of the human genome with the functions that correspond to it—to decipher the encoding of a protein involved in enzymatic activity, for example, or in the reception of light by the eye. In this case the analogy with genetics is rather suggestive. In the mid-nineteenth century Mendel succeeded in establishing the laws of heredity in the form of mathematical laws, which correspond in a way to a description of function. He proposed a certain number of regularities in the transmission of hereditary characters, in their "behavior" over the course of generations. Later the material, structural bases of these laws of heredity were gradually discovered. First came chromosomes. The American zoologist Thomas Morgan demonstrated that easily stainable corpuscles in the cellular nucleus of the fruit fly *Drosophila* exhibited a behavior over the course of the reproductive cycle that was similar to that of the hereditary characters described by Mendel. Just as the characters of yellow and green color are disjoint in the seeds of garden peas, so too there is disjunction within chromosomes. They contain the hereditary determinants of characters, genes, which form a well-defined linear map over the length of each chromosome.

Molecular biology, with the work of Avery and then of Watson and Crick, next identified the chemical material of which genes are made: a very long fiber of deoxyribonucleic acid (or DNA). Then it became a question of matching up the sequence of elementary chemical beads—base pairs—that comprise it with that of the amino acids that form the primary structure of proteins. From the structure of the gene it became possible to infer the structure of the protein it encodes and then to "understand" its function. One can, for example, understand the enzymatic function that determines the green or yellow color of the garden pea seed. The global hereditary character of the color of the seed or of the flower whose transmission Mendel described in formal terms was henceforth understood in a fundamental way through the deciphering of elementary mechanisms. One can even detect an environmental influence in the expression of certain genes, which directly concerns the neurobiologist.

Ricoeur: All this seems perfectly clear to me.

Changeux: If it is clear at the genetic level, why shouldn't it be clear in the case of the relation between the neural structure and organization of the brain, on the one hand, and its mental functions on the other?

Ricoeur: My reservations have nothing to do with the facts that you recite but the uncritical use that you make of the category of causality in passing from the neuronal to the mental. The question is whether it is possible to extend the notion of correlation from the semantic to the ontological plane, which is to say to the level of ultimate explanation. I propose we adopt the term *substrate* to denote the relation of the body-as-object to the body as it is experienced, and therefore of the brain to the mental. "Substrate" is a term associated with the Greek heritage of causality, of course; more precisely, with the Aristotelian theory of four causes. Aristotle distinguishes between the material cause, formal cause, efficient cause, and final cause. Under the head of material causality comes the role of stone in relation to a statue, which the artisan works (efficient causality) with a view to decorating a temple (final causality). I refer to material causality only in a limiting sense, to indicate a cause sine qua non, in order to resist the extrapolations of the Churchlands' brand of eliminativist monism.

In my own discourse this resort to the term *substrate* serves as a corrective with regard to the semantic liberty that the scientist takes when he says, for example, that such-and-such a neuronal complex produces such-and-such mental effects. Against the effective causality that you advocate I oppose substrate causality, in the limiting sense I have just indicated. I quite willingly grant that it constitutes nothing more than a sort of *cache-misère,* a presentable cloak worn to cover up the shabby clothes one wears underneath while traveling the uncertain path that leads from semantics to ontology. In order to maintain the concept of substrate within the framework of the logic of correlation, I would propose coupling it with the concept of indication. I therefore propose that we say that the brain is the substrate of thought (in the broadest sense of the term) and that thought is the indication of an underlying neuronal structure. Substrate and indication would thus constitute the two aspects of a dual relation, or correlation.

Changeux: I do not see that your use of the term *substrate* illuminates the problem. In fact, I think it creates an ambiguity. Is it restricted to connectional anatomy? Why not then employ the descriptive phrase *neural network*? Does it include activity or not? The discourse of the neurobiologist, which bears upon *three* distinct aspects—anatomical (neuronal connections), physiological (electrical activities and chemical signals), and behavioral and mental (action *on* the world and *internal* reflective processes)—seems to me much clearer.

Ricoeur: The last term in your list of these three aspects is a mixed one, combining the behavioral and the mental. The term *substrate* operates in a critical and nondogmatic manner, by contrast, and serves as a warning against the confusion that can creep into all mixed expressions of this type. The problem is really how to devise a uniform and consistent discourse.

Birth of Neuropsychology

Changeux: I have always clearly distinguished, it goes without saying, between *actions on the world* and *internal* operations that are not immediately manifested by such actions. Just so, I am going to try to demonstrate the consistency of my position by reviewing the five principal advances that enable us to imagine establishing an effective correspondence between psychological functions, physiological data, and nervous anatomy. The first of these, as I have just mentioned, derives from the study of animal behavior and its extension to man in the form of projective, purposive activity.

The second, and perhaps more important advance, is due to Paul Broca (1824–1880). At the 18 April 1861 meeting of the Anthropological Society of Paris, Broca demonstrated the first rigorous correlation between a lesion of the middle posterior part of the frontal lobe of the left hemisphere of the brain and the loss of speech, or aphasia. This moment marked the birth of a new discipline, neuropsychology. Its aim was to establish a structural-functional relation between a definite neural territory and a particular psychological and/or behavioral dysfunction, ranging from sensory perception (for example, color vision) to the ability to write or to plan actions.

The description in 1914 by Joseph Babinski (1857–1932) of a curious problem of perception, which he named anosognosia, is particularly pertinent for our discussion.[14] The patient is paralyzed on the left side as a result of a cerebral injury. The doctor asks him: "How do you feel?" "Fine." "How is your left leg?" "Fine." "Can you raise your left arm?" "Of course." And the patient raises his right arm. Not only does the patient not perceive the affected cerebral hemisphere, he denies the very existence of a peripheral problem, showing no emotion, and even accusing the doctor of exaggeration and error. The patient has lost the conscious capacity to integrate half of his body with the conscious perception of his body as a whole, with his image of his own body. He is liable even to attribute to another person the parts of his own body that are paralyzed!

Ricoeur: If I may, let me briefly interrupt here. I do not doubt that the category of material causality is applicable to the relation between the neuronal and the mental in the case of dysfunctions, because here we are dealing with an immediately identifiable relation of causality sine qua non. Things seem to me much less clear, however, in the case of normal function or, as I like to call it, felicitous function. The underlying neuronal activity is silent in a way, and the notion of a causality sine qua non applies more indirectly for lack of a signaling indication by the mental in the direction of the cortical. Whereas, in the case of dysfunctions, I am directly informed of the existence of the underlying bodily function, and the objective knowledge that I have of it becomes part of my practical experience of my body through therapeutic action. In the case of dysfunctions, the "if, then" relation operates in an open and visible way: if I lose my sight I no longer see. From this I conclude by direct inference—or rather I do not conclude, I feel—that I see with my eyes.

Changeux: I wouldn't go so far as to say that I see with my eyes. Instead, I would say that I need my eyes in order to see. One speaks, for example, of the "eye" of a connoisseur of art. But one really ought to speak of his brain, which is to say of his memory of the paintings he has seen and of his ability to judge how a work that he contemplates compares with others that he has committed to memory.

Ricoeur: No, one is right to speak of the connoisseur's eye rather than his brain. On the level of ordinary experience it is acceptable to say "I see with my eyes." But indeed it is much more difficult to say what "with" means when it comes to the cortex. I see with my eyes, because my eyes belong to my bodily experience, whereas my brain does not belong to my bodily experience. It is an object of science. That is to say that the "with" does not function in the same way when I see with my eyes and when I think with my cortex. It is an equivocal "with," I would say. Whereas "to see with my eyes" is an experience of one's own body.

Changeux: Just the same, the case of agnosia is very interesting since it does not come within the framework of your commentary on dysfunctions. In fact the agnosiac *denies* suffering from any problem whatever. Nor is the normal subject aware of the contribution of his cerebral cortex when he thinks. In both cases an external intervention can lead the subject to "objectivize" his perceptual capacities, to overcome failures, perhaps even to function more felicitously. I find Peter Brook's play *The Man Who,* based on the book by the neurologist Oliver Sacks, especially poignant. There is nothing dehumanizing about it. Neurological observation even brings an additional element of humanity.

Anosognosia is triggered by localized lesions of the somatosensory areas of the right hemisphere. By "somatosensory" is meant that which concerns the perception of muscles, of the skeleton, of the skin—the perception that the subject has of his or her own body. In the aftermath of such a lesion one notes a serious disturbance in the subject's image of himself. The perception of the body therefore assumes the integrity of the somatosensory areas. I don't say that this region is the unique seat of the image of the body. But the lesion does introduce a cleavage, which neurologists call "dissociation," within the overall perception of the body as a whole.

The classical conception of phrenology, according to which our cerebral cortex is a mosaic of independent regions, each of which possesses an innate and irreducible psychological faculty, therefore had to be substantially amended. Functional specialization of cortical areas does, of course, exist, as I have already mentioned. But these areas are interconnected with each other in very rich ways. They can group themselves in quite vast, much more global functional ensembles.

Ricoeur: We learn from this that there is a certain relationship between the structure of the brain and the psyche, but it does

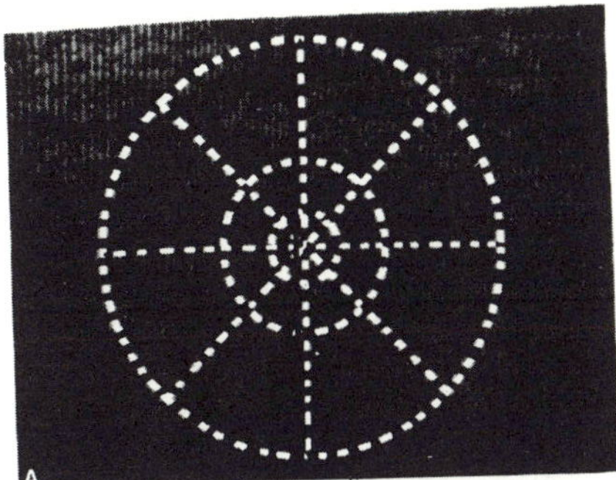

FIGURE 2.4. Homology of form between a geometrical visual stimulus and the state of activity in the primary visual area V1 of the cerebral cortex in the rhesus monkey.

The activity of the cortex is observed by autoradiography. Repeated stimulation of an eye leads to an increase in the activity of the neurons of the visual cortex. The active neurons incorporate a radioactive analogue of glucose, 2-deoxyglucose, which is processed as if it were glucose in order to make up for the loss of energy associated with the increase in activity. After exposure to the stimulus, the brain is soaked in a fixative liquid and the primary visual areas are then dissected and put into contact with a photographic emulsion. The development of the photographic plate reveals black stains that coincide with the distribution of the radioactive neurons. It is remarkable that the radiating structure of the stimulus and its concentric circles are once again found in its neural "representation." From R. B. Tootel, M. S. Silverman, E. Switkes, and R. L. De Valois, "Deoxyglucose analysis of retinoptic organization in primate cortex," *Science* 218 (1982): 902–904.

not tell me what the relationship is. Can this relationship be formulated in a unified discourse? If so, will it be an extension of the discourse of the sciences or, following the example of Descartes's sixth *Meditation,* a third discourse?

Changeux: Let's speak in terms of research that tends toward the integrated discourse we are trying to construct.

Ricoeur: But is our command of this discourse as complete as our command of the discourse that is peculiar to neuroscience?

Changeux: No, of course not, but this is precisely what is at issue. What is at issue is knowledge, progress.

Ricoeur: I share your opinion. But it is a question, too, of interdisciplinarity.

Changeux: Let me mention another aspect of the disturbance of self-image that accompanies certain lesions of the frontal cortex. When the patient is asked to name his hands, his legs, his thorax, he is unable to do so; he can no longer name them.

Ricoeur: But the cortex will never figure in the discourse of one's own body.

Changeux: For an extremely simple reason: there are no sensory endings in the cerebral cortex, whereas there are in the rest of the body. When we have a headache, we do not feel pain in our neurons but rather in the meningeal envelope that protects our brain. One can introduce a scalpel in the brain and remove a piece of the cerebral cortex without the subject feeling pain. Moreover, most surgical operations on the brain are done with the patient awake. Precisely in order to prevent the essential functions of his cerebral cortex, such as the use of speech, from being altered, the surgeon talks with his patient. The surgeon asks the patient to describe what he feels, to pronounce words, to think about something while the operation is taking place. Consciousness occurs in the brain, but we have no conscious perception of our brain!

Ricoeur: I do not understand what it means to say "consciousness occurs in the brain." Consciousness may know itself—or not: this is the whole question of the unconscious—but the brain will forever remain an object of knowledge; it will never belong to the experience of one's own body. The brain does not "think" in the sense that thought conceives of itself. But you, as a neurobiologist, conceive of the brain.

Changeux: Of course—but thought cannot conceive of itself without the brain!

Brain Imaging

Changeux: The brain is an object, but one that commands everything else and that is responsible for both the perception of my body and the production of representations that allow it to be described. Even if I do not perceive my brain, naturally I do conceive of it—I can describe it on the basis of representations that I form in my brain. I even conceive of my brain on the basis of observations that I can make of my own brain no less than that of another person. To consider the question more closely, I come now to the third advance, brain imaging. In the course of recent decades, new observational instruments have literally revolutionized the study of the brain by opening a window on what might be called the physics of the soul. They include positron emission tomography (PET) and functional magnetic resonance imaging (fMRI), as well as new developments in electroencephalography. These methods re-

veal a differential distribution of the electric
activities of cerebral regions that characteristic
the psychology of the subject. It becomes possi
images of the mental states of another person a
first place, one's own mental states.

Ricoeur: You assume here a physical notion of an i
ample as the optical projection of one object u
but to have an image in the sense of imagining, t
thing different—it implies absence, the unreal.
whole phenomenology of the imaginary, develope
and others.

Changeux: The phrase "medical imagery," I grant you,
the word *image* in the sense of a picture book or a

Ricoeur: Somebody reads the picture book.

Changeux: In this case it is the scientist who reads these
in the brain of another person or possibly in his own.
terprets them as an observer in relation to his own brai

Ricoeur: The observer makes a mental operation on a phy
object.

Changeux: The observer records, examines, and interprets
state of activity of populations of nerve cells that are found
the observed subject. Let us ask the subject, for example,
look at a white wall, then a somewhat complex painting, sa
an abstract work by Piet Mondrian or even a landscape o
Claude Lorrain. In the first case, the image will be restricted
principally to the cortical areas to which the optical pathways
directly project back, the primary visual areas; in the other,
secondary areas associated with the primary ones are actively

mobilized. One obtains therefore on the screen of the device a representation of the material states of activity of the brain while the subject is seeing, and one identifies the areas differentially mobilized by the sight of a white wall or a landscape. At this stage, a correspondence is established between a psychological activity and a state of activity of cortical neurons. The projection of a Mondrian-style figure on the primary visual cortex is strikingly similar to the original, although slightly distorted (figure 2.4). It undergoes, to use D'Arcy Thompson's terms, a relatively modest mathematical transformation at this level, but a much more complex one when one goes back up as far as the frontal cortex to the areas of secondary association.

But one can go still further. PET scans provide images of the brain associated with actual or imagined suffering. It even records the pain caused by illusory burns. These are typically static images but still permit us to see "more" than the psychiatrist or psychologist can. Anticipated improvements in the resolution of these techniques in space and time will make it possible to establish still closer correlations with the dynamics of thought and the development of emotional states. Characteristic images of depressive states have been obtained, and, quite recently, hallucinatory states of schizophrenics have been able to be recorded (figure 2.5).

Until now it was possible to conceive of these hallucinations only through a subject's account of them. If we had a PET scan of Theresa of Avila's brain during her mystical ecstasies, we could determine whether or not she had hallucinations and whether or not she was the victim of epileptic fits. Pascal was also the victim of hallucinations. From time to time the entire left part of his visual field was invaded by flames.

Ricoeur: When he said, "Joy, joy, tears of joy!"—that was something entirely different! To use the notion of hallucination in a

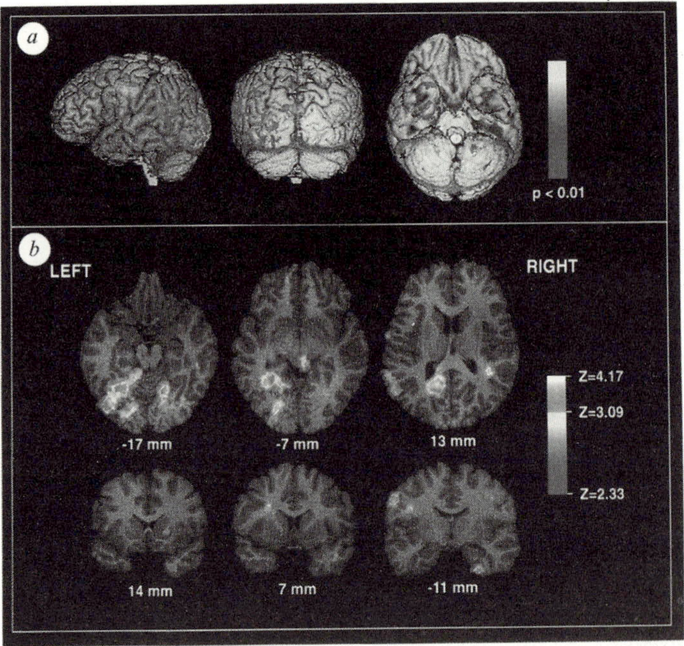

FIGURE 2.5. Functional neuroanatomy of visual and auditory hallucinations in a schizophrenic patient.

The images were obtained using a PET scan to measure cerebral blood flow. The patients, who are relaxed with their eyes closed, press a button when they are stricken by hallucinations. The patient recorded here was a twenty-three-year-old right-handed male who had never undergone pharmacological treatment. He was afflicted with visual hallucinations (seeing bizarre scenes in color in which heads separated from bodies rolled through space) and auditory hallucinations (the isolated heads talked to him and gave him orders). The cerebral images show that the hallucinations are accompanied by activation of areas of visual and auditory/linguistic association as well as of a complex set of subcortical networks. From D. A. Silbersweig, E. Stern, C. Frith, C. Cahil, A. Holmes, S. Groontoonk, J. Seaward, P. McKenna, S. E. Chua, L. Schnorr, T. Jones, and R. S. J. Frackowiak, "A functional neuroanatomy of hallucinations in schizophrenia," *Nature* 378 (1995): 176–179.

categorical way amounts to having a rich neuronal discourse and an impoverished psychological discourse.

Changeux: Except that in the *Mémorial*—found after Pascal's death, sewn into his clothes, containing the famous phrase you mention—the word *Fire* in capital letters appears after a first paragraph that ends with the words "from about 10:30 at night until about 12:30," which can be interpreted as indicating the period during which he had his visions. There follow rather incoherent snatches of text with religious references that recall the symptoms of epilepsy of the temporal lobe described by the late Norman Geschwind.[15] Surely at this moment Pascal experienced a spontaneous evocation of memory traces concerning the religious tradition of his childhood, the intellectual atmosphere of his adolescence, holy scriptures he had meditated upon, rituals he had participated in with great emotion. These memories can be stored in the neighborhood of the temporal lobe or in connection with it, which could explain their recall during the crisis. The content of these memories moves us because it attests to a human experience that the organization of the human brain allows us to preserve in memory.

However this may be, positron emission tomography makes it possible to identify "subjective" hallucinatory states that escape the will, and to distinguish them from the conscious acts of thought that are subject to it.

Ricoeur: What sort of reality do you identify by using the term *states?* One sees, of course, that these are hallucinations and not "conscious acts of thought." But *what,* then, does the hallucinatory mode give access to? Only the statements of the patient seem capable of answering this question—in other words, an account, a fragment of discourse.

Changeux: The fourth advance is due to electrophysiological experimentation. This involves a different experimental approach from imagery, which remains still quite macroscopic, with a resolution of only a few millimeters. Electrophysiology makes it possible to isolate particular states of activity of individual nerve cells, whose size varies between a tenth and a hundredth of a millimeter. It is known that, in the rat or the monkey, when one penetrates a neuron with a very fine microelectrode, whose tip is on the order of a thousandth of a millimeter, it becomes possible to record the electrical activity of this specific cell. If it is found in the primary area of the visual cortex (V1), where the visual pathways issuing from the retina enter the brain, an increase in the frequency of electrical impulses may occur when the animal simply opens its eyes. The result agrees with the images obtained using positron emission tomography. If we now move the electrode to an area located in front of the primary area, called V4, we find that its lesion, in man as in the animal, leads to an alteration of color vision.

At this level, the microelectrode captures several types of activity of individual neurons. Certain cells respond to definite wavelengths of light; they react "primarily," which is to say in direct relation to the physical parameters of the environment registered by the retina. But the British neurophysiologist Semir Zeki discovered other, more sophisticated neurons mixed in with these cells that correspond to color as the subject sees it (figure 2.6). The experiment has been done in parallel in humans and monkeys. It is known that under certain conditions where the composition of light varies, the color that one sees changes little or not at all. We conduct this experiment all the time—when we see that the color of an orange is always orange, for example, whether we observe it in the

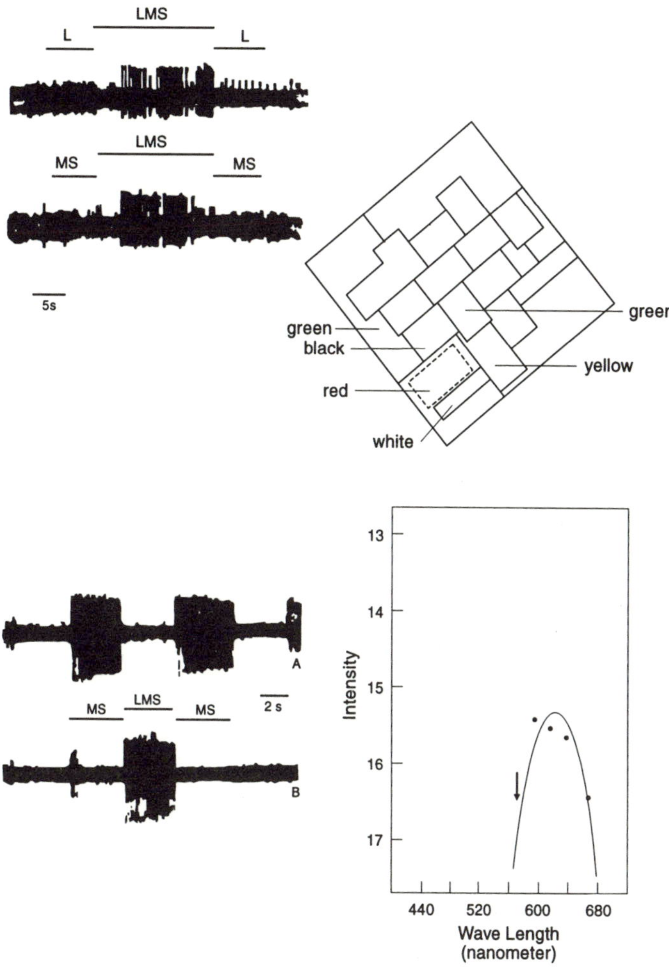

FIGURE 2.6. Color neurons in the visual area V4 of the cerebral cotex of the macaque.

The two recordings shown make it possible to distinguish a cell coded for color (above) from a cell coded for long wavelengths (below). The color neurons correspond here to the red rectangle of a patchwork of colors on the condition that the entire surface of the picture is illuminated by incident light containing all wavelengths (LMS). The cell does not respond here when the scene is lighted ei-

morning when the sun is at the horizon, at noon when the sun is at its zenith, or at night in artificial light. This is the paradox of the constancy of colors, already recognized by Helmholtz in the nineteenth century. A remarkable coincidence is observed between the electrical activity of color neurons and color as the subject sees it. In all conditions in which the subject sees red, for instance, the neurons that correspond to this color are activated. Therefore the brain reconstructs color. It creates, by its state of activity—

Ricoeur:—what we are going to call "color" in mental language.

Changeux: Yes, in the psyche. The methods of the neurosciences here permit a very direct connection to be made between actual mental experience and recorded physiological activity.

Ricoeur: And this is what creates a problem rather than a solution. Can mental experience be "identified" with the observed neuronal activity?

Changeux: For me this poses no problem in principle. In fact, it represents a very important conceptual advance in my field.

Ricoeur: We have only succeeded here in detecting a point of intersection between the neuronal and the mental. The nature and the meaning of this intersection continue to be problematic.

---

ther by long wavelengths (L) or by medium and short wavelengths (MS). The red rectangle is surrounded by white, yellow, and green rectangles that possess a heightened reflectance for medium wavelengths and take part in the "construction" of the perception "red." Specific neuronal responses are obtained at wavelengths between 575 and 675 nm, with the highest intensity of response occurring at 640 nm. From S. Zeki, "The construction of colors by the cerebral cortex," *Proc. Roy. Inst. Great Britain* 56 (1984): 231–258.

Changeux: I would say that it amounts to a major point of contact for the future orientation of the neurosciences, an attempt to put what is subjectively experienced into precise relation with objectively recorded neuronal activities.

Ricoeur: The correspondence you talk of establishing is actually a dual correspondence: on the one hand, within your experimental field, between structure and function; and, on the other, between this whole field and, let us say, the view the subject holds about himself and his body. It is not only the first sort of relationship that poses a problem for me, but also the second one as well.

Changeux: Here the function is precisely established by the subject's own view of his perception of colors!

Chemistry and Mental States

Changeux: The fifth and final advance has been made in chemistry. Our perception of the external world—subjective experience—can in fact be altered by many chemical agents. The best known are the psychotropic drugs—so-called precisely because they act upon the psyche. The most commonly used ones are the benzodiazepines, molecules that constitute the active principle of tranquilizers and sleeping pills. They act to calm the disquiet, anxiety, and depression that assail us unpredictably when events of the external world come to disturb our daily life—mourning, professional failure, family conflicts, unemployment, and so on. In fact, these personal emotions are signals, produced by evaluation systems inside the brain and selected by evolution, that warn the subject of a difficulty needing to be overcome. Similarly, pain—for example, the pain that follows a burn—warns us of the danger of fire; it may itself be chemically removed, not by a tranquilizer but by an analgesic such as aspirin or, when the pain becomes unbearable, morphine. Tranquilizers and analgesics *intervene* in a mode of transmission of signals in the nervous system that employs not electric impulses but the chemical substances called neurotransmitters that I mentioned earlier. Certain neurons in our brain liberate neurotransmitters that have an excitatory effect, as in the case of glutamate: they trigger or facilitate the production of electric impulses in the target neurons; other neurons liberate a neurotransmitter such as gamma-aminobutyric acid (GABA), which reduces—indeed eliminates—excitation, on which account they are called inhibitory. All of them act on specific receptors, specialized molecular "locks" that recognize and translate the chemical signal into an electric signal. The first to have been identified is the acetylcholine receptor, which has also been shown to be associated with nicotine. Hundreds more have been identified since. All of them are macromolecules—the allosteric proteins I described in our previous conversation.

It has been well established for some years now that commonly used tranquilizers—the benzodiazepines, for example—amplify the effect of GABA on its receptor. They facilitate the overall inhibition of cerebral activity by assisting the inhibitor neurotransmitter found in our brain and so producing a "tranquilizing" effect. Similarly, morphine relieves pain by attaching itself to specific receptors of substances—peptides in this case—that are also produced by our brain, enkephalins or endorphins. Morphine takes their place on the receptor, but acts in a more stable and prolonged manner than the endogenous substances. These receptors are themselves distributed among the cells that directly or indirectly participate in the transmission of pain signals and block this transmission. In both cases the transition from a subjective state of anxiety or of physical pain to a more comfortable subjective state of well-being is controlled by a simple chemical agent.

Hallucinations constitute a final and particularly striking case. I have already mentioned that the PET camera allows us to "see" into the brain of the schizophrenic. Hallucinogenic mushrooms, LSD, and mescaline, which provoke visual hallucinations that in general are very colorful, also act on specific receptors of neurotransmitters. One thinks in particular of the receptor for serotonin. Auditory hallucinations—internal voices, usually harmful ones—are one of the diagnostic criteria of schizophrenia. Certain powerful pharmacological agents, such as neuroleptics, make such hallucinations cease in a few hours. The receptors involved belong to the family of receptors of a neurotransmitter to which we shall return: dopamine (see figure 3.6).

The quite spectacular subjective effects of these chemical agents are explained on the basis of the important regulatory function of small groups of neurons whose cell bodies are found at the base of the brain and whose endings are variously distributed throughout quite vast cerebral regions. This makes it possible to "irrigate" extensive ensembles of nerve cells, so to speak, and in this way to chemically regulate conscious states (figure 3.6).

On the basis of these five advances, and of the essential but still fragmentary data they have provided us with, it seems to me that we can try to create and use a common language to put objects of the external world and mental objects of the internal world into correspondence with each other.

Toward a Third Kind of Discourse?

Ricoeur: I apologize for having interrupted you with a series of brief comments that may have broken the thread of your exposition of these five crucial advances in experimental neuroscience. I would like to say, first, how grateful I am that you, a neurobiologist, have not laid emphasis upon computer-based simulation. The argument you make in *Neuronal Man* against the input/output model of the brain seems to me highly instructive for our discussion, for it raises a barrier between machines and living organisms. It is here that I side with Canguilhem, who points out in *La Connaissance de la vie* that living creatures organize their environment, something physical bodies cannot be said to do. Second, I believe that we ought to proceed carefully with regard to this question of the correlation between the neuronal and the mental. I propose that we take as our point of departure what seems to me the primary use of the notion of correlation, namely to refer to a link between organization and function.

Organization characterizes the neuronal base, which itself comprises a variety of levels. Neuroscience traverses these levels in two directions: it follows, on the one hand, a descending course—which may be called reductive in a purely methodological sense of the word, without any definite ontological implication—that ends in the cellular structure of the neurons and their synaptic functioning. In the upward direction, on the other hand, your science takes into account the connections between neurons as well as their hierarchical arrangement, their distribution over cortical areas, and finally those interactions that assure the overall connectivity of the brain; it is in terms of this organizational hierarchy that neuroscience classifies distinct yet interconnected functions. Now these functions are themselves detected in many ways, and their classification is established in accordance with the tacitly accepted codes of scientific practice.

Intimately associated with this neuronal base are three groups of phenomena: first, in the case of deficits, one distinguishes lesions and dysfunctions generally—clinical symptoms; next, behaviors induced by direct stimulation of such-and-such a cortical or cerebral area; finally, chemical interventions, drugs, and so on, to which you were referring just now. It seems to me that there is already a great deal to be said here with regard to the conditions of observation, which are so far removed from what goes on in an unregulated situation, where it is not the experimenter but the subject who has mastery and control of the environment, who chooses signals that are meaningful for him and, on this basis, constructs his own environment.

Organization and function jointly occupy a place that may be called foundational in a sense of the word that later in our discussions will prove to be charged with considerable critical consequence, particularly when we come to tackle the question of the biological foundations of ethics. For the moment let me emphasize that I understand the term *foundational* or *fundamental* in the sense of a seat, a basis or support, leaving open the ontological question of the brain's ultimate causality. Considered strictly at the level of neuronal investigation, these twin concepts, organization and function, seem to me to fully authorize the use of the term *support* or *substrate.* Thus organization may be said to be the substrate of function, and function the sign of organization.

Things seem to me less clear, however, when under the head of function you introduce elements that come within the purview of related sciences such as experimental psychology, ethology, or comparative biology with its evolutionary perspective. A whole series of phenomena thus comes to be placed under the term *function* that makes neuroscience a constellation of sciences rather than a single science. I think therefore that we need to restrict ourselves to the primary sense of correlation as a link between organization and function, and to concern ourselves with the question of clinical or laboratory observation.

Changeux: Yes, and this raises a difficult question having to do with the relation between the observer and the observed subject. The observer, taking advantage of the latest technological methods for observing the brain—imaging, electrophysiological recording, the action of drugs, various other techniques—develops structural data about the subject that he will be able to relate to the subject's "experience" such as this is described by the subject. But the observer is himself liable to have the same experience as the subject, a different experience, or a similar experience to which he will also be able to refer. In his joint capacity as observer-observed, he will be able to produce mental states that will allow him first to observe, and then to interpret, the mental states of another person.

Ricoeur: In a phenomenological reading of this situation, the subject is aware of having an object in front of him. By contrast, in a scientific reading, the subject also becomes one of the objects: he enters into an object-object relation; but in this objectivized situation, you have suspended the subject-object, an intentional relation that does not come within the view of neuroscience.

Changeux: It seems to me that it certainly does. Indeed, I think that a naturalization of intentions can be attempted.

Ricoeur: This is the whole problem: it seems to me that to carry out this program you have to borrow correlations from sciences adjacent to neurobiology in the strict sense, sciences that you group together under the aegis of neuroscience in the plural—the neurosciences. The observer you describe resorts to experimental psychology in order to observe human behavior under experimental conditions that he controls. On the other hand, owing to ethical obstacles, human experimentation is limited; experimentation is therefore principally done on animals, the results of which are then extrapolated on the basis of carefully tested criteria. Under these circumstances, critical reflection ought to be brought to bear upon the discrepancy between the artificial conditions of laboratory research and the physical and social environment in which human beings ordinarily find themselves. The correlation between neuroscience and the world of experience becomes problematic.

We cross another still more problematic boundary when we come to the cognitive sciences, which construct formalizations and consider symbolic systems—chiefly linguistic systems—as their primary frame of reference. My position here will consist in moving away from formal approaches of this type in the direction of actual experience, which itself rests on an exchange of intentions and meanings. And this reply, which is what sets phenomenology apart from the cognitive sciences, leads me to turn the question around: can intentions in fact be naturalized?

Changeux: This is one of the problems already posed by Comte, which gave rise to a very lively debate. The naturalist theory, so important in traditional positivism, has been revived by the possibility of examining psychological facts as physical facts, and therefore of introducing the method of the experimental sciences in psychology. What I propose to attempt is a naturalization of intentions that takes into account *both* the internal physical states of our brain *and* its opening to the world with reciprocal exchanges of meanings, exchanges of representations oriented as much toward perception as to action. Today, at least in the few cases I have presented, I think that observational methods make it possible to obtain physical facts about subjective psychological states. A physics of introspection may even be possible. Are we in agreement on this point?

Ricoeur: In humans a function is not reducible to an observable behavior. It also—and often mainly—involves verbal reports or accounts. These accounts concern what the observed subject feels, which is to say sensory phenomena, whether motor or affective, that the scientist labels mental states or events. A verbal, declarative component is immediately included in the protocols of experience. The experimenter cannot avoid attaching credit to these reports, even though he may seek to control them by reference to others, as in the case of memory and its train of false recollections. But no matter how careful an experimenter may be, he will still need to have recourse to other verbal reports to develop his analysis. When he attempts to establish a correlation between neuronal—or, more broadly, cerebral, humoral, or corporeal—structures and a mental function, he will have to consult ordinary experience.

Ordinary experience does not exactly coincide with what scientists include under the term *introspection*. Language forces us to escape private subjectivity. It is an exchange that rests on several assumptions: first, the certainty that others think as I do, see and hear as I do, act and suffer as I do; next, the certainty that these subjective experiences are at once unsubstitutable (that is, you cannot put yourself in my place) and communicable ("Please—try to understand me!"). One may speak intelligibly of having comparable impressions while watching a sunset, for example. There is indeed such a thing as mutual, even shared, comprehension. This sort of comprehension is, of course, open to doubt. Misunderstanding is not only possible, it is the daily bread of conversation; but it is precisely the function of conversation to correct misunderstanding as far as possible, and to seek the *Einverständnis* of which Gadamer and the partisans of hermeneutics speak. There is a hermeneutics of daily life that gives introspection the dimension of an interpersonal practice. Here we are far from introspection in Comte's sense. What is usually called introspection is only an abstract moment of this interpersonal practice. And even in its most internalized form it still consists, to recall

Plato's expression, in a dialogue that the soul holds with itself. This is what I find expressed in the phrase *for intérieur*, one's heart of hearts—literally, a "forum" in which one speaks to oneself. This heart of hearts has its own particular status that it would appear you will never succeed in explaining in your science. And so my answer to your question is no.

Changeux: Why do you say "never"? I cannot imagine any scientist saying, "I will never succeed in understanding." My hope is that we will be able to discuss plausible models of self-regulation; to discuss testing the internal consistency of plans of action, even where the action contemplated remains "virtual." Nonetheless, I share your interest in the concept of ordinary experience and interpersonal practice, of continuous and reciprocal causation in the organization of our cerebral productions. By way of example, neurobiologists are interested in the false memories that ordinary conversation, the media, and the false views of revisionist historians are apt to put into our heads without our knowing it.[16] It is now possible to critically examine the way our heart of hearts functions and to inquire into its private deliberations. A self as vacillating as ours demands more careful examination.

Ricoeur: I do not at all exclude the possibility of progress in scientific knowledge of the brain, but I wonder about our understanding of the relationship between such knowledge and actual experience. At this stage of our debate, I would say that we can understand either a mental discourse or a neuronal discourse, but that their *relation* to each other remains a problem because we have not managed to locate the link between the two within one or the other. We find it enormously difficult to devise an alternative, a third discourse.

3 — The Neuronal Model and the Test of Experience

The Simple and the Complex: Questions of Method

Jean-Pierre Changeux: I would like to propose to you a model of mental objects that I think makes it possible to establish, although still only hypothetically, an objective relationship between the psychological and the neuronal with a view to submitting it to the verdict of experience. The observer who uses the devices I have mentioned to describe and interpret the mental states of the observed subject brings together facts, constructs a model, and then tests the model. This is my approach as well.

Paul Ricoeur: And it is entirely coherent within its own field.

Changeux: The observer tries to relate three great domains: neuronal networks, the activities that occur in such networks, and finally attitudes and behaviors, which is to say internal mental states and reasoning strategies as well as plans of action. In fact, this method is not noticeably different than the one followed by Descartes in the *Treatise on Man*. In addition it incorporates a projective relation between the external world and extremely complex neural architectures.

Ricoeur: You continue to operate within the framework of a correlation between organization and function, and therefore well within the bounds of a consistent discourse.

Changeux: The attitudes studied may be explicit attitudes toward the world but also implicit mental states that are not immediately manifested by acting upon the world. One of the great advances of the neurosciences has been to provide access to what is not necessarily manifested by external behavior. Where until recently one used words such as *perceived, conceived,* or *experienced,* one may now speak of a mental state in physical terms. In a way the project consists in establishing what might be called a neurobiology of meaning, a physics of the representations produced by our brain as these concern sensory perception, action upon the world, or any intimate state oriented toward oneself or toward the world.

Ricoeur: I am grateful to you for all this because you have dramatized the problem in introducing the mental dimension neglected by other neurobiologists, and so made it still more difficult to solve the problem posed by the relationship between the neuronal—or what I call, for lack of a better term, the neuronal "substrate"—and the mental. But you are dealing only with a psyche found in the psychology laboratory, which may not be the rich psyche of integral experience. Being in the world is first experienced globally. One then proceeds from the global to the particular, whereas the legitimate scientific approach will always be to pass from the simple to the complex: in this respect, there is no isomorphism or term-by-term correspondence between the two planes of experience.

For purposes of analyzing the notion of a mental object, I situate myself not on your plane, of course, but on the phenomenological plane. I believe that what you do in the scientific field you do well, and I have no comment to make about the construction of your neuronal model.

Changeux: The scientific approach is not reducible to the passage from the simple to the complex. The biologist, and in the particular the neurobiologist, who is interested in the higher functions of the brain, likewise tries to move from the complex to the simple—to separate, to isolate, to break down certain complex psychological functions in order to establish a correspondence having some measure of verisimilitude, on the level of causality, between the neuronal and the psychological. The difficulty is enormous when one moves from an apparently indivisible whole, what you call integral experience. This is the problem that neurobiologists currently are facing with consciousness. Consciousness is so all-encompassing a psychological function that deciphering its functional architectures is very hard. Nonetheless researchers are trying to define its regular features, without losing sight of the overall context in which it fits.

Ricoeur: Earlier I wondered whether the mental aspect of your notion of mental objects may not itself be the construct of a particular science, namely psychology, and whether subjective experience does not have rules of comprehension, of interpretation, that resist the functional reduction that allows you to work within the legitimate limits of the correlation between organization and function. In my opinion, the psyche you associate with a neuronal world that is legitimately constructed is itself very much a construct, because the main rule of your science is to develop neuronal architecture on the basis of neurons and synapses. You proceed from the simple to the complex, but the mental world you correlate with the neuronal substrate is very, very simplified—rightly so, perhaps, since this is what enables you to establish the correlation with the neuronal architecture.

Changeux: It is true that science proceeds by devising models that divide up the world into levels of organization, into a few main categories that permit us to penetrate a neuronal and synaptic jungle of staggering complexity. These models don't claim to exhaust all the world's reality! The ambition of the neurobiologist is very limited. The object that he studies is much too complex to be grasped in its totality. To the contrary, he tries through experimentation to isolate a particular function, within a larger ensemble of functions that is difficult to analyze as a whole. While I feel altogether capable of living the "integral experience" of which you speak, this experience does not hold much interest for me at this stage of my career as a neurobiologist. In my spare time I am free to discuss it in philosophical terms; but I am keenly aware of the immense task that remains to be accomplished if we are to succeed in describing it in terms acceptable to the scientific community. In sum, the approach is obviously reductive—but it cannot be otherwise.

Ricoeur: I don't employ the word *reduction* in a pejorative way.

Changeux: It seems to me that one can only proceed by reduction.

Ricoeur: My question really has to do with whether one can model subjective experience in the same way one can model experience in the experimental sense. Can the comprehension that I have of my place in the world, of myself, of my body and of other bodies be modeled without doing damage to it—epistemological damage that entails a loss of meaning?

Modeling serves a genuinely constructive purpose in your field, as it does in the quite heavily constructed field of experimental psychology. But my problem is that psychology seems already to find itself in an ambiguous position by comparison with the incredible richness of subjective experience. Later, when we take up the relationship between the neurosciences and morality, we will consider the biological predispositions to moral behavior. But this lived biology, as it were, will not necessarily be biology in your sense; to say nothing of the spiritual dimensions of experience as a whole. Although modeling is altogether constructive in the domain of scientific knowledge, I wonder if it doesn't have the effect of impoverishing our understanding of the psyche.

Changeux: The scientific approach imposes restraint, caution, and humility; it cannot aim at explaining the whole of the brain's operation at once. I try to explain things step by step, gradually drawing nearer to objective knowledge. Even so I am surprised by your suggestion that modeling is an impoverishing enterprise that causes "epistemological damage" and leads to a "loss of meaning." Indeed, I often quote Paul Ricoeur—"Explain more in order to better understand," as you say—in connection with the human sciences. A model always remains partial, but it points the way to progress in knowledge. What we may expect to gain is considerable by comparison with what might be lost. Why introduce any a priori limitation in the field of neurobiological investigation? What freedom—what joy to be able to sail into the unknown, against its winds and its tides, without regard for prevailing ideologies and systems of thought!

I know, of course, that I won't succeed at once in accounting for the "total experience" that I feel when I look, for example, at the *Bacchus and Ariane* in the museum at Orleans, or listen to Fauré's *Requiem.* (Fauré, by the way, was not a believer.) But what I know about my cerebral functions will not in the least impoverish my understanding of this mental experience. To the contrary. These explanations, as fragmentary as they may be, allow us to see that the "spiritual dimension" of our nature owes nothing to any oppressive or stifling supernatural force. I feel so free! The freedom I feel as a scientist is Spinoza's "free joy," the desire that is realized in aesthetic pleasure—

Ricoeur: I introduce no a priori limitation in the field of your investigations. Far from it! I maintain only that, away from your laboratory, you share with everyone else an experience that lively and immense. You say so yourself, invoking the Le Nain brothers and Fauré. As for joy, the free joy of Spinoza, this comes under another head than that of modeling/refutation: it is a third kind of knowledge. Such joy, I take it, is what inspires the scientist's gradual and open approach as well as our present discussion. With regard to your "march toward the unknown," I have no epistemological hesitation. Much more than this, I very particularly appreciate the contribution neuroscience makes to our debate when it introduces, beyond the genetic composition of functions, the "epigenetic" development of the brain, thus making individual histories of development possible. But that doesn't mean that any advance will have been made in understanding the link between this underlying epigenetic development and the individual history of the human subject. I have no quarrel with you either about the modesty of the project of modeling or about the daring and the courage required to keep on pushing it forward. Indeed, I value this combination of modesty and extreme ambition. But I am not sure that we will have advanced in the understanding of the relationship that concerns us here between neuronal support and human experience considered as an integral whole—let us say, of the relationship to oneself, to others, and to the world.

The Human Brain: Complexity, Hierarchy, Spontaneity

Changeux: Perhaps it would be more prudent to wait until we have examined additional evidence before drawing conclusions. In fact, the model of mental objects cannot be addressed

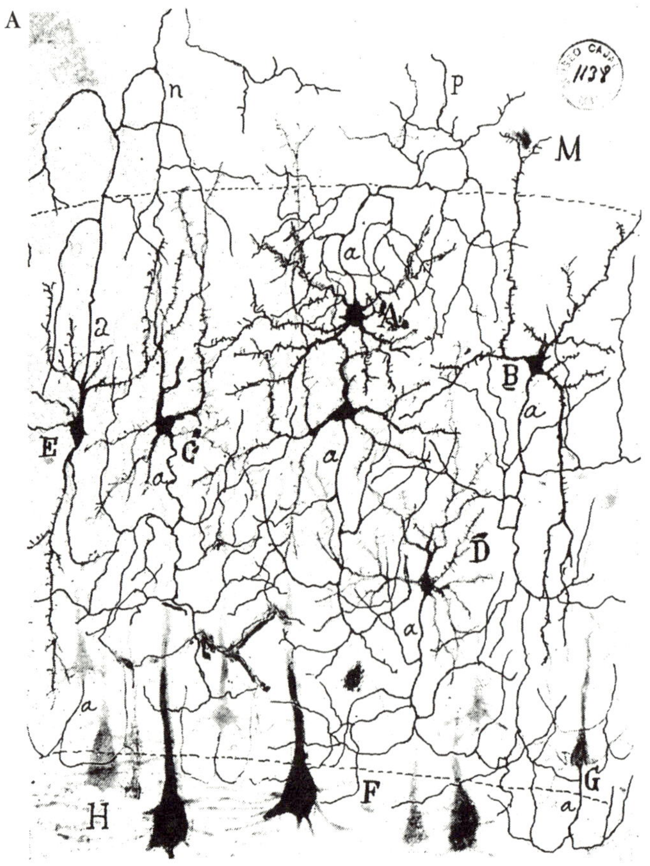

FIGURE 3.1. Neuron, synapse, and neurotransmitter receptor.

A. Original drawing by the celebrated Spanish anatomist S. Ramón y Cajal of different categories of neurons of the visual cortex. Pictured in grey are the bodies of pyramidal cells and in black several categories of neurons with short axons. The dimensions of the nerve cell bodies vary from ten millionths of a meter to some hundreds of millionths. On average, each of the roughly one hundred billion neurons in our brain establishes ten thousand synaptic connections with its many counterparts. (Ramón y Cajal Foundation, Madrid.)

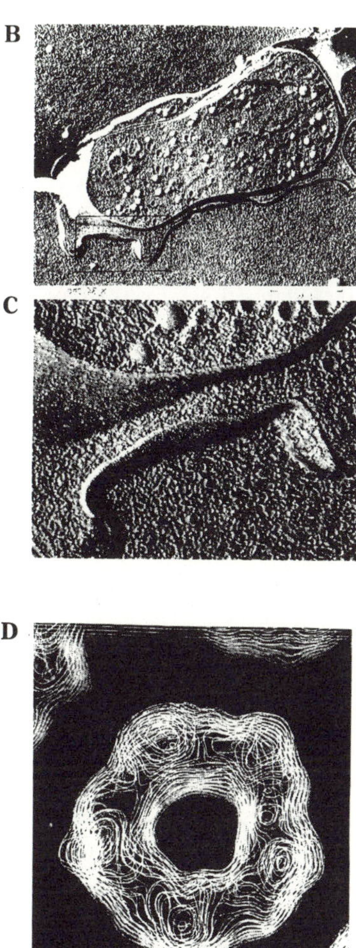

B. and C. Electron microscope image of a very simple synapse between the electric nerve of a torpedo fish (*Torpedo marmorata*) and a cell of its electric organ. The size of the synapse is on the order of a millionth of a meter, approximately the same size as a bacterium. In the nerve endings can be seen the vesicles that stock the neurotransmitter. With the arrival of the nerve influx, the neurotransmitter is released into the synaptic cleft, clearly visible in figure C. It then

without taking into account a number of very important considerations. The first thing needing to be taken into account is the brain's *complexity*. Until recently, no one imagined that our brain might be as complex as the discoveries of modern neuroscience have revealed it to be. As you know, our nervous system is composed of discrete cellular entities, neurons, that form a discontinuous network. These neurons can communicate only by means of synapses (figure 3.1). The notion of discontinuity, as Santiago Ramón y Cajal had conceived it, was combated at the end of the nineteenth century and at the beginning of the present century by dualists who saw it as an obstacle to the notion of disembodied spirit. Several nineteenth-century neurobiologists, including Golgi, believed that a continuous nerve network allowed the soul to function more freely.

In our brain, then, there are one hundred billion neurons, each neuron having on average about ten thousand discontinuous contacts—on the order of 10^{15} contacts in all, about a half-billion per cubic millimeter! This complexity isn't sufficiently appreciated because it cannot be seen with the naked eye while examining the brain; it is microscopic and can be seen only with an electron microscope. Each synapse is about the size of a bacterium. Our understanding of the brain's func-

---

diffuses in this space until finally attaching itself to the membrane of the adjacent cell at the level of the neurotransmitter receptor molecules, whose alignments can be discerned here. (Photograph courtesy of Jean Cartaud.)

D. Molecule of the acetylcholine receptor, a neurotransmitter at the nerve-muscle junction. The maximum diameter is on the order of nine billionths of a meter. The molecule is composed of five subunits, recognizable in this picture. In the brain, very similar molecules also serve as receptors for acetylcholine and for a very heavily used drug, nicotine. (Photograph courtesy of Nigel Unwin.)

tional organization is obtained through the anatomical study of the connections established among individual nerve cells. This universe is extraordinarily rich. What is more, it is not exactly the same from one individual to another, even in the case of identical twins. Exploring this forest of synapses is an endless source of delight for the neurobiologist, but also a cause for despair since the number of possible combinations among all these synapses, assuming them to be of equal weight, is of the same order of magnitude as the number of positively charged particles in the universe. The limits of this combinatoric are expanded still further when the functional flexibility of the connections is taken into account. Stravinsky's brain was able to produce *Le Sacre du Printemps;* Michelangelo's the ceiling of the Sistine Chapel. One therefore has also to understand the rules of organization that such creations brought into play.

Ricoeur: I don't doubt for a moment that when Stravinsky wrote *Le Sacre du Printemps* something went on in his brain. I have never believed that thought functions without a physical basis. The question is determining the relation between the beauty of works of art and the incredible complexity you describe. Even if this complexity were to be enlarged much further than anyone might imagine possible, we would still be going about the matter the wrong way round. My objection has nothing to do with the fact that organization and function are correlated. But to be able to establish such a correlation, appeal has to be made—as I have already said—to a very artificial mental world in relation to a very artificial neurophysiological world. There is no alternative but to construct the neurophysiological; but the construction of the mental that you presuppose proceeds by dismantling and impoverishing human experience, since this is the only way such experience can be constituted as an object of scientific study and thereby correlated

A

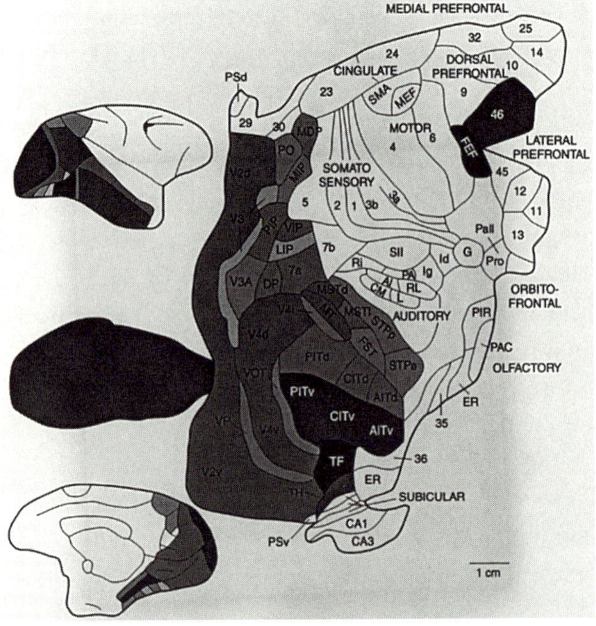
MEDIAL PREFRONTAL
25
32
14
24
10
DORSAL PREFRONTAL
CINGULATE
PSd
23
SMA
MEF
9
46
29
30
MDP
MOTOR
6
4
FEF
LATERAL PREFRONTAL
PO
V2d
MIP
SOMATO SENSORY
45
12
5
2
1
3b
3a
11
V3
PIP
VIP
Pall
13
LIP
7b
SII
Id
G
Pro
Ri
Ig
PA
AI
RL
CM
L
7a
V3A
DP
MSTd
ORBITO-FRONTAL
V4t
MT
MSTl
STPp
AUDITORY
PIR
V4d
FST
PITd
PAC
OLFACTORY
STPa
VOT
CITd
PITv
AITd
ER
CITv
AITv
35
VP
V4v
TF
36
V2v
ER
TH
SUBICULAR
CA1
PSv
CA3
1 cm

B

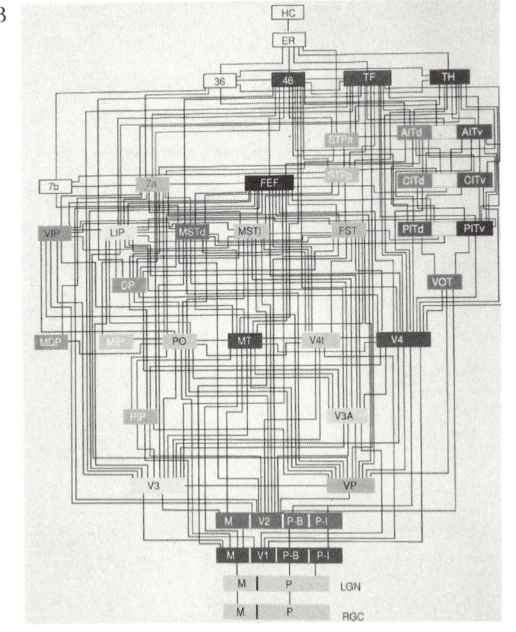
HC
ER
36
46
TF
TH
STPa
AITd
AITv
7b
7a
FEF
STPp
CITd
CITv
VIP
LIP
MSTd
MSTl
FST
PITd
PITv
DP
VOT
MDP
MIP
PO
MT
V4t
V4
PIP
V3A
V3
VP
M
V2
P-B
P-I
M
V1
P-B
P-I
M
P
LGN
M
P
RGC

FIGURE 3.2.

with the neurophysiological. There is nothing wrong with proceeding in this way—it is the way of science; but one must be aware of what one is doing in constructing the mental side of the correlation.

Changeux: We construct the psychological in order to make it into the neuropsychological. Simplifying and critically examining something isn't the same as "dismantling" it. To the contrary, the gain in knowledge is immense; and in doing so we enrich the human experience that we have of ourselves.

Ricoeur: All right. I'll wait to express my reservations about the construction of the psychological until you have finished your exposition of mental objects.

Changeux: The second notion that seems to me necessary to keep in mind before we consider the model of mental objects is the crucial importance of neural architecture: it defines the "capacities" of our brain to produce mental objects. There exists an important element of randomness in the network of connections established in our brain. We owe it to the way in which our brain is constructed, through a process of internal selection. Nonetheless, in its broad outlines, the human brain

---

FIGURE 3.2. Hierarchical and parallel organization of the visual system.

A. Projection of the cerebral cortex of the right hemisphere; the areas involved in the processing of visual information are in gray.

B. Schematic representation of the visual areas and their connections in the macaque, or rhesus monkey, from the retina (RGC), the lateral geniculate body of the thalamus (LGN), and the visual areas (V1, V2, . . .) to the frontal cortex (HC).

From D. J. Felleman and D. C. Van Essen, "Distributed hierarchical processing in the primate cerebral cortex," *Cerebral Cortex* 1 (1991): 1–47.

is quite similar from one individual to another. It follows a constant plan of organization such that one can tell the brain of a chimpanzee from a human brain without any hesitation. This plan is determined by an "envelope" of genes that underwrite, as it were, the universal nature of the human brain. This architecture is still far from being fully understood. One of the most important problems facing the neurosciences today consists in defining cerebral architecture in terms of its invariant features and, with respect to its variable features, the limits of such variability across individuals, and in defining its functions (figure 3.2). For it is the architecture and the functional predispositions associated with it that allow representations to be formed and mental objects to be constructed. It is also necessary to take into account here the two leading principles of the architecture of the brain, parallelism and hierarchy. First, parallelism: our brain is capable of simultaneously analyzing signals from the physical or social environment via several parallel pathways. Thus, in the case of vision, the visual pathways analyze form, color, and movement in parallel. These characteristic features of an object are first separated and later synthesized. The architecture of the visual system is organized by means of a multitude of parallel pathways that, together with auditory, olfactory, and other pathways, permit the brain to analyze the world and to make a global synthesis of it.

The other principle of cerebral architecture is hierarchical organization into levels of integration, which go from the molecular to the cellular, from the cellular to the neuronal, and so on. Van Essen in the United States and Zeki in Great Britain have analyzed these levels of organization in great detail in the case of vision. They distinguish fourteen such levels in the monkey, from the retina to the frontal cortex. The architecture of the brain is therefore at once parallel and hierarchical, on account of which analysis and synthesis occur concomitantly.

guage, with its hierarchy of "codes," ranging from the phonetic to the stylistic, as you rightly point out. Still we have to be careful not to countenance any shifts or confusions of meaning with regard to a single word, as sometimes happens in the human sciences. Here one thinks of terms like "mind," "form," and "nature." Philosophers do not even agree about the definition of "philosophy," for that matter.

Ricoeur: I quite understand that the object of the cognitive neurosciences is to establish a pertinent correspondence between structure and function. But you yourself grant that shifts and confusions of meaning may occur the further one moves away from elementary functions. In the case of psychological functions involving language, I wonder whether the correlation between structure and function isn't being stretched a bit too far. The difficulty that you have in situating yourself in relation to the cognitive sciences suggests that it is. These sciences require much more than simply taking into account the behavioral inventiveness that an epigenetic conception of the brain accompanies and underlies. With the cognitive sciences one sees, in fact, the emergence of a specific vocabulary, governed by a prior agreement about what counts as a scientific object, what counts as the ultimate referent in this field. The cognitive sciences do not lead on to the symbolic, lexical, and syntactic activities of language; these activities are their point of departure. Experience is held to be linguistic by definition. More precisely, the strictest practitioners of these sciences regard cognitive functions as objectively describable in propositional terms. Thus desires and beliefs—to which I would readily add the feelings on which the norms of social and ethical life are built—can be treated as "propositional attitudes" of the form *to believe that, to desire that, to feel that,* and so on. This prior taking into account of language plays a decisive role in the case of memory, for example. Is there a memory

Ricoeur: I understand very well that these levels of integration underlie neuronal architectures, but the question is whether the psyche conforms to such a hierarchical and parallel model. Is there an isomorphism, term by term, between the neuronal and the mental?

Changeux: From my point of view, it is here that the epistemological problem resides.

Ricoeur: This will help us to identify more precisely where a third discourse will come into play.

Changeux: We are trying to create a pertinent and causal correspondence between a particular psychological function and a definite neural structure. The determination of function by structure can only be usefully done if one aims at a level of organization that is adequate to the function. And, as I said in the case of vision, one can go first from the simple analysis of the external world to more complex perceptual functions that involve the subject's personal experience. At the level of the primary sensory areas in the brain, representations resemble external forms; they are isomorphic with these forms. Then, as one rises through the hierarchy, they become progressively more "abstract," increasingly able through the use of language to isolate specific as well as general features; in other words, they form concepts. Other more integrated functions bring into play higher levels of organization, including the prefrontal cortex for the planning of behavior, which is to say intentionality.

Ricoeur: The structure/function relation operates directly in the pure discourse of neuroscience, but more indirectly, for example, at the level of language activities. When I speak I implement a variety of codes: a phonetic code, a lexical code, a syntactic code, and what might be called a stylistic code. But to speak is also to produce a sentence with the intention of saying something about something to someone else.

Changeux: Yes, it needs to be kept in mind that the meaning of the word *structure* as it is employed by structuralists and anthropologists is not to be confused with the meaning I give this term.

Ricoeur: This fits in exactly with my objection bearing on the absence of isomorphism between neuronal hierarchies and corresponding mental hierarchies. How can a unified discourse be created if "structure" and "function" do not designate homologous realities within it? Let's take another example, which I have already mentioned—the notion of capacity. The word *capacity* means "I am capable of," which is to say "I can do something," where I am the one who feels the availability and limits of these powers—*I* can take, *I* can touch, and so on. But the same word will have an entirely functional meaning in the vocabulary of the neurosciences that does not assume that anyone feels this capacity.

What is the relationship between capacity as part of the functional nervous system and the capacity that I feel—*I can, I can't*—and that belongs to my way of being in the world, in my own body, surrounded by bodies that similarly belong to other persons? What is the relationship between a reflective discourse and the notion of "capacity," as you use the term in neuroscience? Mind you, I do not change the subject by changing the example. For structures, on the linguistic plane, become operational only as part of the activity of language, in the form of speech acts, which involve capacities of a remarkable type—the capacity to speak, to produce sentences. This shows how great a discrepancy there is between the use of an expression such as "hierarchical structure" in the two

kinds of discourse, depending how far one is ren elementary functions.

Changeux: I use the word *structure* in the sense of s phological organizations constituted by neurons and nections, in which electrical and chemical impulses I contrast it with *dynamic* acts and operations—proce tivities, and, of course, behaviors. Psychological funct to cerebral organization what, at a lower level, the cata tivity of an enzyme is to the sequence of its amino aci term *psychological function* has been employed by Meyerson[1] and other psychologists who consider the ol their discipline to be a set of functions that express them through a behavior. The object of the cognitive neurosci is precisely this, to establish a pertinent corresponden tween structure and function at one or more defined leve organization. You point out, very aptly, that the word *ca ity* possesses two quite distinct meanings that must not be c fused. One speaks of capacities to distinguish colors, to r or to write; in other words, we dispose of a cerebral orga zation that allows us to do these things. In the field of ethi "capacity" takes on a much more general sense. It includes tl availability of knowledge and means of action, the variou ways of carrying out an intention. In this context, capacity involves high-level functions that depend particularly on the frontal cortex. Believe me, I have no desire to be a prisoner of the closed neuronal world in which you seem to want to lock me up. My purpose is not to go to war against phenomenology; to the contrary, I want to see what constructive contribution it can make to our knowledge of the psyche, acting in concert with the neurosciences. Indeed this is one of the most active fields of research in perception and behavior (with the work of Berthoz and Jeannerod) as well as in certain areas of contemporary philosophy.[2] In philosophy this includes lan-

worthy of the name that comes before the declarative memory that tells a subject that he remembers this or that? Here, it seems to me, we encounter a crisis within the group of sciences to which neuroscience belongs and to which phenomenology stands opposed.

Changeux: Let me reassure you that I have no difficulty whatever in situating myself with respect to the cognitive sciences. To the contrary, I have always favored close collaboration between experimental psychology, the neurosciences, linguistics, computer science, *and* philosophy.[3] For a number of years now I have collaborated with Stanislas Dehaene, a cognitive psychologist by training, in trying to model cognitive tasks. The contribution of the cognitive sciences, most particularly that of cognitive psychology, seems to me undeniable. The introduction of new concepts, and therefore of a new terminology, based on linguistic activities does not run counter to my approach—quite the opposite. The better we understand psychological functions in detail, linguistic functions in particular, the better the fit will be with the neurobiological approach.

Ricoeur: But this is an interdisciplinary enterprise—an attempt to fit together sciences having different points of reference; it does not take place within a given discipline.

Changeux: I agree, and I try to put this perspective into practice.

The third preliminary notion to which I would like to call attention, along with complexity and architecture, concerns the notion of spontaneous activity. Our nervous system is not active only when it is stimulated by sensory organs. We have seen that the brain functions in a projective mode. It is the permanent seat of important internal activities—when one thinks, when one plans a movement, when one hears, perceives, imagines, or creates. These sorts of activity occur when we are awake, but also while we are asleep. They play a fundamental role in the sense that they serve as the basic material for constructing, elaborating, and organizing the representations that will be projected onto the world, thereby making it possible to anticipate the future—to anticipate events that will take place in both the external and internal world. They assure what Merleau-Ponty called the "meshing of my experiences with those of others."[4] These spontaneous activities are manifested already with nerve cells in vitro. A few molecular switches controlling the transfer of ions across the cell membrane suffice. One finds such switches in the "microbrains" of molluscs and insects. They are abundantly present in the brains of vertebrates. But spontaneous activities have not been sufficiently studied by physiologists; nor have psychologists—with a few notable exceptions—taken them into account in their own research.

Ricoeur: Your last remark concerning psychologists interests me enormously. The anticipation of future events has been the object of very interesting research on the part of phenomenologists influenced by Husserl's unpublished manuscripts, which Merleau-Ponty was one of the first to explore. It is not without relevance for our discussion that these explorations bear upon action rather than upon the purely sensory reception of information coming from the environment. I emphasize action, and not only bodily movement, too long considered as a reaction to stimulation issuing from a fixed environment known in advance by the observer. By the term *action* phenomenologists mean the mental schemas that govern motor intentions, which in the final analysis regulate motor commands, observable in the form of bodily movements. These mental schemas are experienced by the subject as basic abilities; that is, as capacities for intervention, which become available once one has learned new physical movements, new maneuvers in the practical sphere. Here one encounters Merleau-Ponty's notion of the *I can*. What the phenomenologist objects to is the primacy assigned to the environment, which the experimentalist considers as a world wholly made up of things from which messages emanate and to which replies are given. It is necessary to step back from the laboratory situation, where experiment assumes an already constituted reality, and take into consideration the role played by the agent himself in building his environment, as Jean-Luc Petit has shown.[5] The human agent does not content himself with being informed about his environment in order possibly to modify it afterward; from the beginning he interprets it and shapes it, or better—to use Husserl's strong formulation, in the last unpublished writings—he constitutes it as the world that surrounds him by projecting onto it the aims of his action and his demands for meaning. This phenomenology of action, in its prelinguistic and (in this sense) preintellectual stage, points in the same direction, it seems to me, as the recourse of the neurosciences to notions such as "choice," "hypothesis," "wager," "prediction," "forecast," and so on. You yourself have just mentioned spontaneous activity. But doesn't this borrow exactly from a psychology that, as you say, remains to be worked out but that, in my view, is to be found in embryonic form in the phenomenology of action, operating at a prelinguistic level?

One can discern, I think, the outlines of a synergistic program allying the phenomenology of behavior with the construction of neuronal models. Phenomenology is in its infancy, it is true, but it seems to me to have an advantage over the neurosciences, which rely on metaphysical anthropomorphisms. In their current usage, words such as *anticipation, choice, wager* derive from the psychology of higher mental operations on the linguistic and volitional level—the level on which the cognitive sciences successfully operate. Phenomenology therefore has had to operate at a level below these higher-level operations; to give bodily intentions their place alongside desire and belief, on which the cognitive sciences concentrate, in order to be in a position to establish a suitable relationship with the neurosciences, which in this respect seem to me to be at a stage that is more programmatic than experimental. The price to be paid, on both sides, for such an extension of the correlation between organization and function is an abandonment of the primacy of representation in mental activity; paradoxically, this primacy seems to me a residue of Cartesian dualism, transposed to the neuronal field. The world is not wholly made before the brain projects upon it, as you say, the representations that it has organized. What really has to be considered is the pragmatic constitution of what Husserl called the life-world (*Lebenswelt*) rather than the projections of the brain upon a world supposed already to have been organized. In this sense, the object constructed by psychologists around the idea of representation is impoverished by comparison with integral experience. But this experience accords a major place to anticipation. Anticipation is a characteristic of shared experience.

Changeux: I think that we are speaking the same language with regard to several points, despite our different points of departure. We both reject the input-output model of cerebral function common to cybernetics and information theory. This mode of analysis is still found in some neurophysiology laboratories, which record nervous responses when the animal, typically anesthetized, is subjected to external stimuli. Recordings are now more and more frequently made when the animal is awake and attentive, in continuous and mutual interaction with its environment. This is particularly the case with "motor intentions," which moreover can now be directly observed in humans by means of cerebral imaging. Thus Decéty and his colleagues have shown that distinct cortical (and subcortical) regions are mobilized by the sight of a moving hand, the mental image of the movement of one's own hand, and preparation for executing this movement.[6] Motor preparation, the observation of action, and motor imagery nonetheless share certain levels of representation. In particular, they have access to an internal model of behavior that corresponds to the aim and consequences of an action. This access is also necessary for the observation of actions when the aim is to imitate such actions. The prefrontal and premotor cortex are among the regions shared by these three operations.

I have adopted the projective schema for several reasons; some of them may be related to Husserl's insight in the late unpublished writings, with which I am not familiar. First, we live in an "unlabeled" universe, one that does not send us coded messages. I have already protested vigorously against the conception, cherished by many mathematicians, of a Platonic world teeming with preestablished forms and ideas—an illusory starry sky decorated with true propositions, harmonious rhythms, and maxims of good conduct.[7] In fact, we project exactly these "aims of action and demands for meaning" onto a world that has neither fate nor meaning. It is with our brain that we *create categories* in a world that possesses none, apart from those already created by human beings.

Another reason for my adopting the projective schema is that when our brain interacts with the external world, it develops and functions according to a model of variation-selection[8] that is sometimes called Darwinian.[9] According to this hypothesis, to which we shall return later, variation—the generation of a diversity of internal forms—*precedes* the selection of the *adequate* form. Representations are stabilized in our brain not simply by "imprint," as though it were a piece of wax, but indirectly via a process of selection. Contrary to what you say, the moment has not come to abandon the notion of representation, which in this context has no dualist connotation. We are far from the Cartesian schema, a schema that on the functional plane is nearer that of cybernetics. I am in agreement with you, however, in according a major place to anticipation in experience of the world. And when I employ this term, following Tolman and Decéty, I know what I am talking about on the experimental plane, without having to appeal to any "metaphysical anthropocentrism."

Ricoeur: I find that you employ the term *world* too freely. The world is not only the immediate environment; it is the horizon of a total experience. This notion of horizon is perhaps exactly what is eliminated in the construction of the mental object in order for this object to furnish an equivalent to what you have constructed in the neuronal field. You are obliged to take the object as it has been reduced by the psychologist—justifiably enough by the standards of his own field. What I mean is that the psychologist himself has already pulled back from the world, and his construction is lacking by comparison with the rich experience of being in the world.

Changeux: But our ambition is simply to advance our knowledge of the brain and its functions, to establish models that make it possible gradually, and hierarchically—with, therefore, nearer and nearer "horizons"—to better understand how our experience of the world comes about.

Ricoeur: I would add, then, to the notions of complexity and hierarchy that of spontaneity, with all it implies in the way of an opening onto the horizon of the world. I understand that, within this opening, you are forced to choose between possible objects of study in order to advance in an orderly fashion, but I would say that in doing this you enrich our knowledge of the underlying neuronal structures without clarifying the notion of a neuronal substrate.

Changeux: As I've already told you, I find the term *substrate* ambiguous and without much operational utility for the researcher. Obviously everything depends on the definition that one gives it.

Ricoeur: The word *substrate* does not aspire to the status of an operational term. It is a critical concept, like *basis*—one refers, for example, to the "neurophysiological basis" of a particular function. It aims only at limiting any explanatory claims that might be extrapolated from transdisciplinary research. It is in this critical, limiting sense that one speaks of the enormous richness of human experience, which includes, among other things, aesthetic experience and mystical experience; that one speaks of the substrate of human experience as a process of neuronal function that is astonishingly open to the multiplicity of levels and modalities of experience. "Substrate" therefore signifies that without which such experience would not be possible.

Changeux: Just the same, I think we should be careful about employing an overly general term that might be used to legitimize some amalgamation of the aesthetic and the irrational.

Mental Objects: Chimera or Link?

Changeux: Given the premises just described, I define a *mental object*[10] as a physical state of the brain, which mobilizes neurons recruited from various defined areas or domains (parallelism), belonging to one or more defined levels of organization (hierarchy), such that they are mutually interconnected or "re-entrant."[11] This neuronal assembly, as the Canadian psychologist Donald Hebb named it in 1949, is identified with the dynamic state of activity (number and frequency of impulses,

A

B

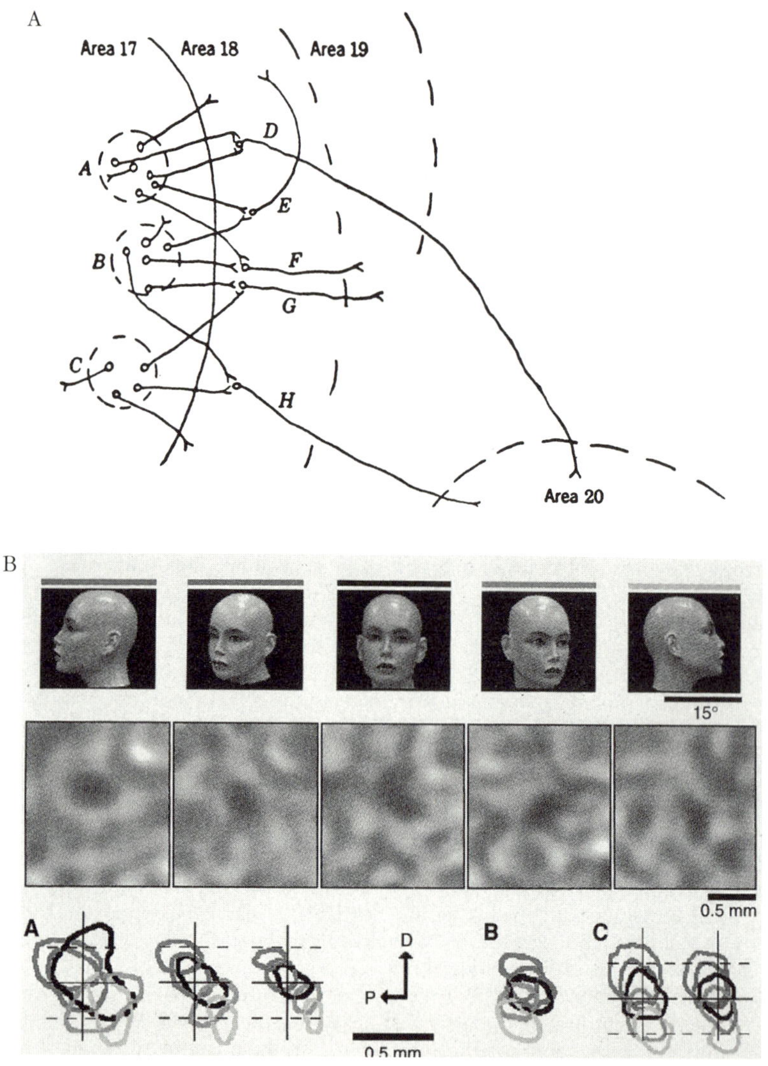

FIGURE 3.3. Mental objects.

A. Illustration of the concept of neuronal assemblies and their growth proposed by the Canadian psychologist Donald Hebb in *The Organization of Behavior: A Neuropsychological Theory* (New York: Wiley, 1949), 67–68. Areas 17, 18, 19, and 20 are the primary (V1) and secondary (V2, V3, V4) visual areas. Hebb's diagram illustrates

free concentration of neurotransmitters, and so on) that in turn is correlated with a topologically defined and distributed *population* of neurons and connections (figure 3.3A). A mental object is a representation that codes a natural sense—a meaning that "represents" an external or internal state of affairs (figure 3.3B). A mental object possesses meaning. This meaning is itself acquired through selection in the course of the child's epigenetic experience of the external physical and social world and in the course of adult communication, in particular through what Wittgenstein called "language games," or else is already coded in the neural architecture that characterizes the species. The number of possible combinations—and therefore, to use your term, of objects of meaning [*objets de sens*]—is considerable.

Ricoeur: I would like for us to pause for just a moment and examine the word *code,* because it is one of the words that shuttles back and forth between the two discourses. It may actu-

---

the distributed character of such an assembly with "convergence as well as spread of excitation" and reciprocity of connections between distinct areas.

B. Observation by optical imaging of activity in the inferotemporal cortex of the monkey evoked by the representation of the same face from different angles. The image is obtained, without a staining agent, by using light reflected at 605 nm: under these conditions, presumably as a consequence of the change in the oxygenation level of the hemoglobin in the capillaries of the brain, the intensity of the reflected light decreases and the nervous activity forms a dark patch. This patch moves in a systematic manner, here downward, during the rotation of the face. Images obtained from the same hemisphere are shown in (A); in (B) and (C) images from two different hemispheres. From G. Wang, K. Tanaka, and M. Tanifuji, "Optical imaging of functional organization in the monkey inferotemporal cortex," *Science* 272 (1996): 1665–1668.

ally be a fragment of the third discourse we seek to construct. A code—for example, the phonetic or lexical code of a natural language—is inert so long as it is not integrated as part of a speech act that actualizes a capacity of which I have vivid experience, an *I can*. But there is nothing that corresponds to this *I can* in a neuronal assembly, which, however open it may be, remains just that—an assembly. Here we find ourselves in the presence of an amphiboly or, if you like, an ambiguity of the word *code*.

Changeux: By "code" I mean the matching up of an external state of affairs, an object, a situation, on the one hand, with a neuronal organization and the state of activity that invests it on the other. This term is also used by analogy in the case of genetic information. One says, for example, that the base sequence of a gene's DNA *codes for* the sequence of amino acids that constitutes a protein possessing, for example, an enzymatic function. By extension, one says that the gene encodes such a function. This may be a misuse of language. But I want in any case to find a way to say that this set of neuronal activities, which exhibits a well-defined geography and is very richly connected with other sets of neurons in our brain, has an *indication function*—or, better still, that it materially, physically possesses meaning (in Saussurian terms, a signified). It would correspond to state C in the schema proposed by Fred Dretske[12] and Joëlle Proust:[13]

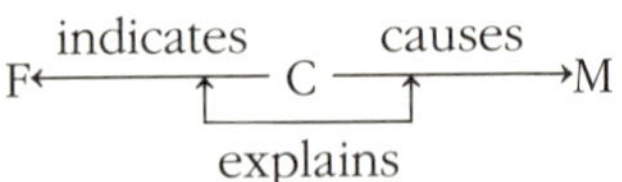

where F is an external state of affairs and M a behavioral outcome. The problem of neural coding is less obvious. One doesn't expect a simple topological relation as in the case of the genetic code. The paradox consists in the fact that, despite the fact that the architecture of the brain as a whole is preserved from individual to individual, variability is considerable from one brain to another. This variability, as we know, is the result of the epigenetic mode of development of neuronal connectivity. Philippe Courrège, Antoine Danchin, and I have shown that, once the network is established, the same entrant message can stabilize *different* patterns of connection and nonetheless lead to the same input-output relation.[14] In other words, the geography of neurons that code for a given meaning does not resemble a deck of playing cards. A mode of *functional relations between types of connections* is nonetheless preserved that will overcome the connective variability (figure 3.4).

Ricoeur: Here we are faced with several discrepant uses of the word *indication*. These are tolerated by current usage, I think, or at least they were before semioticians (and, later, philosophers of mind) redefined the term. To indicate, according to the dictionary definition, is to "make [someone] see [something] in a precise manner, by a gesture, a sign, a marker, a signal." Among the more technical meanings: "to make (the existence or character of) [a being, an object, an event] known by serving as a sign." This leads us back to the noun *indication:* "An apparent sign that indicates [something] with probability." Current practice thus licences a rather unconstrained usage, not forgetting the gesture of showing (i.e., with the index finger). A variety of more or less precise restrictions on philosophical usage of the term are worth noting, however. Husserl, at the time of the *Logical Investigations,* accorded a weak sense to indication by contrast with the cognitive force of the sign proper: "distinctive marks" (canals on Mars, for example, or fossil bones) have indicative value in that they *motivate* belief in the reality of the thing designated.[15] Peirce,

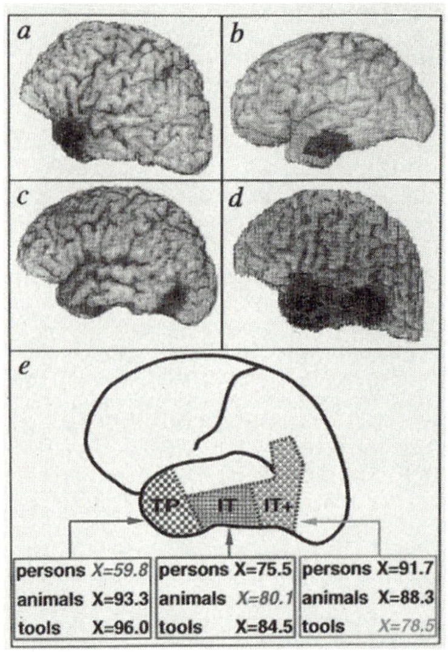
a
b
c
d
e
TP
IT
IT+
persons X=59.8
animals X=93.3
tools X=96.0
persons X=75.5
animals X=80.1
tools X=84.5
persons X=91.7
animals X=88.3
tools X=78.5

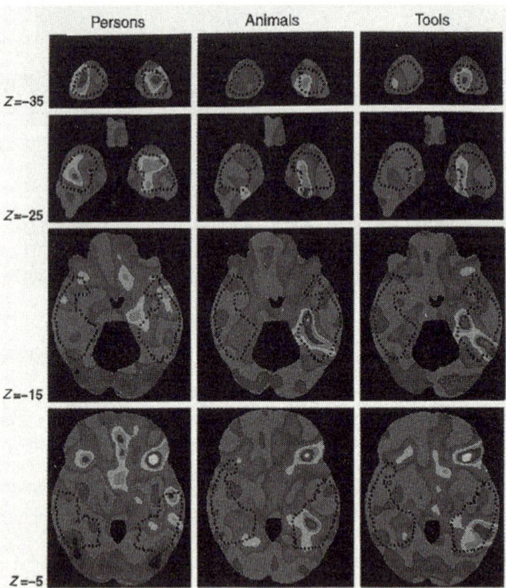
Persons
Animals
Tools
Z=-35
Z=-25
Z=-15
Z=-5

FIGURE 3.4.

to the contrary, emphasized the solidity of the causal link between the "index" and the thing indicated in his famous theory of signs.[16] The index—the symptom of a disease, for instance—is determined by its singular object by virtue of the relation in which it stands to the object. In this respect the index is opposed to the icon and to the symbol: the index is a sign that would immediately lose its character if its object were suppressed (the hole of a wound, for example, and a gunshot).

Indication, according to semiotic theory, consists in a very strong link founded on a commonality of nature and a causal relation. It is in a related sense, and in agreement with Dretske and Proust, that you yourself appeal to the category of indication. But you go further, since for you neuronal reality materially contains the sign. You make it sound as though the psychological experience of what is signified and the cortical

---

FIGURE 3.4. Lexical geography.

Differential activation of topographically distinct regions in the cerebral hemispheres during recall of words designating individual persons, animals, or tools.

(Above) The analysis of spontaneous lesions reveals that two regions of the temporal cortex are involved in the recall of words: the left temporal pole (TP) and the inferotemporal region (IT). The lesions shown in (a) lead to a selective loss of recall of personal names; in (b) of animal names; in (c) of names of tools; and in (d) of all categories. In (e) the average results of word recall are given for the three groups of subjects having lesions in the regions indicated.

(Below) Brain images obtained by PET scan corroborate the lesion analysis and show that different regions of the brain become active when a subject is asked to give a name to computer-generated images representing photographs of known persons, animals, and tools.

From H. Damasio, T. J. Grabowski, D. Tranel, R. Hichwa, and A. Damasio, "A neural basis for lexical retrieval," *Nature* 380 (1996): 499–505.

activity that corresponds to this experience are identical, which risks abolishing the distinction between the sign and what it signifies. By contrast it is the semantic heterogeneity between the mental phenomenon and its cortical basis that I stress by making the former the index of the latter, in a sense that best illustrates the nosological notion of symptom and the clinical notion of diagnosis. Returning from the mental to the neuronal reality that underlies it would thus constitute, in the interpretation that I give of the notion of indication, a fragment of the third discourse that we are trying to develop. In this framework, indication would constitute the reverse counterpart of the notion of substrate or basis, the condition sine qua non that takes us from the neuronal to the mental.

I therefore suggest that the relation of indication may be one of the structures that makes it possible to pass from one discourse to the other, but we must be quite aware that it involves overcoming what I see as an ambiguity.

Changeux: The notion of overcoming ambiguity might be suitable, since we are trying to find a term that characterizes this attempt to establish a correspondence between the two. I think that the word *identity* is not a good choice because one does not identify a structure with a function. It is rather a question of a determining relation: a structure determines a function, keeping in mind that in the present case this relation is established by learning. The term *indication* may not actually be the best one. At all events what I am going to try to do—

Ricoeur: I do not object, so long as we do not naively use words whose ambiguity has gone unremarked.

Changeux: It is for this reason that I use the term *mental object,* which, though it may not necessarily be adequate, designates in an objective way a singular physical state internal to our brain.

Ricoeur: I would say—in all seriousness—that this mental object is poorly constructed indeed, insofar as you are taking a term that belongs to the discourse of mind and transplanting it in the discourse of neurology.

Changeux: The concept of mental object defines a unique entity located where the two discourses meet. To use Spinoza's terms, I would say that there is a "substance" conceived in two "aspects." In fact, the term *mental* belongs to the psychological sphere, and the word *object* belongs, as it were, to the physical and, by extension, the neural sphere. The term *mental object* therefore links the two.

Ricoeur: Then it's an illegitimate term.

Changeux: Yes, but intentionally illegitimate! It draws attention to itself because it is synthetic. Moreover, it has been used by a number of psychologists, including Ignace Meyerson, whom I mentioned a moment ago.

Ricoeur: Let's say instead that it's a hybrid.

Changeux: Yes, it's a hybrid term that links the two discourses.

Ricoeur: You are saying, then, that it's necessary to employ a hybrid vocabulary. Once again, this was Descartes's problem in the sixth *Meditation*.

Changeux: But Descartes in his last years never solved it.

Ricoeur: Let us say that he succeeded in clearly posing the problem, thus breaking with medieval tradition.

Changeux: He posed the problem but didn't solve it, as we saw earlier. Why don't we try together? The only risk we run is that we may not succeed—not of being hounded by the Inquisition!

Let us then examine the results of studies done on the recognition of faces in the monkey and man. A monkey is presented with the image of a face. The neural activity of the monkey's temporal cortex is recorded. Certain cells respond to the presentation of a face, which may be that of a man but also that of another monkey. If one removes the eyes from the projected image, the electrophysiological response diminishes in frequency. One may say that the neurons participate in the formation of a mental object that mobilizes the temporal cortex and possesses an internal representation of this face. It even becomes possible using optical imaging to "see" this representation at the level of the temporal cortex and to observe its displacement according to the angle at which the face is seen (figure 3.3B).

Ricoeur: Something happens in my brain, and when you tell me what happens in my brain, you add to my knowledge of the base, of the underlying neural reality; but does this knowledge help me in trying to decipher the enigma of a face? Do you believe that you understand the faces of others in the street, in your family, because you know something about what happens in their brain?

Changeux: Of course. I understand not only the type of face to which I attach a name but also its expression, the emotions that it communicates, its ethical choices. On the basis of observations of both experimental psychology and the analysis of lesions, Young has distinguished a complex set of successive steps leading to the recognition of a familiar face.[17] The accordance of an image with memory traces, stored in units of visual recognition, entails their activation and so gives access to information about the person's identity and, finally, to his or her name. We frequently find ourselves in a situation where we recognize the face of an acquaintance while the name remains on the tip of our tongue.

Ricoeur: Here I confess to being perplexed. Earlier I have had occasion to express my perplexity in the case of dysfunctions, deficits, lesions, and so on. Objective knowledge of the causes of such disorders may improve our understanding of the situation experienced by the patient, in particular through a therapeutic intervention that ideally the patient ought to understand, accept, and integrate with his daily behavior. But what of successful behaviors—felicitous behaviors, as I have called them? How is objective knowledge to be integrated with daily understanding? This is the problem raised by your example of the understanding of faces: what does knowledge of the brain add here?

Changeux: This knowledge will, I hope, permit us to better understand others, to know how to introduce greater harmony in human relations, to recognize "others" as belonging to a single humanity.

Ricoeur: Greater harmony would be obtained by changing something in our mutual experience, not by acting on the brain.

Changeux: But our mutual experience unavoidably involves *our* brains. It will not happen, of course, by acting directly on the brain but indirectly, through dialogue, the exchange of ideas, deliberation, and access to various external resources—but also to resources internal to our brain. I will come back to this point later. The sad experience of camps of ideological reeducation, as well as the techniques of behavioral modification and mind control practiced by certain religious sects, serves to remind us that the brain is manipulable. It therefore seems essential to understand that the human brain cannot be manipulated to do anything one wants—that there exist neural constraints on its operation. No one would suppose that it is possible to learn to speak Chinese without an accent overnight. Knowing the limits of what a responsible individual can do will permit us to better understand and better achieve what you call felicitous behaviors. I know that a foreigner cannot be expected to speak my language fluently, because language learning is subject to neural constraints, but he is nonetheless a human being like you and me. In antiquity, as you know, the foreigner who did not speak the language of a city was considered a barbarian lacking human status. Certain societies systematically regard the foreigner as "bad," a "monkey," a "louse egg," as Lévi-Strauss observed in *Race and History*.[18]

Ricoeur: Regarding your idea of neural constraint, which covers successful, felicitous functioning as well as dysfunction, I ask the following question: does a better knowledge of neural function help me somehow better understand interpersonal relations? I have no idea.

Changeux: My answer is yes. An experiment performed by Jacques Mehler and his team is very instructive on the level of interpersonal relations (figure 3.5).[19] It involves a comparison of cerebral activity, recorded by a PET camera, in a person who understands one language but not another. For example, a Frenchman who has lived in France all his life is asked to listen to a story in Tamil. Activation of the auditory areas is noted. Then he is made to listen to a list of words in French. Other areas are activated in addition to the preceding ones,

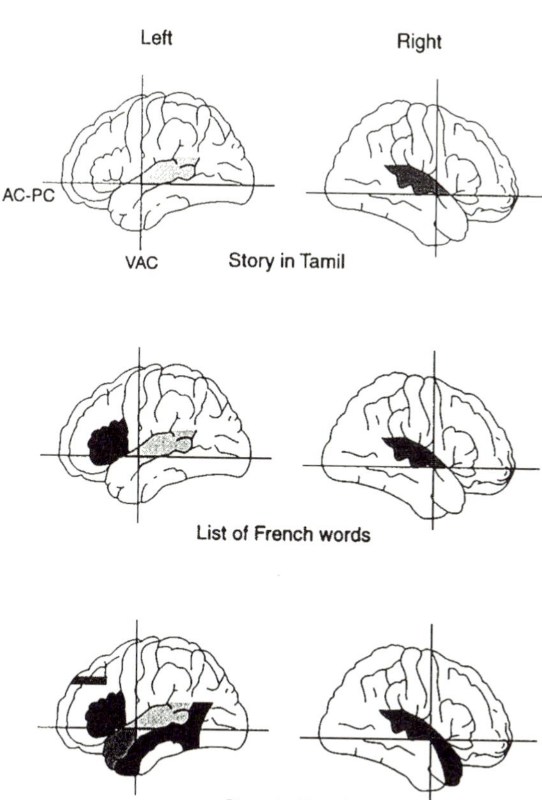

FIGURE 3.5. Brain images of language comprehension obtained with a PET camera.

When a French-speaking subject hears a story in Tamil, a language he does not understand, only the auditory cortexes are activated. When he listens to a list of words in French, which he understands, a large region of the left frontal cortex becomes active. Finally, when he listens to a story in French, a large number of brain areas are activated in the temporal and frontal regions of the left hemisphere. From B. M. Mazoyer, S. Dehaene, N. Tzourio, V. Frak, N. Murayama, L. Cohen, O. Levrier, G. Salomon, A. Syrota, and J. Mehler, "The Cortical Representation of Speech," *Journal of Cognitive Neuroscience* 4 (1993): 467–479.

particularly in the frontal region. Finally, a story is told to him in French, and it is observed that a large number of regions in the cerebral cortex are switched on. When the subject listens without understanding, activity is restricted to the auditory system; when he understands, his brain finds itself invaded, as it were, besieged with activity.

On the other hand, the resolution of imaging methods is now such that one can distinguish between the activation of different cortical regions when the subject hears (or sees) words having different meanings. In the temporal cortex (figure 3.4), cerebral imaging and the analysis of lesions reveal that distinct cortical areas respond differently to faces, animals, fruits and vegetables, inanimate objects, technological artifacts, musical instruments, scissors, watches, pens, what have you.[20] The more objects of meaning involve abstract and general concepts, rules of conduct, relations between oneself and others, the greater the contribution of the frontal and prefrontal areas. The hierarchical advance from the perceptual to the conceptual is accompanied by a progressive mobilization of primary sensory areas, associative areas, and finally prefrontal areas. There exists a geography of understanding, as it were, in our cerebral cortex. Concrete images mobilize primary and secondary sensory areas for the most part while concepts exhibit a much more extensive connectivity. The isomorphism with objects of the external world is progressively lost, giving way to more formal, more abstract representations. Conversely, these higher, more "abstract" representations projectively mobilize first associative areas, and then motor areas, with a view to acting in a definite way upon the world.

Ricoeur: The experiment you describe shows the activation of different cortical regions, but not the specific neuronal assemblies that correspond, for example, to the comprehension of a story in Tamil. Without this detailed knowledge, one can hardly speak of a "semantic geography"—the adjective designating the content of meaning, not merely the presence or absence of neuronal activity. Lacking such a map, we'll have a hard time characterizing the sort of comprehension the cerebral cortex has of itself.

Changeux: Perhaps not. For one thing, we establish a different and particularly pertinent cortical geography for hearing than for understanding. Hearing is topologically much more restricted than understanding. The images obtained nicely illustrate the root meaning of the word "comprehension"—derived from the Latin *cum prehendere,* "to take with"—since a whole constellation of cerebral areas is seized simultaneously when comprehension occurs. The images obtained so far are still somewhat static. But the development of new technologies now makes it possible to follow their dynamics, the way they unfold over time. We have at our disposal physical traces of how meaning is accessed. As Wittgenstein emphasized, meaning is *in* understanding! Isn't our purpose to understand others better in order to better be able to help them? In my view, *mutual understanding* is one of the fundamental activities of ethics and the normative approach.

On the other hand, what is true for language is also true, by implication, for a particular system of cultural representations, of legal and ethical rules. If, on his arrival in France, you ask a Tamil who does not understand French to respect the laws of the French Republic, he won't be able to. You could, of course, translate them for him, but even so he no doubt would have difficulty assimilating them, having been raised in a cultural environment having quite different religious, moral, and legal traditions than our own. The reason he has trouble adjusting to our laws is that he has not internalized them during the course of childhood. A considerable period of time will be necessary before he learns them and comes to feel at ease in a new cultural system. And he may never lose his accent, which as you know is an important factor in discrimination.

Ricoeur: What are learning, understanding, translating if not experiences belonging to the domain of common experience? Does mutual experience owe something to the knowledge that you now provide me with?

Changeux: I simply mean that we dispose of objective evidence of a subject's comprehension or lack of comprehension, evidence that is external to his subjectivity.

Ricoeur: This is in fact something important, but I don't see that such objective evidence is capable of increasing our understanding of ourselves and others.

Changeux: I can at least decide if the person whom I am observing understands the other's language or not. I can have access to this information without having even to ask the subject, without the subject having to express himself in words. This information, it seems to me, is very important for our knowledge of others and our understanding of their motivations. It also poses formidable ethical problems, as I mentioned at the outset of these conversations: what am I to do with information about others that is obtained independently of their own will? In possessing objective information about someone's state of comprehension—information that is not accessible by immediate means of verbal exchange or even visual examination of a person's face—an important ethical barrier is breached.

Ricoeur: What is the nature of this objective information? It seems to me that you conflate two things: observation of the activation of neuronal zones, which still falls far short of a knowledge of the mechanisms involved in another's language, and signs of comprehension in the observable behavior of another person; this is indeed a matter, as you say, of information obtained independently of the other person's own will. But such information concerns only the underlying neuronal activity. And even if a semantic geography were possible, as you suggested a moment ago, the question becomes whether it would enrich ordinary comprehension of dialogue or non-dialogue. How can the intersubjective knowledge that every one of us has be enriched—and, if necessary, rectified—by the fact that I know more about what goes on in the brain?

Changeux: In "ordinary" life, to use your term, the practical consequences are potentially very great from the legal point of view. French criminal law makes a fundamental distinction as to whether or not a subject is insane or not at the moment of a crime. He is sent either to a psychiatric hospital or to prison. Everyone is familiar with the case of Althusser.[21] One can imagine being able one day to distinguish the characteristic cerebral images of the state of insanity from those of a state of criminal responsibility. Similarly, recent work by Daniel Schacter and Eric Reinman suggests that one can distinguish the cerebral images of a subject who tells the truth from those of a subject who lies. In the one case, current representations coincide with memory traces, but not in the other.

Ricoeur: The ethical applications or extensions are in fact particularly convincing in all cases of dysfunction, breakdown, deviance, and so on. I therefore believe that objectivation is not a defect—I support the relationship between explaining and understanding. Improved knowledge of neuronal bases or substrates will probably enrich mutual comprehension in the case of dysfunctions and certain types of deviance, as in the case you have just mentioned of lying. In all these cases, objective explanations can be integrated with intersubjective comprehension.

Changeux: I don't think that it is necessary to limit oneself to the distinction between the normal and the pathological. Lies, alas, are a part of everyday life; they even constitute a characteristic of humans by comparison with nonhumans. Furthermore, apparently normal behaviors may not be normal. Do you regard a scientist who conceives and develops an atomic weapon in peacetime without any qualms as a deviant or a hero? That's a good question!

Ricoeur: One must make a distinction: moral deviance—lying, for instance—poses a different problem from that of pathological dysfunction, which involves a reorganization of behavior in relation to the environment; the breach of lying affects the fiduciary relationship on which communication rests. As for the behavior of the scientist who helps build an atomic weapon, this is still another problem that touches upon the technological applications of science.

Is a Neuronal Theory of Knowledge Possible?

Changeux: Before taking up these questions, I would like you to join me in a rather ambitious attempt to sketch the outlines of a neuronal theory of knowledge. Knowledge, after all, has been one of the privileged themes of philosophers from antiquity until our own time. For Democritus and the atomists, perception was understood as a "touching at a distance" through "emanations," "simulacra" that detach themselves from visible objects and penetrate inside us. Thought was considered to be of the same nature as sensation and organized on the basis of these simulacra. "In reality," wrote Democritus, "we know nothing for certain, but only that which changes according to the disposition of our bodies and according to that which penetrates it or that which resists it." I like this formulation, which seems to me close to the critical attitude of the scientific researcher, who remains cautiously aloof from certitudes and revealed truths; it stands diametrically opposed to the Platonic doctrine of Ideas, an invisible reality of divine origin where true knowledge is found, access to which proceeds through an ascension of the spirit, by means of contemplation or *theoria*. Let's try to follow in Democritus's steps, why don't we, while taking care to avoid strictly empiricist theories according to which knowledge is a matter of imprints, or "impressions," of the environment.

In thinking about this problem it seems to me that we must start from a central hypothesis, namely, that the brain acquires knowledge through a process of selection.[22] "To think is to make selections," as William James remarked. But we ought first define the environment, the "world" that the human child will explore in order to know and learn in order to recognize. Initially this will be the physical, chemical, and biological universe, the sky, the earth, the plains and mountains, plants and trees, fish, birds, and monkeys. This universe is intrinsically empty of meaning and intention. As I remarked earlier, it does not come already labeled. It is important to stress that knowing cannot be reduced to recognizing, to "reading" categories already established in nature; it consists first of all in establishing categories. An earthworm "sees" only a very small part of its subterranean universe. What it comes to know is limited to what its minuscule brain allows it to represent: soil that is loose and damp soil, light (which it flees), a sexual partner for reproduction. The human child already possesses a cerebral architecture peculiar to his own species, which he has inherited from the generations that have preceded him in the course of evolution and which offer him multiple access routes to a material environment infinitely more rich than that of the earthworm (to say nothing of the social and cultural environment in which he grows up and which he organizes—I will come back to this point in a moment). The human child's brain dramatically enlarges the universe of "representables," and therefore that of knowledge as well. His first cognitive activity will be to make categories, to classify what he perceives and, in particular, to distinguish the human from the nonhuman.

Moreover, he is born with a very immature brain, whose synaptic network is incompletely stabilized and therefore ready to receive traces of the environment. At birth, even earlier, his brain is the seat of intense spontaneous activity. This is manifested by movements of the arms, hands, and mouth. He clings to his mother's breast. He tries to sit, then to crawl and finally to walk on four legs. Through trial and error his movements become better and better coordinated.[23] He constantly explores what is around him, looking around, fixing his attention and then shifting it by means of neuronal mechanisms that have been analyzed in detail by Droulez and Berthoz.[24] His brain produces mental objects of a particular type that might be called *prerepresentations*—preliminary sketches, schemas, models. These are nonstabilized mental objects—fluctuating "variations" that, according to the hypothesis I am proposing, are identified with spontaneous, transitory states of activity, with multiple and variable populations of neurons capable of random combination. The cerebral regions involved may associate several sensory modalities, and combine the traces of several objects of meaning already selected in the course of prior experience. On the formal plane there develops what Darwinian theories of evolution call a "generator of diversity," whose productions are in some respects comparable (despite obvious differences) to mutations or random rearrangements of the chromosomic apparatus.

What might be called the moment of truth now arrives. The child projects these preliminary representations on the world around him, first through motor acts[25] and then later "mentally." He proceeds by trial and error, trying to spot, to define, to frame, to categorize (the last is the scientific term) the objects and phenomena of the reality that surrounds him. The external world then retroacts on the transient mental state that determined the behavior. Depending on the signal received from the external world, the initial prerepresentation is stabilized or not. A selection takes place—the representation, the pertinent category, is selected. Specialized mechanisms of evaluation intervene in this decision that call into play specific systems of neurons associated with reinforcement and reward (figure 3.6).[26] A trivial example: the sugar that one gives to a dog when he sits up and begs, or the orange juice given to a monkey when he does what is expected of him. But the dog's master is not always present—in fact, he isn't present most of the time. The animal possesses its own internal systems of evaluation. These systems have developed over the course of evolution, are capable of being learned (figure 3.6B), and "automatically" entail a subjective sensation of pleasure or displeasure. The mechanisms of reward are connected with the system of emotions.[27]

According to Panskepp's theory, the affective system is divided into four great subsystems that mobilize topologically and biologically distinct sets of neurons involved in producing the fundamental emotions: *desire/pleasure; distress* (which arises from a disturbance of social bonds); *anger/violence;* and *fear* (figure 6.1). The first system engages specialized neurons that synthesize and release dopamine. Their electrical (or chemical) stimulation brings about a pleasurable sensation. When a rat is presented with the possibility of electrically stimulating these sets of neurons by pushing down on a pedal connected to an intracerebral electrode, having discovered

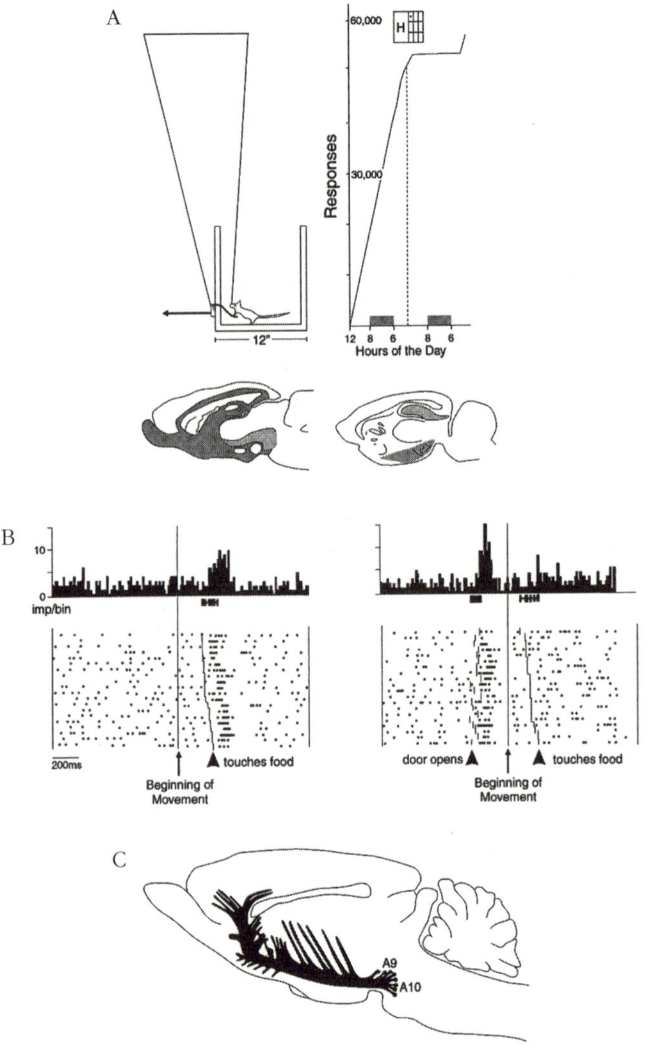

FIGURE 3.6. Electric self-stimulation in the rat and "reward" neurons in the monkey.

A. Device permitting the rat to stimulate itself electrically by pressing down on a pedal that triggers an electric discharge in his own brain (left). The rat ceases stimulating itself only to sleep (right). The

this gesture by chance, it stimulates itself thousands, indeed tens of thousands of times, stopping only to sleep (figure 3.6B). Similarly, if it can administer to itself a chemical substance—a drug, such as cocaine or nicotine—it will become dependent on this substance, which will directly or indirectly stimulate its reward neurons.

On this theory, the return of a positive signal leads to the stabilization of the prerepresentation that provoked it, whereas a negative signal leads to the reactivation of the generator of diversity, the production of new prerepresentations,

---

areas of the brain where the implantation of the stimulus electrode produces a positive reinforcement are indicated in the figure on the left below in gray; the areas producing a negative reinforcement are represented in the figure on the right. From J. Olds, "Self-stimulation of the brain," *Science* 127 (1958): 315–324.

B. Activity of dopamine neurons in the midbrain recorded in an alert monkey exhibiting spontaneous or induced movements. Each line corresponds to a different trial and records the electric response of a given set of neurons. The histograms above give the average for the responses recorded. The graph on the left represents the response recorded when the monkey touches food (a peanut hidden in a closed box): the activity of the "reward" neurons increases the moment it recognizes the food. The monkey learns that, when the door of the box opens, it will have access to the food: the dopamine neurons become active the moment the door opens but not when the monkey touches the food (figure on right). From R. Romo and W. Schultz, "Dopamine neurones of the monkey midbrain: Contingencies of responses to active touch during self-initiated arm movements," *J. Neurophysiol.* 63 (1990): 592–606.

C. Diagrammatic representation of the distribution of dopamine neurons in the rat. Note the modest scale of the nuclei containing the cell and the great divergence among axons reaching the prefrontal cortex. From O. Lindvall and A. Björklund, "The organization of the ascending catecholamine neuron systems in the rat brain as revealed by the glyoxylic acid fluorescence method," *Acta Physiol. Scand.* 412 [supplement] (1974): 1–48.

new tests against experience, and so on. Causal relations, internal to the brain, are therefore established between external reality and mental objects. A neural lexicon is constructed to which the various interlocking levels of organization of the child's brain will contribute. Experiences of the external world are enriched by internal experiences that draw upon still more complex processes of self-evaluation. These processes exploit innate endogenous memories or else memories issuing from prior experiences, learning, and rules of behavior internalized by education. As a result the child will incorporate in his brain the outlines of an account of his personal history that will come to be merged with the social and cultural history of his family circle and of those beyond it.

This still very hypothetical schema follows the Darwinian model in positing a source of variability at each level: a generator of prerepresentations, a process of selection, and then an amplifying mechanism connected with the storage of memory traces that will later be reutilized many times. The individual, in the "narrative" he develops about himself, will use these memory traces—compare them, evaluate them, subject them again to the test of reality—and thus construct "knowledge" about the external world and about himself. In every case this will be a matter of *reconstruction*. Every evocation of memories is a reconstruction on the basis of *physical traces* stored in the brain in latent form, for example at the level of neurotransmitter receptors.[28] But the *efficacy* of such knowledge in his future behavior and mental operations, and in the reasoning for which they furnish the primary material, serves to bring out criteria of truth, of objectivity. Validation will be obtained through personal experience, but also through the scientific community and the accumulated knowledge that it possesses. An increase in knowledge follows. No other human activity is characterized by such cumulative progress.

This, then, in its broad outlines, is my point of view as a

neurobiologist—still a very speculative and conjectural one—with regard to the notion of representation and its application to a theory of knowledge, too briefly sketched.[29]

Ricoeur: The model that you propose is, as you remark in closing, largely conjectural, and therefore still a long way from being experimentally confirmed. It seems to me to contain from the outset a series of presuppositions, the first having to do with the privilege that you accord to knowledge, following Democritus, who in this respect was a Socratic. Now, once again, the constitution of what I join the later Husserl in calling the "life-world" seems to me to involve straight away a practical as well as a theoretical dimension. The first presupposition seems to me to be reinforced by another still more serious one: you avail yourself at the outset of a notion of the environment that is that of a world wholly made up of realities that you define in terms of physics, chemistry, and biology—a world that is already scientifically organized. And it is this same world that you declare "empty of meaning and intention." But it had previously been emptied of meaning and intention by the Copernican, and then the Newtonian, revolution, which effectively left us a dead physical world, as Hans Jonas emphasizes in his philosophical studies of biology. Yet this doesn't prevent you from seeing it as populated with vegetables and animals, before the human child undertakes to "read" it. I quite agree with you that it is by a process of selection that the world comes to be, as you put it, labeled. But on the basis of what? On the basis of what I have just called a life-world—a world in which human beings orient themselves, choose signals that are meaningful for them, and anticipate events with a view to making of it a relatively practicable world, which is to say a habitable world. In this sense it is much more than a universe of "representables" that needs to be raised to the level of something knowable. You yourself, moreover, introduce the notion of prerepresentation, which I find entirely appropriate, but which has to be fleshed out in its affective and practical aspects from the beginning. It is against this background of presuppositions that you construct your neuronal model, which makes room for spontaneous activity with its random combinations and for what the Darwinian theory of evolution calls generators of diversity.

You do not lay enough stress, it seems to me, on the conjectural character of this model. It is characterized also by its coherence, in relation to what is experimentally known in neurobiology, to the hypotheses and facts belonging to sciences associated with neurology, and above all to Darwinian theories of evolution. This model seems to me to have reached the stage of de facto nonfalsification—which, I grant you, is not trivial, and why I do not wish to criticize it on this ground. Every science has a right to allow conjecture to run ahead of verification for a time. It is rather the hybrid character of this conjectural model that I want to emphasize. Here we come back to our earlier discussion of what I described as a semantic amalgamation. What you describe as the moment of truth—a test of experience, which is principally an attempt at categorization—comes under the head of the theory of knowledge and is variously treated by epistemology, experimental psychology, and the cognitive sciences. The same is true of the notion of evaluation, which you quite legitimately associate with the great subsystems of emotions such as desire/pleasure, anger/fear, and so on. You then discuss the contribution made by specialized systems of neurons, without it being clear what "contribution" means here. The hybrid character of your discourse is particularly marked when you refer to systems of reinforcement and reward, suggesting that they play a role in the formation of moral judgments. This hybrid character culminates with the notion of a neural lexicon, which well summarizes the whole enterprise. And so for you everything takes place *in the brain*. The alleged causal relations between external reality and mental objects are said to be "internal to the brain." But your present model displays the same defect as the one put forth by psychologists, who have, under scientific conditions, constructed a conception of representation as an "internal" mental image—in the head, as it is said—contrasted with external reality, itself wholly made and wholly given at the level of knowledge of the physical world. I would like to show what is missing from this representation by comparison with complete and complex experience, with what I call phenomenological experience. And I would like to show what contribution phenomenology makes in this regard by comparison with psychology.

For me, the distinction is actually not so much between psychology and the neurosciences. There may be a prior distinction between psychology and phenomenological experience. The notion of mental objects was used by the psychologist before you used it. You have transplanted in the domain of the neurosciences a notion that is itself a construct of psychology. Constructed in relation to what? First in relation to the notion of intentionality. Consciousness is not a box in which there are objects. The notion of mental content has been constructed in relation to the experience of being led toward the world and therefore of being outside oneself in intentionality. I stand in a very particular relation to the world, that of being born into this world, of being in it. The great advance of phenomenology was to reject the containing/contained relationship that made the psyche a place. Thus I do not at all accept the conception of the "mind"—I deliberately put the word between quotation marks—as a container having contents.

Intentionality introduces the notion of transcendent purpose. I do not interpret "transcendent" in the religious sense of the term; I simply say that I am outside of myself when I see, which is to say that seeing consists in being confronted by something that is not myself, and therefore participating in an external world. I would say therefore that consciousness is not a closed place, about which I might wonder how something enters it from outside, because it is, now and always, outside of itself.

Changeux: Naturally I do not object to the notion that conscious behavior opens, not only onto the external world but also onto other persons. To the contrary, the projective character of the model and the evaluation that accompanies it make possible exactly this "participation in the external world" that you mention. I have emphasized the theoretical and still preliminary character of my propositions, but I think that at least some of them can be subjected to verification—the variability of pre-representations, for example—through the methods of dynamic brain imaging in particular; also the stabilization of pre-representations through the systems of evaluation and reward. But I would like to point out that the contribution of phenomenology, no matter how fertile it may be, makes the experimental problem more difficult.

My only specific comment concerns the word *hybrid,* which is to be understood in the sense of a successful bridging of discourses. Mental objects, for example, are capable of mixing and recombining, or "hybridizing," like chromosomes in genetics—I use the Mendelian metaphor to illustrate the point that there are physical ways within the brain to bridge the two discourses with which we are concerned. As for the notion of "amalgamation," I understand it as preserving one of the meanings of the Arabic phrase from which it derives, *al-malgham,* or "work of union." The meaning this term has in chemistry—of alloy and, by extension, alliance or combination—I do not find displeasing either.

Let us, then, avoid derogatory terms while remaining critical. I agree with Wittgenstein when he says that the aim of philosophy is to clarify our ideas. My scientific proposition is clear, even if my terminology doesn't suit you. There is a very large scientific literature on neurons involved in systems of reinforcement and reward, in particular with regard to their role in drug dependency.[30] We are now able to distinguish specific groups of neurons involved in motivation from those involved in the perception of reward.[31]

Ricoeur: I don't retract my purely epistemological use of the notion of semantic amalgamation, which was not meant to be derogatory. It was intended simply to point out a conceptual ambiguity. This warning against the dangers of conceptual confusion does not stand in the way of interdisciplinary work. To the contrary. Such work begins at exactly the moment when each party recognizes the difference in the other's approach at the level of basic referents: for you, the basic referent is the brain; for me, at this point in our discussion, it is the intentional purpose of awareness. That said, I propose to extend the notion of intentionality in a direction where comparison with your notion of neuronal systems of evaluation, responsible for subjective sensations of pleasure or displeasure, may prove to be fruitful. In fact you deploy a whole theory of emotions that you then associate with the neuronal theory. Now this theory of emotions appeals to a complex typology that has its origins in medieval philosophy and that with Descartes's *Passions of the Soul* and the writings of his followers, Spinoza among them, acquired the status of a veritable semiotics of the passions. These celebrated analyses provide the point of departure for the contemporary phenomenology of the emotions, where the idea of intentionality is extended beyond the sphere of objective representation (sensation, perception, imagination, concept, and so on). In this regard I attach a great deal of importance to Sartre's studies of the emotions. Sartre showed that emotion is both intentional and meaningful. When I am frightened, what frightens is actually opposite me, outside, facing me, and so has meaning for me. This meaning—"frightening," "surprising"—constitutes the correlate of the intentional purpose. This correlate can be considered transcendent. I see you don't like the word *transcendent*—

Changeux: Not at all!

Ricoeur: It's equivocal, I admit. Myself, I avoid it—it's not part of my vocabulary. Husserl employed the word in a purely phenomenological sense to mean that it escaped the internal/external relation, precisely because the notion of intentionality does away with this opposition. The notion of meaning, in turn, adds to intentionality a relation to something other—a relation of otherness. A relation of otherness obtains when something "applies to" or "is applied to." It is absolutely irreducible, one of the absolutely fundamental structures of the lived world.

Finally, after intentionality and meaning, I come to the notion of communication, in the sense of pooling or sharing. It doesn't supplement the two preceding notions, but it derives from the same source, which is to say that intersubjective understanding is a part of understanding in general. Thus we are in the world in the plural, and mutually understand that we understand the world together. We must then reserve the possibility that this understanding of the world, like others, may admit of many degrees. And thus I arrive at the three main notions upon which the construction of your neurological object depends—complexity, hierarchy, and openness.

Changeux: I agree with you on several points—first with regard to participation, the opening of consciousness onto the external world, between the self and the outside-oneself, which I find pertinent. Nor do I dissent from Husserl's thesis of the concrete unity of intentional experience, nor even, for that matter, from the somewhat magical statement that "the inside is outside."[32] All of this is to say that the enterprise of modeling or naturalizing intentions must take into account the reciprocal opening at any given moment of our cerebral universe onto the external world. I see intentionality as an aiming at exteriority, a global but definite representation of the world, a sort of mental framework, a contextualized end—in short, a world in which we have to function and which it falls to us to formalize.[33]

Ricoeur: There is nothing magical about the idea that the inside is outside. Its paradoxical form only expresses in a critical way the rejection of the dual prejudice that makes consciousness an inside and the world an outside. One may also say, in keeping with another use of the preposition "in," that man is in the world; but here the "in" has lost its meaning of spatial inclusion. It becomes necessary then to recover the original and irreducible dimension of otherness. Accordingly, I don't see how one can naturalize this primitive structure, which can be captured only by "suspending" the naturalization of the intentional relation of consciousness to the world implicit in the model of the natural sciences. Let's simply say that I want to restore the notion of representation to its original and rightful place, within the vast phenomenon of aiming at something other than myself.

Changeux: Fine—though it remains difficult to provide a serious experimental basis for the idea that the internal/external relation can be done away with. In this connection, however, I would mention the discovery by Rizolatti of a very particular category of neurons in area 6 of the frontal cortex, known since as "mirror neurons" (figure 3.7). These neurons fire each

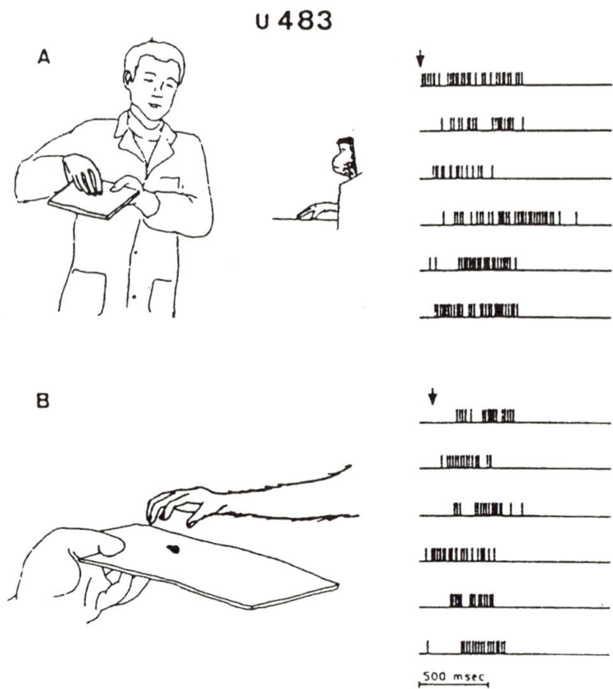

FIGURE 3.7. Mirror neurons of the premotor area (area 6) of the frontal lobe in the monkey.

These neurons are activated both when the monkey grasps a peanut and brings it to his mouth (B) and when the monkey sees the experimenter make the same gesture (A). From G. Rizzolatti, M. Gartilucci, R. M. Camarda, V. Gallex, G. Luppino, M. Matelli, and L. Fogassi, "Neurones related to reaching-grasping arm movements in the rostral part of area 6 (area 6a)," *Experimental Brain Research* 82 (1990): 337–350.

time the animal makes a specific gesture, such as carrying a peanut to its mouth; but the same neurons are activated when the monkey sees the *experimenter* make the same gesture. In other words, the same neurons are involved in perception (from the outside toward the inside) and action (from the inside toward the outside). Since this mediation occurs in both directions, I call it reciprocal. This simple observational fact singularly clarifies the relation of oneself to another.

Ricoeur: Once again we find ourselves at a point of intersection between a discourse that preserves the notion of internal and external in the case of perception, and a discourse that abolishes it. The external is the world the experimenter knows scientifically and controls technologically; it is not the environment that living creatures construct in orienting themselves with respect to it. But it is in such an environment that the one's relation to oneself and to others unfolds.

Changeux: And this relation of living creatures to the environment that they construct is itself the object of a very lively research discipline, ethology—in particular, human ethology.

Understanding Better by Explaining More

Ricoeur: I come now to the possibility of objectifying the relations of lived experience that I have characterized by the notions of intentionality, meaning, and communication. By objectivation I understand the process by which subjective experience, which is always the experience of a subject who feels he exists in the world, is treated as a detached object—detached both from the living being who aims at it and from the horizon of the world that surrounds it. Thus subjective experience, which is always at bottom mine, yours, or his or hers, becomes a doubly separate object that functions within a network of equally detached objects, within a system. This process of objectivation poses a problem for hardcore phenomenologists, who would like to forbid it, and thus cut off explanation from understanding. For my part, I have always argued in favor of a coordination between (experienced) understanding and (objective) explanation. I want to explain in order to better understand. This is why I want to show that this process of objectivation, which makes our encounter and our discussion possible, comes to be part of the experience of meaning. In the experience of meaning, I can detach the signified from the act of signifying. Phenomenology, in the pure form I just mentioned, is very hesitant here; it has retreated to a sort of excessive subjectivization, somehow putting back the intentional *in* consciousness—whereas I would like to show that the possibility of objectifying is contained in the intentional relation, in the relation of significance, and in the communication of meaning to other persons. Each of these levels—intentional, signifying, and communicating—marks a progression in the possibility of objectifying; that is, of detaching meaning from its intended object. I think that this was clearly seen by Husserl when he distinguished the act of consciousness (*noēsis*) from its intended object (*noēma*) in the intentional relation.

Changeux: Could you elaborate?

Ricoeur: When I speak, what I mean can be detached from the act of meaning. Let us take an example in the domain of the emotions, which seems the most unfavorable to such an analysis. When I say that I am afraid, the notion of something that frightens is the object of my fright, and the object of this fright can be shared with others. Above all, it may be detached from the person who is frightened so as to become what is called a "floating signified." This floating signified permits me to develop the whole vocabulary and lexicon of fear. It is legitimate to seek the neurological equivalent of this floating signified, thus detached from its intentional object.

Changeux: But the object that frightens has no meaningful content independent of the representation. Let us take a specific example—a snake. A snake is an object that frightens a bird.

Ricoeur: It frightens me. It frightens you. I may speak of what frightens abstractly as a predicate, as a floating predicate.

Changeux: Therefore the snake is frightening for a person to the extent that this person is familiar with the object represented by the snake.

Ricoeur: What I mean is that I can give a lexical analysis of the word *frightening* without taking into account who is frightened.

Changeux: Just the same this is a very formal analysis.

Ricoeur: Not at all. I can analyze the meaning of the word *frightening* and attribute it to one thing or another. What is interesting is that this word lends itself to a variety of attributions. Here I have in mind the analysis proposed by the English philosopher Peter Strawson.[34]

Changeux: The word *frightening* has meaning only to the extent that it makes reference to a definite organism, to memories acquired by experience of the world or previously inscribed in the genetic memory of the species. What frightens a human doesn't necessarily frighten a mongoose or a scorpion. In this connection I distinguish learning of the signified, as an entry in the mental lexicon, from that of the signifier, which is communicable by voice and sight.

Ricoeur: Thanks to this procedure of objectivation, I am able to perform the inverse operation of compensation—what English analytic philosophers call "ascription," which consists in attributing an act or a mental state to someone. Human understanding, or mutual comprehension, is possible precisely because objects of meaning can circulate from subject to subject. Thus, the property of fright, once attributed to someone or something, becomes frightening for me and for you: both of us are now frightened. In other words, I have attributed a common object, or predicate, to someone or something while roughly preserving its meaning.

Changeux: I think that it is a question rather of the appropriateness of verbal or nonverbal communication, of the appropriateness of the mental objects communicated through language or images.

Ricoeur: I would say that it is a question of the mental objects themselves, which are the product of an extraordinarily complicated operation embedded in a network of intentionality, meaning, and communication, with the added element of a process of objectivation that detaches or uproots the object of its own experience. This process of detachment can always be corrected by that of attribution, of identifying someone or something as a bearer of meaning. I would say then that you have the right to do the following: try to find a neurological basis for this object, constructed in three phases—intentionality, meaning, and communication in the primitive sense of a pooling or sharing. The bridge between these three moments of phenomenological experience and your neurological research resides in two subsequent operations: objectivation, which detaches the object of meaning from its experienced context, and attribution, which ascribes it to a subject capable of saying "I," "you," "he," "she."

My aim is to reestablish on this prior basis the extraordinary complexity and the hierarchy of levels of experience. At an elementary level we have what may be called daily experience—what Descartes described as "the experience of life and ordinary conversation." At other levels we have, apart from scientific activity and the exercise of knowledge, the social and political dimension of practical life, the poetic dimension, the religious dimension—in short, total experience. To do psychology I am obliged to restrict this field, whereas the task of phenomenology is to restore its full scope. Thus the extraordinarily tangled skein of operations that makes it possible to pose the problem from which we set out at the beginning, that of the connection between the mental and the neurological. To pose this problem, it is necessary to show how the "mental" is constructed, which is what I've tried to do. We have to pass once more through the whole series of operations that permit us to remove the mental object from the complete phenomenological field. To understand ourselves, we always need to isolate the content of meaning—what is "signified"—and to submit it to operations of understanding and explanation, which include that of scientific objectivation. And among the objects of science, well, there is the brain.

Changeux: I do not disagree with what you say. To the contrary, I think that neurobiologists, psychologists, and neuropsychologists, in their enterprise of naturalization and experimental analysis, ought very carefully to examine—if they have not already done so—the points that you mention. The hierarchy of levels of experience, the "extraordinarily tangled skein of operations" to which you refer, is entirely relevant to the study of the *complexity* of the functional organization of our brain, which is both parallel and hierarchical.

I share several of your concerns with regard to the question of intentionality. The experimental implementation of what is meant by "meaning" poses a problem, not between us but among scientists. In my opinion it will be one of the principal issues of research in cognitive neuroscience in the years to come. Experimentally, the problem is not out of reach. Positron emission tomography can reveal different maps of cerebral activation depending on whether the subject observes a manual gesture that has a meaning or one that does not (figure 3.8). When the subject observes with the intention of recognizing a gesture that he has stored in memory, a somewhat different distribution of cerebral activities occurs than when he observes with the intention of imitating a gesture. But brain images differ with respect to meaning and non-meaning, no matter what the strategy may be. Differences of meaning and intention become accessible to observation through brain imaging.[35]

As for the problem of the communication of a mental representation or mental object from one individual to another, this is mainly a problem of language, of the relation of the signifier to the signified. Research is now actively being conducted on various aspects of communication. One of the relatively accessible problems is the coding of the signified by the signifier. Saussure himself wrote that "the terms involved in the linguistic sign, concept, and acoustic image, are united in our brain through the bond of association."[36] The ball is in the court of the neurosciences.

Ricoeur: I don't want us to rely only on Saussure here. We know today that a whole section concerning the role of phonetic and lexical structures in actual speech was removed from the first edition of the *Cours de linguistique générale* (1916), which set the terms of the debate that followed. Benveniste remedied the omission by insisting upon the sentence as the principal unit of discourse.[37] Now, in a sentence, someone says something to someone about something. It is necessary then to complete what you have just called "coding" by a theory of speech acts, which comes under the head of language practice.

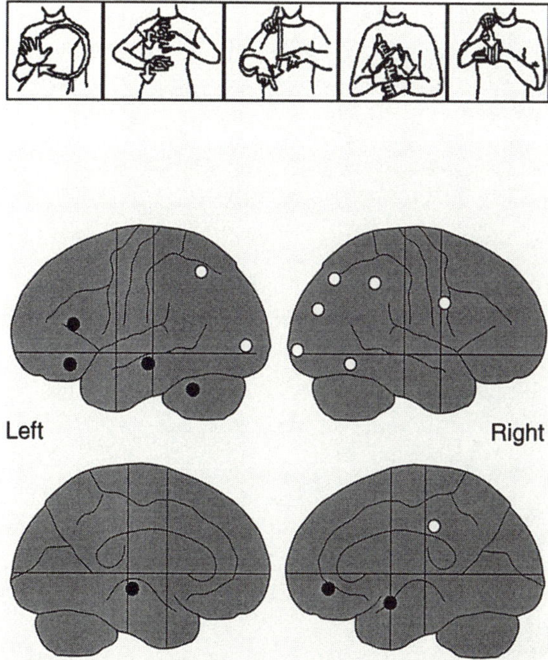

FIGURE 3.8. Effect of the meaning of an action on the activity of the brain.

The states of a subject's cerebral activity are mapped with a PET scanner as he observes, on a video screen, hand movements that have a meaning for the subject (opening a bottle, drawing a line, sewing a button, and so on) or that do not have meaning for him (the gestures of American Sign Language shown in the figure, for example). In both cases, whether or not the movements have a meaning for the subject, he is asked either to imitate or to recognize the movement. The cerebral images differ when the movement is perceived as meaningful or not meaningful, regardless of the strategy employed (imitation or recognition). Actions having a meaning strongly involve the frontal and temporal regions of the left hemisphere. The black dots correspond to meaningful gestures, the white dots to meaningless gestures. From J. Decéty, J. Grèzes, N. Costes, D. Perani, M. Jeannerod, E. Procyk, F. Grassi, and F. Fazio, "Brain activity during observation of actions: Influence of action context and subject's strategy," *Brain* 120 (1997): 1763–1777.

Changeux: Dan Sperber and Deirdre Wilson have introduced the notion of relevance in the communication of objects of meaning.[38] I think that their formalism clarifies and brings out what you call the communication of meaning to other persons. They abandon the standard model of communication due to Shannon and Weaver, according to which a coded message is transmitted through a communication channel to a receiver who somehow decodes it, word by word. They adopt instead a model of inferential communication based on the idea that comprehension of a message involves more than the decoding of a linguistic signal. In human verbal communication, first a framework of thought is transmitted that involves shared intentions and emotions. Each speaker tries above all to recognize the intentions of the other and, within the model thus created, to make use of *relevant* information; that is, to try in the most efficient way possible, and with the greatest possible multiplicative effect, to exploit new information in combination with old.

Newspaper headlines rely on this strategy: in a few words, sometimes a single word, they transmit a strong message that will be understood by readers who are prepared to receive it but that may seem incomprehensible only a few years later. Zola's famous phrase, "J'accuse," takes on its full meaning only in the context of the Dreyfus affair. When you speak of detaching what I call a mental representation from its intended object, you remove it, if I understand correctly, from one intentional frame in order to transplant it in another. Its relevance therefore changes; that is, its functional "connectivity" with the repertoire of other mental representations embedded in the new context changes, and as a result its very meaning changes as well. We are just now discussing, in fact, a neuronal theory of context, intentions, and the operations that our brain carries out upon objects of meaning—what I call mental representations or mental objects.

This capacity of the human brain to communicate intentions, contexts, frameworks of thought through language—but also through gestures, symbols, and rituals—seems to me altogether fundamental. It finds direct application in art. It contributes also to self-evaluation, to judgments about oneself, and leads us finally to consider the question of consciousness.

Ricoeur: The model proposed by Sperber and Wilson may be usefully compared, I think, with Benveniste's linguistic theory, which I contrasted a moment ago with Saussure's overly lexical model. The notion of discourse, centered on the utterance of sentences, implies the notion of contextual relevance on which you insist. A phenomenology of action will add in gestures and all the elements of behavior that contribute to the practical deciphering of the environment. There is much material here for fruitful interdisciplinary research.

4 — Consciousness of Oneself and of Others

Conscious Space

Jean-Pierre Changeux: The activity of communicating, of making oneself understood, occurs among alert and conscious subjects. The problems associated with consciousness need to be approached with care. I will try first to define the notion of conscious space. This may be thought of as a sort of *milieu intérieur*—a neural setting within the brain, still very poorly described by the neurosciences, for operations that are qualitatively distinct from those carried out in the other unconscious parts of our brain and our nervous system. This space is given over to simulation, to virtual action. Its development from lower vertebrates to humans is dazzling. Although it is internal to the organism, it is somehow inserted between the external world and the organism. At this level one finds intentions, goals, plans, courses of action evaluated with constant reference to (at least) four poles involving distinct systems of neurons: actual interaction with the external world—this opening onto the world that you yourself have mentioned; the self and the whole of an individual's history, which takes the form of remembered events, of a narrative reconstituted from one's own life and the memory of prior experiences marked somatically by their emotional tone; and, finally, internalized rules and social conventions, as well as those global conceptions of man and society that each person tacitly carries within himself or herself. Here I recall *your* definition of narration—a concrete example if ever there was one of the operations carried out in the conscious space of the brain—as "deploying an imaginary space for thought experiments in which moral judgment operates in a hypothetical mode."[1] This suits me perfectly. Finally, the philosopher and the biologist find themselves on common ground!

Many neurobiologists (Edelman, Llinás, Crick, Zeki, Dehaene, and myself) and philosophers (Dennett, Searle, and so on) have enthusiastically undertaken the task of modeling consciousness. Among the few sure guides at our disposal are a number of very different systems of neuromodulators that control states of vigilance and attention, of wakefulness and sleep; chemical agents, namely those drugs I mentioned previously that alter our perception of the world and our states of consciousness (figure 3.6);[2] "binding" mechanisms that coordinate states of activity and assure the functional coherence of large groups of neurons;[3] finally, systems of evaluation—systems that may themselves be learned, as studies of the alert monkey indicate[4]—that allow us to pass back and forth from the non-self to the self. Much theoretical and experimental work remains to be done before we can reconstruct the neural bases of consciousness from these data.[5] By contrast, the function of consciousness in the life of the organism seems obvious: it permits a considerable economy in acting upon the world.

Paul Ricoeur: Here again the construction of your neuronal model seems to me to run quite far ahead of its experimental verification—as a consequence of advances in other fields that owe nothing to the neurosciences. You integrate these results while trying to remain faithful to your basic premises. Now, these premises limit the import of the results you have borrowed: rather than look for increased openness onto a world shaped by actual and virtual interactions, you are obliged to say that all this takes place in the brain. The simulation space, you say, is somehow "inserted" between the external world and the organism, while nonetheless being "internal" to the latter. In the same way you speak of modeling consciousness as though it were an accomplished fact. I quite willingly accept your more cautious formula of a "neural basis of consciousness"—but now we find ourselves back to the discussion we had earlier concerning the relation between the neuronal and the mental. The problem is only made trickier by expanding our topic to include what, as a sort of shorthand, we call consciousness.

Changeux: You find that I limit the scope of my analysis by saying that all such activity takes place in the brain. Indeed I do. Here I wish to restrict myself to the field of neuroscientific research, while reserving the liberty of enlarging the subject of debate when the time comes. Two remarks in this connection: one on intellectual practice, the other, more seriously, on a fundamental issue. References by authors in the human sciences to Freud and psychoanalysis abound; you yourself often refer to psychoanalysis in your writings. Research in the neurosciences, on the other hand, is virtually never mentioned by these authors, or else only among themselves. Given a choice between speaking too much of the brain and not speaking of it at all, I leave you to judge who is right and who is wrong!

On the fundamental issue, it would be a mistake to underestimate the importance of the set of behaviors, programs of action, and memories with their various emotional tones that are "wired" in our brain on a long-term basis. As Marx observed, "Men make their own history, but they do not make it just as they please. . . . The tradition of all the dead generations weighs like a nightmare on the brain of the living." This is, in fact, the case—a consequence of all the traces of history and culture internalized in our encephalon. Sperber and Wilson's argument regarding relevance, like your remarks on the importance of context, show that under many circumstances the signals we receive from the external world acquire meaning only in an intentional framework, internal to our brain, whose structure is derived from our immense repertoire of long-term memories. As a result, our brains can intervene effectively in a concerted way—we shall come back to this point in our discussion of ethics later—by exploiting the various resources of the external world, past and present.

Ricoeur: Before we turn to the topic of memory, I would like to come back to your notion of conscious space. Space and time are closely connected in actual experience. Space holds a double interest for phenomenology. Experienced space is, on the one hand, that of one's own body, an extension of the sense organs, felt though postures, movements of our limbs, and when we move about; but also in the bodily depths of enjoyment or suffering. On the other hand, it is the space surrounding us that extends as far as the horizon. The body, in relation to this space external to it, is nowhere; or, rather, it defines the absolute *here* in relation to which there is an *over there,* where you are, and a common space where things have a place and in which we occupy a place and move about. This space is oriented, actively explored, crisscrossed with viable paths and more or less surmountable obstacles—it is, in a word, a habitable space. The role of objective knowledge, then, is to refer this private and common space, this bodily and public space, to an abstract system of places in a geometric and physical space where places become geographic sites, and where *here* and *over there* become any places whatever. It is in this objective space that the internal cerebral setting of which you speak is found, as well as the "simulation space" that concerns each of us. Time, as an aspect of memory, poses a comparable problem. For the moment the neurosciences may be said to regard the brain as a remarkable space "in" which material traces are stored. With the notion of a memory trace, or engram, space and time become more closely related still.

Changeux: We have already considered, through the example of anosognosia, the neurology underlying the perception of one's own body and one's self-image. Similarly, the analysis of lesions in humans, like physiological recordings in animals, leads us to dissociate this "egocentric" perception from the "allocentric" perception of one's body in extrapersonal space, which chiefly involves the parietal lobe. Putting these various systems of geometric coordinates into correspondence with each other involves considerable learning. Their coherence in space and time is tested by means of simulation experiments in conscious space, before finally being realized in the form of actual movements.

The Question of Memory

Changeux: Memory occupies a central place in the consciousness of oneself and of others. More than a century ago, in 1892, William James distinguished two components of human memory. To primary or immediate memory, he held, we owe the perception of time—the immediate past of a few seconds, which is projected against a background of an apparent present. Today we call this short-term, or working, memory. Its capacity is limited: seven units, plus or minus two, rapidly forgotten after about twenty seconds. Secondary, or long-term, memory, is—once more to cite James—"the knowledge of an event, or fact, of which meantime we have not been thinking, with the additional consciousness that we have thought or experienced it before."[6]

In fact, the past knowledge stored in long-term memory in

the form of stable traces is constantly reactualized in the working compartment, where it is held "on-line" while, for example, we search for an address or move a piece on a chessboard. Working memory confers unity and continuity upon conscious experience. But it also includes tacit evaluation and explicit reasoning, with the capacity for projecting prerepresentations on the future, for directing the execution of a task. In man as in the monkey, brain lesions selectively alter working memory. François Lhermitte, for example, has described a kind of "utilization behavior" in certain frontal patients who constantly lose the thread of their thought, seizing and then manipulating every object they encounter, without having any question or definite plan in mind.[7] A frontal patient is no longer able to plan a trip correctly or even put together a meal tray.

Brain imaging reveals that when the normal subject makes a conscious effort to use his working memory, a sustained level of activity manifests itself, within the limits of this memory, in the frontal cortex, specifically in the language area known as Broca's area. Objects of knowledge called up to the working compartment are also recruited from the regions of the cortex where long-term memories are stored: visual areas for concrete images; motor areas for actions on the world; specialized parts of the temporal areas for the recognition of faces, animals, and artifacts, including tools and instruments; a group of areas distributed over the cortex and converging in the frontal cortex for "abstract" concepts. Generally speaking, most areas of the cerebral cortex are involved in a latent form in storing stable traces of explicit memories, which therefore are widely distributed in the brain. They are differentially activated when these memories are called back up to the working compartment. With repetition, recall becomes easier, more "automatic," and the contribution of the frontal lobes gradually diminishes while that of the other regions persists.[8]

The other category of long-term memory, implicit memory, which involves competences and unconscious impressions, operates by means of distinct mechanisms. For example, training the fingers of the hand to produce a motor sequence, as in the case of a musician learning to play an instrument, yields an increase in the surface area of the relevant regions of the motor cortex: new neurons are recruited—to the detriment, of course, of neighboring regions. During the acquisition of implicit memories, a very lively competition develops among cortical areas.

The acquisition of language leaves long-term traces in the brain whose neuronal "inscription" is manifest. Children learn their native language spontaneously through simple immersion in the life of their family and social circle. They also learn, albeit only with effort, to read and write. In the course of the very long period of development that follows birth—in relative terms the longest in the animal kingdom—traces of the mother tongue are indelibly recorded in the developing network of synaptic connections.[9] Also stabilized in this network are the symbolic representations, social conventions, and moral rules that contribute to the formation of individuality and to the singular features of each person.

Brain imaging opens a spectacular, although still limited, window on this neuronal development in the case of bilingual subjects (figure 4.1). The images obtained by functional magnetic resonance in early bilingual speakers show that the distribution of activated areas is the same without regard to language. In late bilingual speakers—those who have learned a second language between the ages of eleven and nineteen—the distribution of activities doesn't change in the sensory temporal areas of language known collectively as Wernicke's area, but it is clearly distinct in Broca's area. A different cortical geography is therefore found to be associated with the late learning of a second language.

Experimental models of learning in the animal suggest that the way in which these traces are registered depends as much on the number and topology of synaptic connections as on their efficiency in transmitting nerve signals. Memory traces are "materialized" in molecular processes that involve, in particular, the neurotransmitter receptors we have already discussed at some length. Bergson, in *Matter and Memory* (1896), had concluded that "memory must be, in principle, a power absolutely independent of matter" and "hence any attempt to derive pure memory from an operation of the brain should reveal on analysis a radical illusion."[10] On this point, however, the great philosopher's intuition proved to be mistaken.

Long-term memory comprises another, somewhat neglected, aspect, namely its emotional component. Memories are in fact often associated with emotional markers: memory traces are evaluated as a function of the pleasure, happiness or unhappiness, or suffering that the subject anticipates. The neurosciences provide a definite basis for asserting a connection between the memorized cognitive representation, the knowledge trace, and the emotional trace associated with this knowledge, which appears to be located at the level of the various pathways that unite the frontal cortex with the limic system, and most especially with a specialized nucleus, the amygdala.

The neuronal inscription of memory traces is thus clear. Much nevertheless remains to be done in order to decipher these synaptic hieroglyphs.

Ricoeur: The case of memory is particularly favorable to the continuation of our discussion. Phenomenology and the neurosciences are in agreement, in fact, with regard to description while diverging with regard to interpretation. Let us consider the problem of description for a moment. It is not by chance that you cited William James in connection with the distribution between immediate memory, understood as working

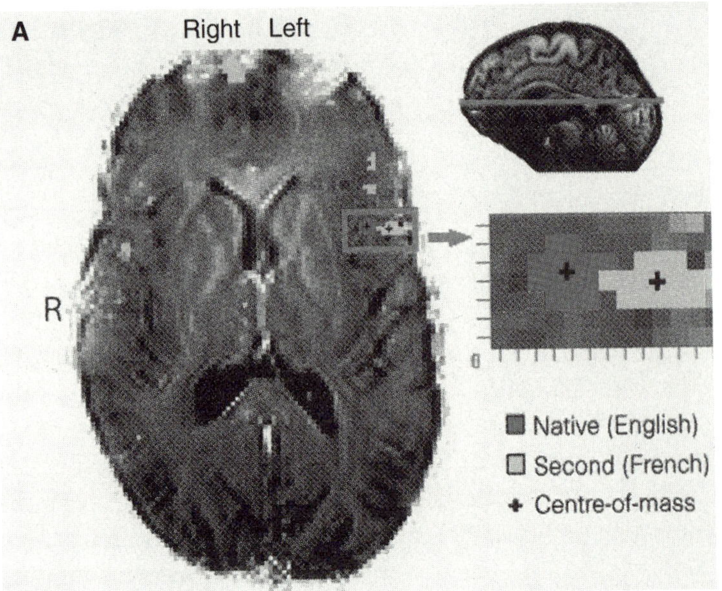
A
Right
Left
R
Native (English)
Second (French)
Centre-of-mass

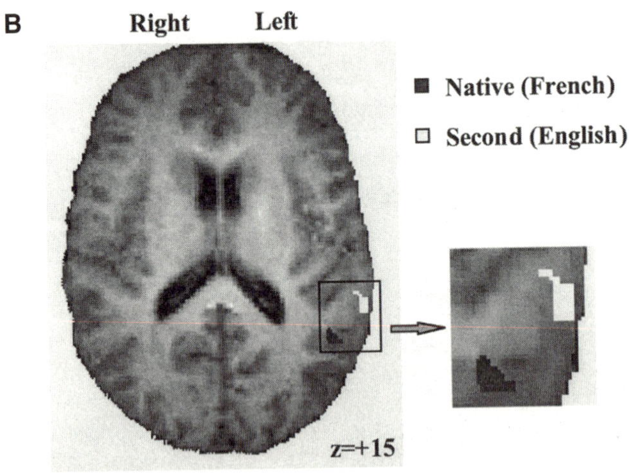
B
Right
Left
Native (French)
Second (English)
z=+15

FIGURE 4.1

memory, and indirect, or long-term, memory. In Husserl's *Phenomenology of Internal Time Consciousness,* one finds a comparable distinction expressed in the vocabulary of "retention" and "remembrance." In the case of retention, the recent past, which has "just" occurred, "still" remains present to consciousness, whereas the distant past no longer plays a role in the present that James calls "specious" and you call "apparent"; it is reached through an interval of time by stepping backward into a time other than the present described as "no longer being," which is to say "having been." You observe that the sense of the unity and continuity of conscious experience depends on working memory—the whole of the duration, I would add, being put together by means of a series of retentions of retentions.

Moving from this observation to consider the question of memory traces, phenomenology may be seen to operate on the plane both of description and interpretation. The descriptive aspect can be examined with the aid of several new pairs of contrasted terms. First there is the distinction introduced by Bergson between "habit memory" [*mémoire-habitude*] and

---

FIGURE 4.1. Differential distribution of the areas of the cerebral cortex associated with native and second languages.

Brain images obtained by functional magnetic resonance during the tacit production of various linguistic tasks (A) and during the comprehension of a particular language (B). In both cases the subjects tested were late learners of second languages. Late learners manifest differences in the distribution of cerebral activity that are not observed in early bilingual speakers. From K. Kim, N. Relkin, K.-M. Lee, and J. Hirsch, "Distinct cortical areas associated with native and second languages," *Nature* 388 (1997): 171–174; and S. Dehaene, E. Dupoux, J. Mehler, L. Cohen, E. Paulesu, D. Perani, P. F. Van de Moortele, S. Lehéricy, and D. Le Bihan, "Anatomical variability in the cortical representation of first and second languages," *Neuroreport* 17 (1997): 3775–3778.

"pure memory" [*mémoire-souvenir*]. For it is one thing to execute a familiar task, for example to recite a text learned by heart; it is another to recall learning to execute such a task. The latter form of memory concerns a singular, nonrepeatable event that occurred once in the past. The relation to time, which I will come back to in a moment, is different in the case of each term of the contrasted pair: in the case of habit memory, the past is acted out and incorporated in the present without distance; in the case of pure memory, the anteriority or priorness of the remembered event stands out, whereas in habit memory it does not. This distinction concerning the relation to time is important for dissociating memory and learning, as against the tendency of the biology of memory to treat the two phenomena as continuous—to remember and to memorize are distinct phenomena.

Another pair of terms concerns the relation between spontaneous recollection and more or less labored recall: one pole is represented by Proust's involuntary memory; the other by an effort of memory, which is a type of intellectual effort and which reduces neither to the association of empiricist tradition nor to calculation. This effort involves what Bergson and Merleau-Ponty call a "dynamic schema" capable of directing memory searches by discarding inappropriate candidates and recognizing the "right" memory. The phenomenon of recognition is itself very interesting, in the sense that the remembered past and the present moment of recall overlap without being identical: the past is not known, but re-known, as it were—recognized.

A third remarkable pair involves remembering as memory of oneself and, at the same time, as memory of something other than oneself. One may speak here of a polarity between reflexivity and worldliness: on the one hand, as the pronominal form of the French verb "to remember" [*se souvenir*] suggests, it is of *oneself* that one remembers; on the other hand, the specific intentionality of memory carries it toward events that are said to have happened, to have occurred. Events occur in the world and are linked to places—the places of memory [*lieux de mémoire*] famously analyzed by Pierre Nora.[11] In the case of the most memorable events, these places are "marked" by collective memory, as a result of which the events linked to them are made memorable; they are inscribed in geographical space just as commemorable events are inscribed in historical time—that is, in the world around us. The connection between reflexivity and worldliness is established by bodily memory, which may itself be immediate or deferred, acted out or represented: it is a self of flesh and blood that we remember, with its moments of pleasure and suffering, its states, its actions, its feelings—which in their turn are situated in an environment, and particularly in places where we have been present with others and which we jointly remember.

Changeux: So far, I agree. The implementation of such a dynamic schema of memory recall by trial and error in terms of a neuronal network seems to me entirely possible and relevant. We will come back to this.

Ricoeur: A final point regarding description: neurobiologists insist on the distinct and derivative character of "declarative" memory, which is structured by language—mainly by narrative. I wonder whether it is possible to escape the connection between memory and language; the link seems so close that, in the case of problems related to a lesion or other dysfunctions, one can hardly do without the accounts of the subjects themselves. Nonetheless, this is a question that Husserl posed in the unpublished writings: does the prenarrative level rise above muteness? Can one join Dilthey, then, in speaking of the "cohesion of life"—and therefore of the coherence that life creates with itself—underlying the narrative coherence of personal accounts? For the moment I leave the question open.

Your reference to time, in introducing the problem of memory, leads me now from description to interpretation. The question of memory traces is unavoidable to the extent that the notion of time involves reference to something absent. Plato was the first, to my knowledge, to have formulated the essential paradox: memory, he says in the *Theaetetus,* expresses the presence of something absent. But whereas, for the imagination, the absent is *unreal* (as Sartre emphasized in *The Imaginary*), for memory the absent is *prior,* marked by the adverb "previously." Prior to what? To the memory that we now have of it, to the account that we now give of it. Of course, memory and imagination constantly interact, in the form of fantasy, among other things; also owing to the tendency to display our memories in images, as on a screen. This doesn't prevent us from expecting our memories to be trustworthy, and our memory faithful to what has actually taken place—we do not demand this of the imagination, which is permitted to dream. As untrustworthy as memory may be, it is all we have to assure ourselves that something previously took place. The past is therefore absent from our accounts in a specific way. Neuroscience introduces the notion of a trace in order to account for exactly this presence of something absent. Preservation, storage, mobilization at the moment of recall—the competence of objective science with regard to these material operations is indisputable.

For my part, I have no trouble integrating your notions of cortical geography and neuronal inscription with the notion of a basic substrate, understood as an indispensable condition. Besides, in the case of dysfunctions, whether due to lesions or something else, knowledge of these neural mechanisms comes to be altogether naturally incorporated with the experience of one's own body, in the form of therapeutic intervention aimed at adapting behavior to a "catastrophic" situation, to use Goldstein's term once again. But the use of such knowledge as a practical matter seems to me more problematic, indeed irrelevant, in the case of felicitous memory—even though the forgetting against which we struggle serves to remind us that such memory is not absolutely felicitous, or fully functioning, since forgetting oscillates between the complete erasure of memories and the blocking of memories that are available but inaccessible. In this regard, psychoanalysis is inclined to suppose that we forget less than we fear we do, and that with effort—Freud's famous "effort to remember"—we can recover and reincorporate whole pieces of memory in a more readable and more acceptable personal history.

Changeux: You mention forgetting. Two psychologists, Hermann Ebbinghaus[12] at the end of the nineteenth century and F. C. Bartlett[13] in the 1930s, were the first to quantitatively analyze the development of memory traces. They measured the rate of forgetting through quantitative and qualitative evaluation of conscious recall. The first method makes use of meaningless syllables; the second, by contrast, of meaningful stories. In both cases the trace undergoes a rapid decline within an hour; then a slow process of forgetting over a period of days, weeks, even months. The trace becomes fragmented. Separate elements disappear, others persist. The recall after several months of a complex story displays modifications, omissions, changes in the order of events and alteration of the details. Recalling a memory trace involves, in Bartlett's phrase, "an effort to understand"—a *reconstruction* based on preexisting schemas and on what has been retained. The agreement with Merleau-Ponty's theses, and even with Freud's "effort to remember," is clear. Nonetheless, to create meaning in the course of restoring memories also risks changing them, falsifying them—quite innocently, of course.

In a pathological context, there are "source" amnesias, often due to age, where the patient can no longer remember when, where, or how a memory was acquired. Recollection in the case of other amnesias is associated with a curious sort of speech containing obviously false, contradictory, bizarre, and in any case improbable information. These fantastic confabulations, typically the result of frontal lobe lesion, are the result of inadequate reconstructions, errors of evaluation in the recollection of memories, and a failure to properly situate them in the context of one's personal history.

In normal subjects, memory *distortions* and implantations of *false* memories frequently occur.[14] Their experimental implementation is simple.[15] One presents the subject with a series of slides depicting a complex event and then reads him an account of the event containing deliberate misinformation; after several other tests, he is finally given a memory test. The result is obvious: not only is a very high proportion of false memories introduced during the misinformation stage, but the subject unhesitatingly believes them. The implantation of false memories in adults, as in children, can have serious consequences. In the United States recently there has been a sort of epidemic of cases of "resurrected" memories involving persons, sometimes undergoing psychotherapy, who think they have recovered long-forgotten memories of childhood mistreatment (most commonly sexual or other violent abuse). Illusory memories can thus be created in vulnerable patients, leading them to invent a false autobiography.[16]

Ricoeur: The contribution made by the neurosciences to the question of forgetting is undeniable and considerable. But it doesn't come to grips with the difficulty I stress concerning the notion of a trace. One cannot ignore the fact that this notion has been a source of formidable puzzles since Greek antiquity. Plato gave it form in the *Theaetetus* with the famous metaphor of the impression (*tupos*), as for example the impression made by a seal on a piece of wax. The metaphor was adopted by Aristotle and Augustine in the guise of the term *effigy* (in the sense of a representation or image). It is not unhelpful to recall the circumstances that gave rise to the metaphor, which grew out of a need to account for an epistemological and ontological scandal connected with the power of false opinion and the fame of the Sophist Protagoras, who (according to Aristotle) boasted of his ability to "make the weaker argument the stronger." How was one to explain the fact of false opinion and Protagoras's renown? Well, by supposing that certain opinions do not coincide with the appropriate impression but are adjusted to fit a "wrong" one, like a person who puts his foot into a footprint that doesn't match. Where, then, is the problem? It resides in the fact that all traces are present to our minds. There is no hint of something that is absent, still less of something that existed previously. It is necessary then to endow the trace with a semiotic dimension, so that it functions as a sign, and to regard the trace as a sign-effect, a sign of the action of the seal in creating the impression. Aristotle tried to improve the metaphor by adding to it the notion of a picture, to indicate a form of writing or drawing (as we still do today in speaking, as you do, of neuronal "inscription"). He then proposed to distinguish two aspects of the picture or inscription: its own features, which in a sense are present in the inscription itself, and its reference to something other than the inscription, to that which the inscription denotes. But the Platonic puzzle was only deepened by interpreting the impression as an image, as a picture or inscription: how is it that such an inscription is itself present and yet also a sign of what is not present, of what existed previously? Are we to hold that the stability of the trace—which is said to remain, to stay, to be left—may itself be observed and that the past remains inscribed in the trace, just as the age of a tree is inscribed in the concentric circles of its trunk? But then it is necessary to appeal to the category of indication, which is a category of the sign, as Aristotle showed elsewhere. Plato himself had done this earlier in treating the impression as a sign of the stamp of the seal. A trace must therefore be conceived at once as a present effect and as the sign of its absent cause. Now, in the trace, there is no otherness, no absence. Everything is positivity and presence.

It is here that phenomenology offers, not a substitute, but a complement. Don't we have, in the actual experience of recognizing a memory sought and found, a paradoxical sense that the absent is present, despite its distance in the past—in short, a sense of the depth of time? Manifested in this instant is the specific intentionality of memory, which Aristotle describes as memory "*of* time." But included in this paradoxical sense of the presence of the absent, of what went before, is the prior passivity of a consciousness *affected* by the event that has occurred. Memory keeps the phenomenal (and no longer merely material) trace of this initial passivity—an experienced trace of attention, of being, affected by the event. The expression of this initial passivity at the level of declarative memory is therefore akin to the sort of testimony, in the everyday sense of the term, given in court or contained in archival documents. Someone says: "I was there. You can believe my account or not, as you like. If you don't believe me, your only alternative will be to find another witness—but his testimony won't be any better than mine." The trustworthiness of memory is at issue here. Don't we have to say, then, that this sense of the trace left by the event and its "stamp" stands in a relation of indication to the neuronal trace, as a sign of its existence—the mirror-image of the relation between the neuronal basis of mental experience and the experience itself?

Changeux: Your remarks link up with the argument of the Canadian researcher Endel Tulving, who has proposed that encoding, storage, and recall form three distinct processes.[17] The encoding of memories is carried out serially. For example, one can register a new piece of historical information about the French Revolution in a pertinent way only if it has to do with an event that occurred in France at the end of the eighteenth century. Encoding is done in context! Storage, by contrast, can be carried out in parallel. For example, the discovery of previously unknown correspondence between Lavoisier and his wife might be committed to memory under the categories "chemistry" and "love life" as well as under "Reign of Terror" (Lavoisier, you will recall, was a victim of the Revolution, executed in 1794). On Tulving's theory, recall is independent. Stimulus words intervene in a definite intentional context to produce hypotheses, in effect, that serve to reassemble traces dispersed in the brain. The convergence between the neurobiological approach and the phenomenological theses of Merleau-Ponty's "dynamic schema" is plain. Recall via reconstruction establishes, in an anticipatory way, the coordinates of a spatio-temporal context in relation to the contents of working memory and the self. In this case these coordinates might be "chemistry" or "Terror." The recollection of memories amounts to an internal test of the coherence of hypotheses about the past, with all the risks this involves (that false memories may be introduced in the process, and so on). The neural modeling of memory recall now seems to me possible. On an entirely different plane, however, the task of the historian now becomes overwhelming. His own memory, though it has evidentiary value, cannot by itself yield an objective reconstitution of the past. This can be attained only through comparison with other memories and the give-and-take of free debate.

Ricoeur: But now we have passed to another use of the notion of a trace, moving from the cerebral or mental trace to the cultural trace or inscription. Here I take up what you have said about the cultural mediation of memory. Inscription proposes a semiological metaphor of wide scope that is limited neither to the neural bases of consciousness nor to the experienced traces of a marking or stamping event. When you refer to distinct mechanisms of long-term memory, you give a new context to the picture metaphor, which is no longer either the brain or the affected being of the subject, but a material support distinct from the body; writing—and, a fortiori, phonetic writing—is itself only one manifestation of the general phenomenon of drawing, which appears in many other forms (cave paintings, body decorations, decorations of clothing and housing, and so on). This is a question not of neurological, but of cultural material. Such inscriptions lend themselves to a shared reading and this whole activity of deciphering and decoding that you mention.

We ought to use the notion of a trace in three senses: to refer to a neural trace; an experienced trace of the initial passivity of affected consciousness; and a cultural trace conveyed by a cultural support external to the body.

Changeux: Of course—but what seems to me important is the notion of sharing and cultural inscription. The two elements can't be separated, for cultural representations are intended to be shared, not only at a given moment in a particular community but across generations as well. Inscriptions in stone, clay, wood, papyrus or paper, and now on magnetic computer disks constitute so many prostheses, as it were, of cerebral memory—prostheses that are remarkable for being more stable than cerebral memory and transmissible from generation to generation. In this connection the exceptional initial plasticity of human cerebral organization should be noted, which makes it possible to draw upon whole regions of the brain in the case of essential activities such as writing and reading. These, however, are relatively recent cultural inventions, considering the whole of human history.

On the other hand, there is a great diversity of categories of representation giving rise to specific modes of transmission in human societies. Sperber has proposed a hierarchical classification of "public" representations,[18] which is to say representations that are capable of being communicated from brain to brain. There are two main types:

- *First-order representations,* which involve objects and facts of the external world (rocks, rivers, plants, animals, human beings), artifacts (tools such as chisels and glasses), and relations between factual representations, such as "The wolf is dangerous" or "The apple is edible." Their diffusion is quite vast. They involve empirical knowledge that is very widely shared and indispensable to the survival of the individual.
- *Second-order representations,* which are located at a higher hierarchical level and involve complex relations among first-order representations, which in turn are the objects of rationalization, conceptualization, and selection.

At least three broad categories of second-order representations can readily be distinguished that are shared within the social group to a lesser degree than first-order, or factual, representations: scientific representations, which constitute the body of objective knowledge about the world whose effectiveness in solving practical problems has been universally recognized by the community of scientists; aesthetic representations, which are intended to communicate subjective messages having symbolic and emotional impact within the social group; and ethical representations, concerning the self in relation to other selves and to the social group to which they jointly belong, that are sustained and validated by a shared way of life. Such representations are distinguished from a whole corpus of social conventions, symbolic systems, rituals, reference texts, and, of course, institutions that vary in incidental ways from one social group to another, depending on their history and geographic distribution. They are also distinguished from delirious beliefs, which fall under the head of mental pathology because they are cut off from intersubjective communication and, as a result, are not shared by the majority of the individuals who make up a given social group. For example, the frightening image of the victims of the bombing of Hiroshima can be perceived by you and me as a common signifier.

Ricoeur: A common signified, you mean.

Changeux: No—photographic images, and the plastic arts in general, it seems to me, are able to do without the distinction peculiar to language between arbitrary signifier and signified. A painting offers itself directly to the sensibility of the viewer. The image mimics, as it were, and the viewer puts himself in the place of the persons it represents, identifies himself with them. This is what allows us to entertain the notion of universalism, perhaps even universality, in intercomprehension—an issue of considerable importance in any discussion of ethics.

Comprehension of Oneself and of Others

Changeux: In the course of our discussion so far you have called attention to one's relation to oneself and to others. I think we are justified in relating it to a cognitive device that is particularly developed in human beings: the capacity of attribution, or of representing the mental states of others, their sufferings, plans of action, intentions (figure 4.2).

In a famous article, Premack and Woodruff asked whether this capacity to interpret one's own behavior and that of others in terms of inferences about the mental states (desires, intentions, beliefs, knowledge) of others is peculiar to human beings. "Does the chimpanzee have a theory of mind?" they

FIGURE 4.2. *The Fortune Teller,* by Georges de La Tour (1593–1652). (Rogers Fund, Metropolitan Museum of Art, New York.) This famous painting illustrates in several ways the capacity, particularly developed in human beings, to attribute knowledge to others and indeed, as here, the absence of knowledge. With a sidelong glance the young woman on the right checks to see that the rich young simpleton's attention is totally concentrated on the fabulous revelations of the old gypsy woman while she cuts his gold chain and her partner steals his purse. In related studies, brain imaging reveals a differential activity of the frontal cortex when a subject reads a text mentioning mental states that disappears when he reads a text about physical states.

wondered.[19] On their view, the word *theory* is justified to the extent that the mental states of others are not directly observable by the subject. They must be represented in hypothetical or theoretical form in order for the subject to be able to make predictions about the behavior of others. This capacity of attribution progressively develops in the baby. At two months, reciprocal communication is established between the mother and child and, at the end of the first year, a coordination of looks is achieved between the child and those around him. The child communicates with gestures and uses his hands to point to objects or situations. He knows how to use visual and auditory information. Finally, he becomes capable of representing intentional relations between the first and third persons.

In the course of the second year, the child sets off in search of hidden objects, imitates various things, plays at make-believe, begins to use language, and refers to memorized representations to interpret perceived events and to respond to them. He appeals to imagination to compare past objects of memory and present reality. He recognizes himself in a mirror (as adult chimpanzees do). Even before the age of eighteen months, babies perceive the suffering of other babies and cry with them. But beyond this age their behavior changes: they spontaneously make attempts to comfort the baby in distress. A "decentering" of the sort proposed by Piaget and Kohlberg occurs. The baby understands that the feelings of others may differ from his own and that his attitude can change them. He imagines the mental states of others in order to act upon them. As Baldwin recognized in 1894, comprehension of oneself develops in parallel with the comprehension—imagined, but real—of others. A clear relation was thus established between self-knowledge and empathy-sympathy.

The Premacks have shown, with the aid of an elegant video animation, that children ten months and older attribute intentions and "human" purposes to extremely simple self-propelled objects (balls of different colors, for example).[20] A caress is positively coded by the baby; a violent shock negatively. The help given by one intentional object to another—in order, for instance, to escape confinement—is evaluated positively; preventing escape, negatively. The baby positively codes the "freedom" of the object to emerge from a hiding place. He attributes an internal cause to intentional objects and assesses the *reciprocity* of a positive gesture (if A caresses B, he expects B to act positively toward A). He values a ball that bounces regularly by comparison with one that takes odd bounces. The very young child spontaneously acquires a system of *moral values* that attaches importance to cooperation and sympathy, and even *aesthetic preferences* distinct from moral values.

From twenty-four months the young child becomes capable of attributing beliefs to intentional objects, whom he now interprets as seeing, wishing, and believing. At four years the child begins to develop a theory of mind. The crucial test is false belief. The child succeeds in imaginatively picturing a situation in which another child does not possess the knowledge appropriate to a new situation, whereas he knows himself to be adequately informed with regard to such situations. He compares two representations: the knowledge he imagines others to have with the knowledge that he possesses.

Autistic children exhibit serious cognitive problems of development affecting social communication and affective contact, empathy, and sympathy. Research done by the English team of Leslie, Frith, and Baron-Cohen suggests that autistics have an altered theory of mind.[21] They do not draw inferences about others from information they have of themselves, operating at the cognitive level of the newborn child.

Various attempts have been made to identify the cerebral correlates of the theory of mind using positron emission tomography. On the basis of psychological tests involving recognition of terms designating defined mental states, various authors have shown that the prefrontal cortex is directly associated with a theory of mind. This is not surprising since the prefrontal cortex is the most recently evolved part of the human encephalon.

Ricoeur: Now you've moved from the notion of inscription to that of cultural representation. It seems to me that this shifts the question from one scientific discipline to another and poses a dual problem: the reception such a view is likely to meet with in the neurosciences, on the one hand, and in the interpretive human sciences, on the other. In neither case is a formula so general as "communication from brain to brain" satisfactory.

First, in your field, it seems to me that there is the problem of being caught between a science that has its center of gravity in neurological biology and a science of social behavior that defines itself as social or cultural anthropology. Each of these disciplines has an interest in retaining control over its own agenda, which consists in two things: on the one hand, the definition of what in either case counts as its ultimate referent—in the one, neuronal organization, in the other, social forms of communication; and, on the other hand, the determination of which procedures are to be accepted as valid within each field, having to do with the elaboration of hypotheses—modeling—and of tests aimed at confirming or disconfirming such hypotheses. As Thomas Kuhn showed, rules of acceptance assure that a paradigm will prevail so long as new facts resistant to the dominant model do not force a revolution in paradigms. If a given domain of knowledge is assigned to a particular discipline, an interdisciplinary consensus needs to be reached with regard to zones of encroachment, as it were, in which results can be compared and, possibly, found to be complementary. In the absence of such interdisciplinary collaboration, no science appears capable by itself of resolving the problems posed by neighboring disciplines. The recourse to such collaboration seems to me justified by the hegemonic tendency of every scientific discipline to redefine the aims of adjacent fields in its own terms.

This, in my opinion, is what you have tried to do with regard to social anthropology. The notion of social representation may figure in the lexicon of the neurosciences (along with its famous companion, the mental object), but it also figures in the lexicon of the cognitive sciences as well as in that of cultural anthropology. Now, this term suffers from a serious ambiguity. Sometimes it is used to refer to an internal image that the neurologist takes to be constructed by the brain as an active response to information received from the external environment already described by the other natural sciences; sometimes to refer to desires and beliefs that the cognitive sciences formulate in propositions of the form "X desires that," "X believes that," and so on; and sometimes, finally, to social structures immediately defined by their function in communication. These cultural representations, you say, are intended to be shared. The classification proposed by Sperber within the framework of his discipline is altogether pertinent, together with the various extensions you have proposed in the direction of the ethical representation of oneself and of others, and of oneself in relation to others. But you continue to exploit the ambiguity of the word *representation*. This ambiguity is enlarged further when you appropriate the results of neighboring sciences, such as the psychology of child development, citing the work of Piaget, Köhler, and the Premacks. I do not know whether these researchers pose the problem of the neuronal inscription of the behavioral phenomena that they describe. The attempts to identify the cerebral correlates of the theory of mind you mention in closing fill me with the same reservations that I expressed earlier in connection with mental objects.

Changeux: I'm surprised by the step backward that this conclusion represents. On the one hand, with regard to the topic of mental objects, our previous discussion led us, first, to overcome the ambiguity you mention. Was this effort wasted? Next, we reached agreement on the necessity of research that you call interdisciplinary and I call multidisciplinary, which is to say research that is open to new scientific discoveries, particularly in the neurosciences. Perhaps progress in the sciences of the brain arouses fears of hegemony. This is certainly not my view. At our present stage of development it seems to me more productive to try to promote joint advance through dialogue and the exchange of information than to concern ourselves with setting an agenda.

On the other hand, I am not interested in language games involving the word *representation*. I am much more interested in advancing research on issues of substance than in debates over formal questions. Contrary to what you suggest, Piaget (to say nothing of the Premacks) showed a real interest in neuroscience and in the neuronal inscription of learning. On the occasion of his debate with Chomsky on language and learning,[22] Piaget devoted an entire section of his opening remarks to the "biological roots of knowledge"; and in an epilogue even integrated into his own thinking on the subject the theory of functional epigenesis through selective stabilization of synapses that I had laid out.

It seems to me that fruitful links can also be established with anthropology and sociology. There are, of course, certain dangers from the philosophical point of view in giving social representations the status of high-level mental objects. In overstepping the boundaries between disciplines one naturally exposes oneself to the charge of illegitimate interpretation—but one also risks making important discoveries!

The notion of *habitus,* in the sense proposed by Pierre Bourdieu, is an example of the sort of bridging concept (and not merely bridging word) that may prove to be useful in the various disciplines that he brings together. Bourdieu's concept links the notion of learning with that of the imprint of the social and cultural environment, quite specifically in the context of the social representations we've been discussing. He defines *habitus* as a system of acquired dispositions, practices, and representations that are permanent, generative, and organizing.[23] I understand it in terms of the model of language acquisition, where learning plays a decisive role in mobilizing innate neural structures that are peculiar to the human species. The importance of neuronal processes of learning in Bourdieu's analysis is such that he explicitly mentions, in his *Méditations pascaliennes,* "the strengthening or weakening of synaptic connections."[24]

Finally, the first neuropsychological investigations of the frontal lobe, contemporaneous with the discovery of language areas by Broca in 1865, illustrate the anchoring of moral behaviors in cerebral organization. In 1868 Harlow described the case of a New England railroad worker, Phineas Gage, who survived a serious lesion of the anterior part of the brain resulting from an accident in which a huge tamping iron passed clear through his skull.[25] Among the subsequent changes to Gage's personality, Harlow noted that he became "fitful, irreverent, indulging at times in the grossest profanity which was previously not his custom, manifesting but little deference for his fellows."[26] After the accident he no longer took into account social conventions, ignored morality in the broad sense of the term, and made decisions that ill served his own interests. Subsequent research on the frontal lobe confirmed Harlow's observations, leading the Russian neurologist Alexander Luria to call the frontal lobe "the organ of civilization." It is therefore a matter of urgent concern that we continue to encourage research on the neuronal inscription of representations, and in particular on ethical representations of oneself and of others.

Ricoeur: I don't at all mean to say that Piaget and Chomsky have shown no interest in biology. Myself, I am as interested as you are in problems at the intersection of scientific disciplines, which, like you, I do not wish to see become intradisciplinary problems. To your plea on behalf of work in neurobiology concerning the neuronal inscription of social representations, I respond with an exposition, which I offer in a constructive spirit, of the critique that phenomenology proposes of the notion of representation—a notion that scientists and philosophers too often take for granted. On the one hand, from a purely critical point of view, phenomenology challenges the idea that there exists a replica, in the mind, of some external reality belonging to a wholly finished world. In other words, considering mental ideas as actual pictures that are painted "in" consciousness poses a problem. Here we encounter the misleading Cartesian heritage of a soul populated by ideas, which later became representations in English empiricism and, subsequently, Kantian idealism. The most strenuous criticism of this view is due to Heidegger. For him, the most fundamental relation in the world is that of care (*Sorge*), which comprises a whole range of elements, from the passive feeling of individual beings to prelinguistic and linguistic comprehension, including all attitudes relating to the passage of time (anticipation, rehearsal, and so on). The implications of this notion for our discussion are complex, and the type of ontology associated with Heidegger's *Dasein* could be adapted to our purposes only with difficulty. Let me mention just one of the many adjustments that would be required, with a view also to proposing a more constructive version of the crisis of representation. I referred to it earlier, in our discussion of mental objects, in proposing a shift away from the theoretical plane (in the meantime, I note, you have made reference to the chimpanzee's theory of mind) toward the practical plane. The new discipline that has been constituted around the notion of action lays out a vast course parallel to the one you have just sketched with regard to representations: one would find, first of all, activities of orientation and prehension together with chains of motor intervention, which help to configure the world as a navigable milieu, marked out with paths and strewn with obstacles—in short, as a habitable world. The sometimes tentative, sometimes dazzling sketches of the later Husserl, contained in his final unpublished papers, nourished and amplified the intuitions of his last great work, *Die Krisis,* devoted to the life-world (*Lebenswelt*).[27]

Changeux: The contribution of the neurosciences to an understanding of the notion of action is potentially considerable. I have already mentioned Rizzolatti's "mirror-neurons" and the research into preparations for action, and imitations of action, that exploit new techniques of imaging and electrophysiology.[28]

Ricoeur: The excellent studies of cultural representations that you mentioned a moment ago would in any case find an appropriate framework in the description of how people experience the world and behave in relation to it. An important intermediary step would be to consider a hermeneutics of culture, such as the one proposed by Clifford Geertz, the great connoisseur of the cultures of the third world, which it would be interesting to compare with Sperber's cultural anthropology. Geertz seeks actually to enter into conversation with his subjects, to share their view of the world and to understand how they see themselves interacting with it. A philosophy of action, supplemented by a hermeneutics of culture, could therefore provide the interdisciplinary discussion we seek with an interpretation of social representations in terms of exchange. Besides, I think that the shift I propose from the theoretical to the practical will prove to be useful and fruitful when we pass from epistemological to moral problems.

Changeux: I agree with this turn toward practical experience—I include in the term *mental object,* of course, motor programs, plans, and internal states oriented toward action. Our debate illustrates the complementarity of philosophical reflection and attempts at formalization in theoretical neurobiology. Philosophy reveals what is at stake with the work now being done in the fields of neuroscience and cognitive psychology, points out the difficulties associated with it, and rightly emphasizes its excessive simplification. The crucial issue remains intentionality—and the question we posed earlier: can intentionality be naturalized? The answer to this question appears to be yes. Both of us understand intentionality as the highest level of representation, which orients human behaviors and defines our plans of action, our projects—indeed our conception of the world.

Ricoeur: I don't want to let the notion of intentionality be confined within that of representation. Just now I've argued in favor of a shift from the theoretical to the practical plane. It is not only a question of enlarging the field of inquiry to projects, plans of action, and voluntary intentions but also of exploring the most primitive dispositions of a subject who orients himself in the world, discovering in it the seat of the dispositions and humors that affect him and of the powers that he exercises—some of which constitute a bundle of basic abilities that make possible the learning of new abilities. This enlargement amounts to a shift in point of view that calls for a theory of action, because what we call representation also involves a power, a capacity, that we experience in the feeling *I can*. It is this *I can* that carries the scope of intentionality beyond itself. Through the *I can,* and perhaps still more through the *I think,* I am over there—I am not in my head, I am next to things outside of me.

Changeux: The genesis of intentions and their realization in programs of action can be interpreted within the framework of a projective-style model of the functioning of the brain. Intentional activity is continually exhibited in the alert subject. It is grafted on to a basic emotional activity, essential to the survival of the organism—motivation. The dominant intention at a given moment corresponds to a sort of formal general plan, a stable representation at the upper hierarchical level, that encompasses intentions as well as more restricted, more definite programs while allowing them a certain freedom regarding the details of their realization. These dispositions have even been implemented in the form of a virtual neuronal organism, within the very limiting framework of a task that involves the frontal cortex: the Tower of London game (figure 4.3). Can the principle of this model legitimately be extended to cover more general cognitive processes?

For example, at this very moment we share the same intention of pursuing our discussion and moving it forward, while permitting ourselves the liberty of arguing in an unprogrammed manner. This intention will remain stable for a few hours, until hunger and family obligations destabilize it in favor of some other intention. But if in the meantime the roof catches fire, our common intention will immediately be destabilized, our dialogue interrupted, and we will leave the room at once.

Ricoeur: Naturally I have taken intentionality in a much more encompassing sense, since there is intentionality in emotions as well as in projects and perception. Intentionality is not reflection, but the general character of consciousness directed toward the other. I would like to take this occasion to point out that the indiscriminate use of the word *consciousness*—sometimes in the sense of reflection, sometimes in the sense of awareness, or else of intention—is responsible for pointless debates such as the one that has raged over the phenomenon of the "split brain." One hears neurobiologists attribute an al-

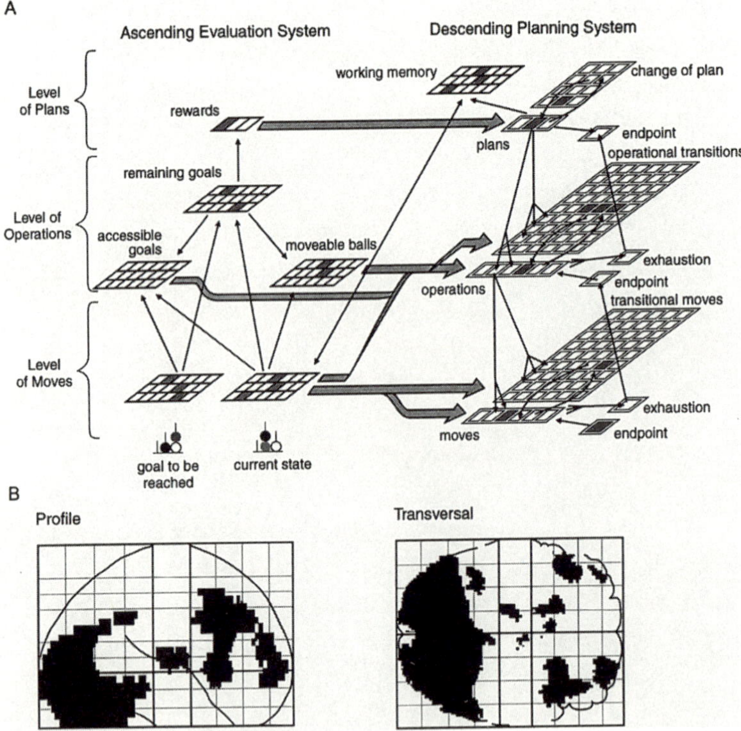

FIGURE 4.3. Brain evaluation mechanisms and the Tower of London test.

Our nervous system contains multiple interlocking regulatory systems that allow us to perform evaluations. The model of a "formal organism" devised by Dehaene and Changeux successfully passed the Tower of London test, a mathematical game in which success depends on the integrity of the frontal cortex. The subject has before him three vertical rods of different heights that can accommodate one, two, or three balls of different colors. He starts with a particular configuration, for example, three balls superimposed on the long pole in the order blue-white-red from the bottom up. The game consists in reaching a target configuration in a minimum number of moves, for example, an arrangement of two balls in the order blue-white from the bottom up on the long rod with the red ball on the medium pole. The subject develops strategies that, depending on the

ternate consciousness to one or the other cerebral hemisphere. The right or the left hemisphere is said to perceive without the other's knowing it, the other hemisphere being blind or in a latent state. Leaving aside the sort of semantic confusion that I am forever denouncing, the notion that consciousness might be assigned to one or the other hemisphere is mistaken. For one thing, it doesn't take into account the problem posed by the verbal reports that subjects make in the course of tests and other types of interrogation to which they are submitted (in experimental and clinical circumstances quite far removed from those of ordinary conversation). One

---

target arrangement, may be very simple and visible at a glance (such as blue, white, and red distributed over each of the rods) or, on the other hand, more difficult to construct and requiring intermediate displacements of the balls. The model represented in (A) postulates that these intermediate strategies are interlocked and subject to evaluation at several different levels, ranging from a global evaluation of how far a particular intermediate arrangement remains from the desired configuration to more local evaluations that correspond to individual displacements aimed at achieving the target arrangement. Even with an extremely rudimentary model it is possible to implement a hierarchy of evaluations. The one shown here is a very simple neural network model of reasoning that includes the "intention" of reaching a goal. From S. Dehaene and J.-P. Changeux, "A hierarchical neuronal network for planning behavior," *Proc. Nat. Acad. Sc. USA* 94 (1997): 13293–13298.

B. Brain images obtained from a subject presented with the Tower of London test. The initial activation of the prefrontal cortex is accompanied by the activation of occipital and parietal areas involved in analyzing the course of the game. Lesions of the prefrontal cortex produce a systematic deficit in the discovery of solutions to Tower of London problems. From R. S. J. Frackowiak, C. D. Frith, R. J. Dolan, and J. C. Mazziotta, eds., *Human Brain Function* (San Diego: Academic Press, 1997).

ought then to ask who is talking. Certainly not a half-brain, but someone who, from the clinical point of view, disposes only of half a brain in a dominant state of activity and of a single cranium in a single body. Otherwise one wouldn't speak of a person with a split brain. What in this case is called "consciousness" implies the notion of identity.

Here is where things become confused. The question of identity is in fact one of considerable difficulty; but popular psychology, which is riddled with preconceptions, acts as though unity and plurality are simple matters to explain. Ordinary experience is associated with, and sometimes actually conveys, a cultural history generated by literature, philosophy, and religions. The notion of personal identity is a particularly striking example of the interlocking of ordinary experience with the millennial history of a culture. This is why the status of the notion of identity oscillates between presumption and demand, to the extent that it goes on being weakened by the test of time or threatened by comparison with other cultural identities—when it is not being manipulated by ideologues or exalted by utopians. Philosophers, whether they are named Locke, Hume, or Nietzsche, traverse a minefield here that they have ended up making still more chaotic. To say nothing of literature—of authors from Montaigne to Musil and Proust! Writing makes even more problematic what ordinary conversations manage to keep at a bearable level of discordant compatibility. In this respect, cognitive science and phenomenology find themselves in the same boat.

Anyone who has read the psychiatric literature can understand why Patricia and Paul Churchland mockingly ask whether assigning fragmentary personalities not only to each of our cerebral hemispheres, but also to groups of mental functions correlated with disjoint neuronal architectures, doesn't amount to counting how many angels can dance on the head of a pin.

Mind or Matter?

Changeux: The debate over naturalizing intentions leads us inevitably to examine the scientific use of the word "mind" [*esprit*] and, as a result, to return to the question of materialism. I have sometimes been criticized as a vehement materialist, something obviously I don't wish to be called. Georges Canguilhem, during a debate at the Society of Philosophy in Paris prior to the publication of *Neuronal Man,* characterized my position—one that is shared by many neurobiologists—as methodological materialism.

A naturalist approach, which, as Joëlle Proust says, "recognizes as legitimate only the objectifying methods and explanatory thinking ordinarily recognized and employed in the natural sciences,"[29] cannot make reference to occult forces or to mysterious origins. As Spinoza argued, and after him Comte and Carnap, the seeker after knowledge must forego any appeal either to metaphysics or to anthropocentrism and adopt the mode of thought that is characteristic of the experimental sciences. For someone who works on laser radiation or silicon chemistry, this isn't hard to do. But the situation is different for the neurobiologist. The myth—traditional in Western culture—that there is an immaterial and immortal "Spirit" [*Esprit*] that governs our destinies is still firmly anchored in our ways of thinking today. And even if the Holy See has rehabilitated the scientific work of Darwin it had previously condemned, allowing that the theory of evolution is "more than a hypothesis," it is careful to stress that "if the human body has its origin in living matter that preexisted it, the spiritual soul is immediately created by God."[30] Since the death of vitalism, and despite the advances of molecular biology, the brain remains the privileged site of conflicts between science and faith. It is important, all the more since these conflicts may be obscure, that we pay attention.

The elaboration of scientific theories finds itself continually submitted to the verdict of reality. Nonetheless no scientist can deny that he carries with him a "general conception of the world," to use Karl Popper's expression, or a "spontaneous philosophy," in Althusser's phrase, which includes both an intrascientific element deriving from the "spontaneous" daily practice of science and a more diffuse extrascientific element that represents a number of convictions or beliefs such as the ones I've just mentioned. To detect coherence among the various interlocked levels of organization that make up our brain requires that we make an effort to overcome the mental barriers that dominant beliefs seek to establish at one level of complexity or another—from the molecule to the neuron, from neurons to groups of neurons, or from neuronal groups to higher-level neuronal groups—whether this level is internal to the brain or part of its opening onto the world. In the unceasing struggle for greater intellectual rigor and coherence, surely appeal to some Spirit (with or without a capital S) is not necessary. Is it here that one passes from methodology to ontology? I leave it to the professional philosopher to decide. However this may be, it seems difficult to escape a materialist conception of the world, even if the word offends or displeases. The specter of "materialist" ideologies, and their legacy of violence and oppression, are remembered by all. The materialist who seeks pleasures and material goods outside any morality is greeted with derision. But one must not forget the very strict ethics of the materialist philosophers of antiquity and of early Buddhism.

In the event, as Olivier Bloch has emphasized, even if materialism is as old as philosophy itself, historically it has been suppressed as a clandestine and subversive doctrine.[31] No doubt it was found frightening, for its subversiveness is that of the free spirit—the laughter of Democritus before the tears of Heraclitus, the gentle irony of Spinoza, the stinging satire of Diderot;

but also because it is a critical, lucid, and rational form of thought, and because it leads to a particularly demanding wisdom, to a humanism that asks man, and man alone, to define his destiny, and to construct it using the resources of reflective knowledge. The responsibility that this approach to life imposes is much heavier than allegiance to any spiritual teacher.

As Alain Berthoz has pointed out, neurobiologists are themselves in part to blame for the widespread prejudice in favor of a militant dualism: "We do not manage to persuade [others of our view] because we do not know how to describe the complexity of the brain. . . . We supply too simplistic, and above all too static, an image of the brain in order to provide a glimpse of its mechanisms. We must show its complexity, but we must show it in simple terms."[32] This is the price to be paid for a reasoned, consistent, and responsible materialism.

Ricoeur: I note your defense of a reasoned and responsible materialism, which supports the objections that I raise against the temptation to slip from the semantic into the ontological. Any attempt to cross this threshold seems to me condemned to reach an impasse of absolute indecidability. In this connection, a great part of the debate concerning reductionism, emergentism, eliminativism, and connectionism—chiefly in the English-language literature—strikes me as hopelessly contradictory. Eliminativism, in particular, seems to me guilty of a reckless slide from the epistemological to the ontological. Connectionism, on the other hand, in the guise of an antidualist, monist, materialist ontology, constitutes to my mind a plausible thesis so long as it restricts itself to postulating the unlimited extension of the field of neuronal connections; in this regard, it is perfectly compatible with the most cautious position one finds in the cognitive sciences, namely the view that appeal to a neural-level referent is not pertinent for work in these fields. Once again, the choice between monism and dualism goes beyond the bounds of the debate between the neuronal sciences in the broad sense and the reflective, phenomenological, hermeneutic philosophy on behalf of which I am arguing.

That said, I wish to respond to your remarks regarding the term *esprit*. For my part, I do not use it to refer to some sort of spiritualism. This does not prevent me, however, from referring to "spirit" in a phenomenological framework, just as English-speaking philosophers and researchers do from another perspective in looking to build a philosophy of "mind" in the tradition of Russell. The word *esprit* seems to me endowed with a polysemy that is very rich on the plane of subjective experience. It has three main usages. First, that of spirit, in the general sense of the mental, including the various features I have mentioned—intentionality, meaning, communicability, and mutual understanding. This is roughly the sense intended by the English phrase "philosophy of mind," allowing for the particular connotation given to the term "mind" by the neurosciences. It also designates what medieval writers placed under the head of the transcendental: that which aims at the true, the good, the just, the beautiful. This later became the problem of understanding with the Cartesians and, with Kant and his followers, the problem of thought or *Denken*. The transcendental level is that of the guiding or regulative functions governing the activities of knowledge, action, and feeling. It is over the origin and status of these regulative ideas that rationalists and empiricists are divided.

Changeux: That is, an intentionality that takes the social into account. I rather agree with this much, though I do not use the term *transcendental,* whose use in French is ambiguous and liable to be exploited for various ideological and religious purposes.

Ricoeur: I understand "transcendental"—which, as I explained earlier, is not to be confused with "transcendent"—as a critical term in the Kantian sense. Finally, there is a third use of the word *esprit,* designating what I would call a level of inspiration.

Changeux: I must part ways with you over this last notion, which as far as I am concerned is insufficiently precise. The first two uses of the word *esprit,* in the sense of "mental"—which includes intentionality and the conventions of meaning and mutual recognition—I do not hesitate to associate with research in the neurocognitive sciences, without feeling obliged to use the term myself. The notion of guiding functions of reference, which you characterize as transcendental, I include as part of the experience of human beings, their history, the evolution of their culture—as an element of sociology and the human sciences in general. But the third use, which you describe as associated with inspiration, does not in my view correspond to any well-defined concept.

Ricoeur: This notion belongs, I should say, to integral experience. Why do you dismiss a part of human experience?

Changeux: I don't dismiss it; I do without it in this form.

Ricoeur: You lock it away in an ontology that I reject.

Changeux: No, no—I don't lock it away; to the contrary, I leave things open. Ideologies and dogmas are the jailers. Scientific research is an incessant and unlimited quest for truths; it's as open as anything can be. I challenge the notion that "integral experience" introduces any new principle, apart from signaling the abandonment of the *emendatio intellectus* in favor of an experience that can only be incompletely described at this stage of our knowledge, but that has nothing mysterious or ineffable about it.

Ricoeur: I am not arguing in favor of a spiritualist ontology. I have no need of one in order to define the third modality of what I call *esprit,* which is to say the inspirational function. I am not the master of this function—I am the beneficiary of it. Just the same I do not go beyond experience because I do not identify experience with experimentation, nor do I reduce it to an objectifying function. Experience, even of the most theoretical kind, includes an inspired dimension. Here I am thinking not only of the various expressions of religious feeling but also of the Platonic praise of *mania*—"madness," "enthusiasm"—as well as "genius," praised by Kant himself in his theory of aesthetic judgment and later by the German Romantics. Earlier, at the outset of our conversations, I mentioned Charles Taylor's argument in *Sources of the Self,* which, under the rubric of moral sources, places on the same level the Judeo-Christian heritage, that of the Enlightenment, and that immense romantic tradition that runs through lyric poetry, music, and speculative thought.

Changeux: What a lot of bric-a-brac! Madness, aesthetics, the Judeo-Christian tradition—this confirms my doubts about the coherence and autonomy of your third level of meaning. What's more, this level doesn't seem to take into account a fundamental datum, namely evolution—the evolution of species as well as of cultures.

Ricoeur: Evolution surely gives rise to a progressive enriching of experience. I will even grant you that our brain has probably developed in such a way that it is capable of giving us access to an experience as powerful and as profound as the folly that Erasmus famously praised.

Changeux: I think that you introduce a sort of finality, or purpose, in evolution—

Ricoeur: No, it is simply that I stand in a broad phenomenological tradition, which I don't want to let you disfigure because you haven't yet found its equivalent.

Changeux: I do not mean to disfigure it. I simply wish to proceed with caution—the caution of the scientist who tries to avoid appealing to immaterial forces or to ambiguous principles that seem purely imaginary. The inspiration of the poet, like that of the scientist and, I dare say, that of the philosopher, consists in seeking—through the functioning of his brain, which includes his experience of the world—the knowledge that humanity has acquired over the course of thousands of years of history, and the wisdom of the thinkers who have lived on our planet.

Ricoeur: But human experience isn't only scientific. Moreover, scientific activity can be approached from two different points of view. From an epistemological point of view it rests on the relation between modeling and verification/refutation. But from the pragmatic point of view it is one practice among others, a theoretical practice alongside not only technological practices but also ethical and political practices—and, for that matter, aesthetic and spiritual practices in the third sense of the word *esprit*.

Changeux: I have never considered human experience as "only scientific." You are well aware of my interest in artistic creation, in music and the plastic arts. You know the importance that I attach to it in my personal life. Nonetheless there is nothing ineffable in the creative work of the artist that would justify making of it a third level superior to the others, as Nietzsche wished to do. I have a completely different view of the activity of the artist, whose actual practice resembles that of the scientist, requiring a great deal of hard work, a heightened sensitivity, a lively intelligence and a capacity for apperception (or self-consciousness in Diderot's sense), a feeling for the relationships between forms, lines, and colors, an original imagination, a flawless rationality, and the desire to convey a message of ethical or political commitment. When one thinks of all those artists from Michelangelo to Van Gogh, including Mozart, who ran up against the incomprehension and hostility of their contemporaries, one thinks above all of their courage and spirit of sacrifice.

I would replace your third level by the more down-to-earth notion of *conatus,* the joyous effort and striving of the creator. This quite terrestrial enterprise makes no appeal to any extrahuman inspiration or mystical ecstasy whatever. The brain of the artist holds center stage here, and the finished work results from a long process of trial and error in which the history of the work itself is merged with the artist's own personal history and, of course, the history of the art he practices.[33]

I am delighted nonetheless that you place art on the same plane as what you call the "spiritual." We are, in any case, in the presence of works that involve human activities of the highest cognitive level, in a perspective that is at once individual and historical.

Ricoeur: It is permissible to assert, in a programmatic way, that neural connectivity will one day be able to be extended to cover behaviors structured by language, symbols, and norms. But is this correlation demonstrable given the present state of research?

Changeux: No, of course not; but the potential resources of the neurosciences should not be underestimated.

Ricoeur: But what, then, will it prove? That cerebral activity underlies all mental phenomena? This is the working hypothesis of the neurosciences! The reproach that I would bring once more against your program is that it groups together under the banner of neurobiology all related disciplines without taking into account either the variety of the respective referents of these sciences or of the variety of their styles of research—instead of leaving it up to interdisciplinary collaboration to create a synergistic relation among these fields, with each member of the constellation being free to compete with the others for hegemony. That said, I do not at all pretend to detach the psychological level of organization from the neural level. I say only this: either reference to this neural level is not pertinent to an understanding of the operations being considered, or we have no knowledge of this neural level whatever.

Changeux: It is not because knowledge is limited that one must refuse to formulate hypotheses based on what is known. The neurobiological field is only very incompletely explored; but I can't say that it won't be completely explored one day. One must not confuse the unknown with the unknowable. For me, nothing is unknowable—this is a term I excluded from my vocabulary long ago. The aim of the scientist consists in moving forward, in trying to explore worlds that are still unfathomed and that may even seem to be unfathomable, such as the universe of social representations.

Ricoeur: You come back to the notion of social representation, which we started to discuss earlier. To try to get beyond the problem of representation, I would like us to shift our attention to the twin notions of disposition and predisposition. Indeed, it seems to me that the main concepts you employ are representation—of mental objects—and predisposition.

Changeux: You're right. Let us move on, then, to consider the question of the origin of the human brain's predisposition to ethical deliberation. Your yourself have written that moral values are not "eternal essences"; instead they are linked to the preferences and evaluations of individual persons, and ultimately to the history of human customs. Whence my question: is it possible to pass from the evolution of species, a genetic phenomenon, to cultural evolution via the epigenetic neural evolution of each individual? To pose the problem of evolution amounts in my view to showing that a science of normativity can exist, a science of human beings that aspires to be among the most distinguished of all sciences, to which the neurosciences may have something to contribute. Why refuse to science, and in particular to the neurosciences, the possibility of contributing to the development of an authentic science of morals?

Ricoeur: That is what we now need to discuss.

5 — The Origins of Morality

Darwinian Evolution and Moral Norms

Jean-Pierre Changeux: The next stage of the course we have set for ourselves consists in examining how far neural predispositions to moral judgment can be understood on the basis of the evolution of species.

In antiquity and the Middle Ages, the physical world and the living world were conceived as fixed and harmoniously organized—worlds in which the design of the Creator and his generosity and goodness could be detected. Living creatures composed a "great chain of being" in which each species had its place, from the simplest to the most complex, with man at the apex. This idyllic conception of a finished world, in the formulation given it by John Ray in *The Wisdom of God Manifested in the Works of the Creation* (1691), remained influential in the writings of Bernadin de Saint-Pierre a century later, incorporating the Platonic thesis of "universal essences" that served as organizing principles for all living things.[1]

Lamarck's theory constituted the first important rupture with this conception. In 1794, at the age of fifty, having devoted his life to the attentive observation of plants and molluscs, he began to work out a "theory of descent," presented in his inaugural lecture at the Museum of Natural History in Paris six years later. According to this revolutionary thesis, living species are related to each other through reproduction, slowly diversifying over the course of successive generations. To explain the diversification of species, Lamarck proposed that acquired characteristics are heritable. This idea has now been totally abandoned. Shortly afterward, however, in *The Origin of Species by Means of Natural Selection* (1859), Darwin imagined a plausible and still accepted mechanism for the phylogenetic origin of living species, allying the idea of common descent with that of a spontaneous, directly heritable variability on which natural selection operates. The consequences of this remarkable intellectual revolution are still not fully assimilated today, one hundred fifty years later. The implications, with respect to systems of belief and ethics, are immense. It is a question quite simply of replacing a static world, created by God, with an evolving world having neither cosmic teleology nor purpose. Thus the reign of an unlimited anthropocentrism came to an end. All essentialist reference to a divine "plan" was replaced by a populationist perspective founded on the purely material process of natural selection, which consists in the interaction of undirected variation and opportunistic reproductive success, indeed even random stabilization.

Ricoeur: Let me make it clear that I do not at all subscribe to the "idyllic and completed conception" of John Ray and Bernardin de Saint-Pierre, the absurdity of which has been exaggerated, however. I find myself faced, as you do, with the problem raised by the work of Lamarck and Darwin. Far from attenuating the evolutionary thesis, I join Stephen Jay Gould in trying to deepen it in order to dramatize as far as possible the problem that you and I jointly pose of the neural predispositions to moral judgment. Let us carefully review Gould's argument in *Full House,*[2] a book whose subtitle in the French edition—"The Myth of Progress"—is not insignificant for our purposes. He argues that, in many variants of Darwinism, randomness is corrected by the view of a progressive development in the direction of the human, which occurs by chance, of course, but nonetheless in accordance with a visible, ascendent pattern. For Gould, it does not suffice to eliminate finality; its residual form, progress, needs to be eliminated as well.

Why should this extreme position be of interest to us in discussing the natural disposition to normative behavior? The view that Gould proposes is one of a universe in which life is entirely dispersed. In this world, minority populations detach themselves from the crowded branches of the tree, generating new stocks that themselves branch, eventually giving rise to *Homo sapiens* as a random variation. This radicalized version of Darwinism would appear to suggest that the picture of life as a dispersed phenomenon has nothing to contribute to an understanding of morality, considering not the actual existence of morality but its *normative significance*. I try, then, to interpret Gould's resistence to the idea of progress in the following way: it is because we are here, as human beings, posing the question of the meaning of morality, that we can read the spectacle offered by the diversity of living things backwards, as it were—going back from our own time to the beginnings of life. We thus choose, from the profusion of lines of descent, those lines that, serially arranged, point toward the human. It is therefore retrospectively, by means of a tacit look backward to what came before, that we conceive of the process of selection and, in trying to make sense of it, draw up the genealogical tree of the human species. Along the way, as Gould remarks, we quietly forget that bacteria continue to constitute the most stable, numerous, and indestructible population on earth. We forget the immense multitude of fishes, remembering only the species that are capable, as he says, of "landing" on our shores. And, in the course of this forgetting, we relinquish the memory of all our ape-like cousins and other hominoids who stand outside the line of *sapiens sapiens*. What then does Gould do? He forgets our forgetting—forgets the looking back that retains only that which led, in a random way to be sure, but nonetheless a progressive way, to man. What meaning can a world have for us that is not only without purpose but without progressive evolution? It signifies the ruin of the very idea of descent, in the sense of progressively "coming from."

What does this imply for our discussion? Two things, I think. First, the reminder that it is because man exists, and poses the question of meaning, that the directionlessness of evolution troubles us. Evolution has meaning—or rather doesn't have meaning, at least with regard to the positing of norms, the very purpose of which is to compensate for the meaninglessness of nature—because man is capable of inquiring into nature. Second, there is the suggestion that all questions concerning a natural disposition to morality are retrospective questions, the posited norm looking backward in search of precursors. Whether or not nature knows it, responsibility for imparting a bit of order to nature falls to us.

Changeux: Absolutely. It's up to us to put it in order. But your support for Gould's ultramaterialist claims surprises me. Doesn't the radical abolition of all divine intervention in evolution, and in particular in connection with the evolutionary origins of *homo sapiens,* stand in contrast to the reference to the "Great Code" of the Bible that runs through your work?[3] Indeed, you insist firmly on the "bracketing, conscious and resolute, of the convictions that bind me to biblical faith."[4] In any case I am eager to know what position theologians take with regard to Gould's theses.

Ricoeur: Do I have to reiterate the point of my opening remarks? I do not pose the problem of divine intervention in evolution at this level of discourse. As for my treatment of the theme of the "Great Code," it occurs in response to Northrop Frye in another context, that of the literary interpretation of Jewish and Christian canonical texts that tell a story involving a divine intention and the recalcitrance of a people that recognizes itself as chosen. That ancient sages saw in this story of the divine and the human a mythical account of origins, on which dogmatists later constructed a pseudoscience, does not concern us for the purposes of this discussion.

Changeux: It may not concern *you,* but it concerns everyone who wishes to keep informed in a critical and objective way with regard to the growth of knowledge. In his popular works and public statements, Gould vehemently defends the importance of random variation in evolution—an essential concept in the thought of Darwin and, nearer our own time, Jacques Monod. I subscribe to this point of view, of course, along with contemporary evolutionists. It seems to me useful to try to develop it in scientific terms, keeping in mind the fact that the models proposed by evolutionary theorists are inevitably difficult to confirm because they bear upon past events. My position is nonetheless more nuanced than Gould's.

First, it seems to me unjustified to claim, as Gould does, that we forget bacteria and insects and everything that seems removed from our direct ancestors. As Monod remarked, "What is true for the colon bacillus is true for the elephant."[5] I would go further, with François Jacob, and include the vinegar fly, the *Drosophila,* which provided the biological material for the demonstration of Mendelian genetics.[6] We possess in our genes, in our cells, a heritage that goes back to the origins of life. This constitutes one of the best proofs of the filiation of species. Jacob insists on the remarkable genetic diversity of bacteria, as of insects, in the living world. This, however, must be compared with the altogether remarkable *epigenetic* diversity of human beings, which assures that no individual (even if it is a clone) is identical to its neighbor. Tobias has noted that, throughout the course of the descent of man, individual variability is very modest in species of "savage" pri-

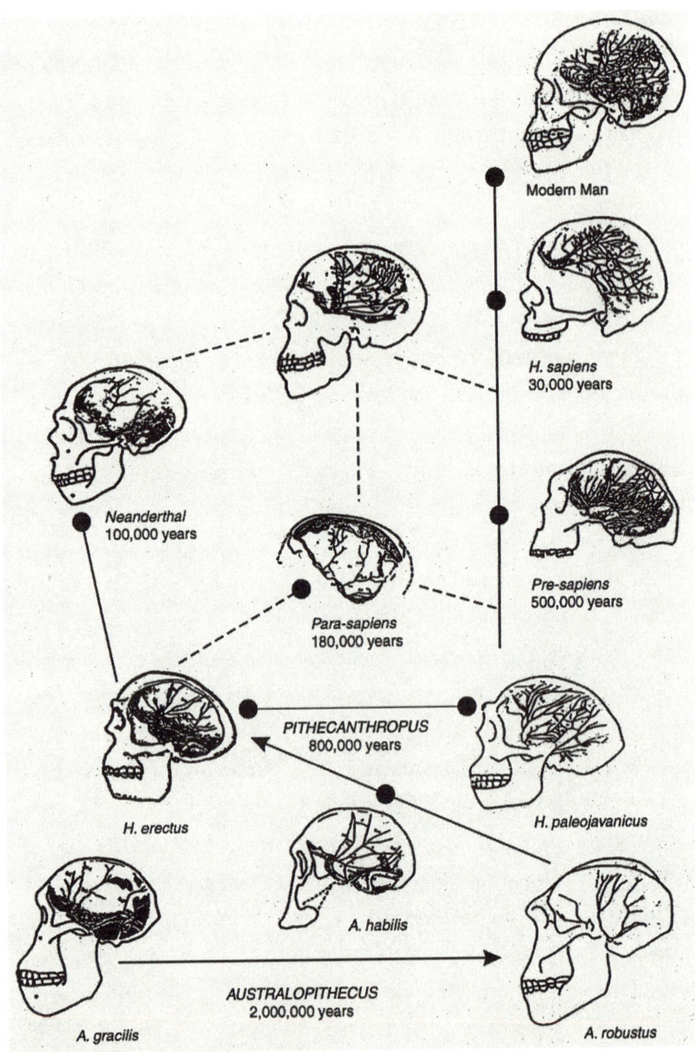

FIGURE 5.1. Morphological evolution of the human brain.

Roger Saban has closely analyzed the impressions made by the vessels of the meninges (or membranes covering the brain and spinal cord) on the internal wall of the skull in contemporary adult humans and during the development of the child. He then compared them with impressions obtained by endocranial casting from the skulls of

mates and grows in importance with *Homo sapiens* and the rise of civilization.[7] The considerable variability found in the case of the human brain, which contributes to the complexity of its organization and to the diversity and the richness of its functions, probably played an important role in the origin of the human species.

Second, does the random variability of the genome suffice to construct a reasonable model of the genetic evolution that preceded *Homo sapiens sapiens*? In his popular works Gould underestimates the difficulty of the problem posed for evolutionary genetics by the undeniable increase in complexity of the brain over the course of the last four million years, an increase that is manifested by the very rapid expansion of the prefrontal cortex and language areas (figure 5.1). (I am completely opposed, by the way, to using the word *progress* to describe this evolution.)[8] Such complexity is very poorly defined in terms of the relation of the genome to neuronal organization; it must not be either underestimated (as in the case of Gould) or overestimated (as in the case of Teilhard de Chardin). On the other hand, the genetic differences that bear specifically upon the organization of the brain, from Australopithecus (or from the chimpanzee) to man, are small and still difficult to identify. The overall divergence in genetic sequence

---

various human ancestors, from *Australopithecus* to modern man. It is remarkable that the topography of the parietal meningeal vessels of *Australopithecus robustus* (having a cerebral capacity of 520 ml) resembles that of the modern newborn. The distribution of vessels in the earliest humans, *Homo habilis* (with a cerebral capacity of 700 ml), is similar to that of a forty-day-old child and that in *Homo paleojavanicus* (1,000 ml) resembles that of a one-year-old child. From R. Saban, "Image of the human fossil brain: Endocranial cast and meningeal vessels in young and adult subjects," in J.-P. Changeux and J. Chavaillon, eds., *Origins of the Human Brain* (Oxford: Clarendon Press, 1995).

is very modest—on the order of 1 percent. It must be hoped that current research on the sequencing of the entire human genome will give us a clearer idea of what this difference involves. The elucidation of the mechanisms responsible for the embryonic and postnatal development of the brain will also help. Whatever the outcome, it appears plausible to suppose that the extremely rapid evolution of mankind's ancestors must have drawn upon elements of social life—language, so-called moral behaviors, and so on—that in turn acted upon it.

A third nuance: Gould argues that cultural changes are founded on Lamarckian inheritance. This underestimates the selective character of long-term memory storage and the degree to which randomness enters into the process of recall, demonstrated by the pioneering research already mentioned of Ebbinghaus and Bartlett, to say nothing of Freud. The role of selection mechanisms, which intervene at the level of cerebral memory in cultural transmission, is still quite underappreciated.[9]

Finally, on an entirely different plane, I would like to respond to your remarks concerning the retrospective view that the biologist takes of human origins. Why should such a thing be thought alarming? The biologist does not differ in this regard from the astrophysicist, the geologist, or the historian, who likewise look back toward the origins of the universe, the continents, and the recent past. Of course, no scientist escapes the influence, whether he is aware of it or not, exercised by the cultural, social, and historical context in which he lives when he develops hypotheses—any more than the philosopher does when he marshals his arguments. The difference, which we have both pointed out more than once, is that scientific hypotheses are continually submitted to the verdict of facts and to the permanent—and forever merciless—criticism of the scientific community. The incessant questioning of such hypotheses radically differs from the theologian's retrospective consideration of foundational texts.

Ricoeur: The sort of looking back I have in mind has nothing to do with the theologian's relation to foundational texts. The retrospective view I am talking about issues from the position of a moral subject who, in positing himself, posits a norm.

Changeux: Natural selection has operated on the random variability of the genome during the course of evolution, stabilizing dispositions that are sometimes reflected by our normative choices. It may be helpful to review certain theses that have singularly influenced thinking in this domain and given rise to tenacious prejudices. Natural selection is considered to be synonymous with blind and brutal competition. Life in a state of nature is seen as dog-eat-dog, a form of gladiatorial combat; and the morality revealed by God on Mount Sinai as having been given to men, as Calvin taught, to tame their fundamentally sinful nature. If one accepts these theses, it is hard to see how a morality of benevolence and friendship, indeed of love, could derive either from natural selection or from a neutral sort of evolution in which chance prevails.

But let us reread Darwin, and most especially the Darwin of *The Descent of Man* (1871).[10] Here he says that the moral sense finds its origins in the animal under certain conditions. First, sympathy. Next, memory: "As soon as the mental faculties had become highly developed, images of all past actions and motives would be incessantly passing through the brain of each individual; and that feeling of dissatisfaction, or even misery, which invariably results . . . from any unsatisfied instinct, would arise, as often as it was perceived that the enduring and always present social instinct had yielded to some other instinct."[11] The faculty of language is also a condition of the existence of the moral sense. Finally, habits are necessary as well—sympathy and the social instinct being considerably strengthened, he says, by habit.

Again according to Darwin, the development of moral norms occurs on the basis of man's "instincts" in a "very crude state." To the extent that his self-control, feelings of affection and sympathy are strengthened by habit, and that his ability to reason becomes more lucid, making it possible to more soundly evaluate the justice and the judgment of his fellows, man feels prompted to adopt certain rules of behavior, independent of the pleasure or pain he momentarily feels. Darwin rejected moral philosophies that rest on egoism, such as those of Hobbes and Spencer, as well as those founded on the principle of the greatest happiness, such as those of J. S. Mill and the utilitarians. He proposed instead, following two thinkers of the Scottish Enlightenment, David Hume and Adam Smith, a theory according to which man is subject to "an impulsive power widely different from a search after pleasure or happiness; and this seems to be the deeply planted social instinct."[12] Instead of searching for the "general happiness," man has in view the general good, or the prosperity of the community to which he belongs. "As man advances in civilization, and small tribes are united into larger communities, the simplest reason would tell each individual that he ought to extend his social instincts and sympathies to all the members of the same nation, though personally unknown to him."[13] But "as man gradually advanced in intellectual power, and was enabled to trace the more remote consequences of his actions"[14] and to express them through the faculty of language, and as man's "sympathies became more tender and widely diffused, extending to men of all races, to the imbecile, maimed, and other useless members of society, and finally to the lower animals—so would the standard of his morality rise higher and higher."[15]

And that led naturally to the rule: "Do unto others as you would have them do unto you."

For Darwin, the origin of this "golden rule" was to be found in the moral evolution that took over from biological evolution, and sometimes became mingled with it, through an adaptive process that he borrowed, surprisingly, from Lamarck. Considering the biological evolution of mankind's ancestors, classical sociobiological theories of course exclude any inheritance of acquired characteristics. They interpret the genetic evolution of altruistic traits at the level of the individual on the basis of genetic mechanisms directly related to kinship or to the reciprocity of individual altruistic behaviors.[16] Certain authors are wont to speak of "selfish genes."[17] I don't subscribe to such views. Recent work by Elliott Sober and David Sloan Wilson offers an alternative, or at least a complementary, mechanism to selection operating upon the individual.[18] They have reintroduced the notion of *group selection,* which favors cooperation within the social group at its highest level of organization. This idea has been applied by the American anthropologist Christopher Boehm to the analysis of hunter-gatherer societies.[19] Such societies possess a highly egalitarian ethic that, in an evolutionary context, works against an increase in individual fitness to the detriment of the other members of the group. Boehm has shown in theory that altruistic behaviors that are good for the group can develop despite the fact that they diminish the relative fitness of altruistic individuals in the group. Even behaviors that are neutral on the individual level, but beneficial for the group as a whole, can be stabilized. Under these circumstances, altruistic behaviors and compassion would no longer run contrary to nature; they would point *in the same direction.* They would prolong by nongenetic means, and with a much more rapid dynamic, a suspended genetic evolution.

Evolution therefore offers us a human being who possesses not only a moral sense but also all the predispositions of moral evaluation necessary to ethical deliberation, including the capacity of representation, the function of attribution as it concerns others and oneself (or, reversing your terms, "the other as oneself"), and the function of evaluation.

Ricoeur: You consider the Darwinian evolutionary schema at the point where man becomes differentiated from the other primates. You are looking, then, for an origin of the moral sense in the animal. And in fact you see a morality of benevolence and friendship, even of sociality, derived from natural selection. But you can do that because you have isolated, among the behavioral traits of animals, those that function as "conditions of existence" for the moral sense. Once again, then, as a result of a retrospective search that moves from a supposedly constituted morality, the behavioral traits that anticipate morality come to be assigned undue significance.

Changeux: Frans de Waal has recently given many examples of this kind of behavior in several animal species, in the chimpanzee in particular.[20] He reports that very early in life chimpanzees adopt caring behaviors when one of their group is wounded, and even make efforts to comfort one another.

Thus a young trisomic rhesus monkey named Azalea who, owing to her handicap, exhibited few grooming activities *toward* others was herself, by contrast, the object of greater than average grooming *by* others after eighteen months (figure 5.2). Thus too, after fighting, reconciliation most often occurs through sexual manifestations. And again, phenomena of emotional *contagion* are occasioned by signs of suffering, as if the golden rule already existed in embryonic form and, of course, without any explicit linguistic formulation.

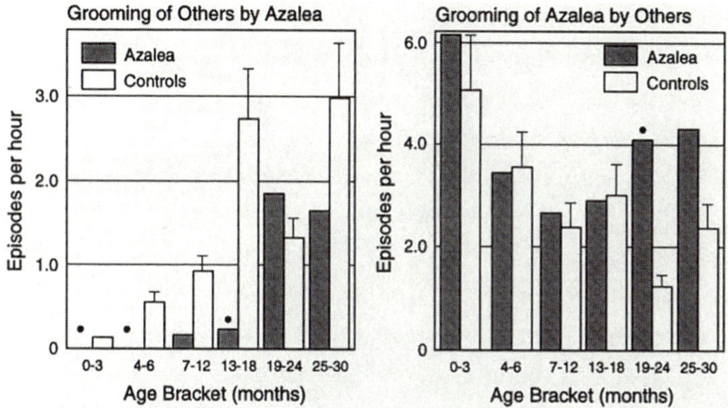

FIGURE 5.2. Reciprocal grooming behavior of a young trisomic female rhesus macaque.

The grooming activity of Azalea toward others remained lower than that of others her age until she reached eighteen months. From that time on she was the object of greater than average grooming on the part of female counterparts her age. From F. de Waal, *Good Natured: The Origins of Right and Wrong in Humans and Other Animals* (Cambridge, Mass.: Harvard University Press, 1996).

Ricoeur: Hold on! I don't contest the facts presented by Frans de Waal in the admirable work you mention. Nonetheless I would say that it is in a climate of friendship for animals, particularly chimpanzees, that he was able to collect and assemble the patient observation reports that make his work an invaluable document. If a slight excess of anthropomorphism may be detected in his descriptions, which correct Konrad Lorenz's overemphasis on aggressiveness, this only confirms my argument that we always interpret animal behaviors from a human perspective. The mild anthropomorphisms that punctuate de Waal's book testify to the situation in which primate specialists and, more generally, ethologists find themselves, looking to discern in animals behaviors that sketch forms of moral conduct that have already been named on the human level. Such a work supposes that a set of names—a lexicon—has already been created for feelings, behaviors, indeed rules of sociality. Once more, a kind of retrospection is presumed. This looking back is tacitly assumed by any reconstruction of processes of "derivation" or, to use Darwin's term, "descent" (in the sense of descending a slope that the ethologist has already climbed in silently looking back over the past).

To come back to the conditions that Darwin lists—sympathy, memory, feeling, habit, and above all language—one might say that we start off from these predispositions but that, first, we go back to them in order then to trace the path of descent. Thus one might say, following Darwin, that the golden rule has its origin in moral evolution, which takes over from biological evolution. For "has its origin" I would substitute "searches for its origin." One searches for what in biological evolution prepared the way for the golden rule. But this rule had first to be formulated, following the example of humanity's greatest sages.

And afterward one recognizes in moral evolution a "taking over" where there is simply a profusion of lines of descent, a small number of which will be retained in the reconstruction of the stages considered to be intermediary. That the prior recognition of the golden rule conditions the identification of its origins and course is confirmed historically by the incessant lending and borrowing between biological theory and sociological theory. Thus it was that the apology for competition and the struggle for life won the approval of Darwin himself during a period of unrestrained capitalism in the last century; and it is because we are now concerned, at the end of our own horrible century, to make sympathy prevail over aggression that we notice and emphasize signs of sympathy and sociability, for example among chimpanzees. It is therefore owing to a sort of *trompe l'oeil* effect—the forgetting of our own moral questioning—that we are now able to set compassion on the side of nature or against it. Apart from our moral questioning, however, nature does not move in any direction.

Changeux: Let's be careful not to slip from methodological criticism into assertion of an ontological claim. To be sure, the prior knowledge of the golden rule constitutes an important step in the historical analysis of the origin of moral norms. This, it seems to me, is indispensable to any scientific undertaking. It is necessary first to recognize a thing's existence before posing the question of its origins. One may compare this search for the origins of moral rules with the search for the origin of species. Theories of evolution couldn't be worked out until a systematic classification of species had been established by Linnaeus, Buffon, and the young Lamarck himself. Similarly, the recognition of the golden rule in present-day human societies precedes any attempt to inquire into its origins.

Lamarck, an illustrious scientist whom I do not hesitate to rank among the greatest of all thinkers, devoted the first half of his life to observing, describing, and classifying plants and mollusc shells in an essentialist framework of natural theology that saw species as "fixed." At the age of fifty he looked back over the course of his work up until that point. Six years later, having been appointed to a professorship at the Museum of Natural History in Paris, he delivered his inaugural lecture on 11 May 1800 on the topic of "animals without vertebrae."[21] The library of the museum conserves the scrawled manuscript notes in which he set down the first thoughts about evolution: moving evidence of a look back to the past that revolutionized current thinking. Was his conception of biological evolution also influenced by the ideas of the French Revolution? Even if it were, his theory proved to be so adequate and so fertile that it hardly matters!

The attempt to reconstruct the biological ascent of the higher vertebrates and man benefits today from the immense progress that has been made in molecular genetics. Modern techniques, which allow the genealogical tree of a family to be analyzed (with the aim, for example, of establishing a prenatal diagnosis in the case of a serious hereditary problem), are now used to search for our evolutionary origins. These techniques provide unbiased confirmation that Neanderthal man is only a cousin of modern man.

The search for the origins of the golden rule, recognized to be common to many human societies and often conceived in an essentialist framework, can also be submitted to comparative examination by looking at various present-day civilizations as well as to evolutionary analysis using the tools of paleontology, ethology, and anthropology. A new discipline known as cognitive archaeology,[22] the aim of which is to reconstitute the mentalities and social organization of prehistoric civilizations, stands also to contribute to this line of research.

I do not agree with you when you turn to the analysis of the historical development of Darwin's ideas. The idea of sociability and sympathy in the chimpanzee and primate societies does not date from the present day; it is already found in works on animal societies written at the end of the nineteenth century, such as those of Alfred Espinas[23] and George J. Romanes.[24] Since that time it has also inspired political thought, particularly in opposition to the campaign led by Spencer to extend the notion of the struggle for life from biological competition to social life.[25] In the history of ideas, of course, certain arguments and theories may fade away while others reappear in a new context. There are quite interesting evolutionary processes to be analyzed in this connection—but one needs to exercise caution when it comes to revisionism in this domain.

Identifying the golden rule in human societies, through

recognition of its antecedents in the animal, attributes no particular direction to evolution. On the contrary, it allows us to carry out an inquiry into origins free from metaphysical prejudice—which is to say, to make such an inquiry objective. You pass from methodological criticism over into ontology in saying that, apart from our moral questioning, nature does not have a direction. It is not a matter, in any event, of giving "meaning" to nature or evolution as Teilhard de Chardin did, or even Hans Jonas, but of moving forward in search of the origin of moral rules, availing ourselves of all the tools that contemporary science offers us—in particular the anthropological and historical sciences.

Ricoeur: I don't see myself as having slipped from methodological criticism into ontology in saying that the diversity of living things, in Gould's sense, is morally neutral or, better, morally undecidable. This is the implication of his book's subtitle; he is arguing against the myth of progress insofar as it constitutes an ontological residue in the evolutionary theory of the birth of morality.

The First Structures of Morality

Ricoeur: The problem of moral intentions forces us to look into the formation of what Charles Taylor calls "strong evaluations," in which he sees the first structures of morality. You yourself introduced the notion of evaluation only a moment ago.

Changeux: Yes, in the context of a theory of learning.

Ricoeur: I don't understand what it can mean to say that a brain evaluates. A person—a someone—evaluates.

Changeux: It compares a plan, an intention—

Ricoeur: Evaluation is a matter of contrasting the good and the less good, of saying that this is better than that.

Changeux: That is exactly what I would call deliberate moral judgment: the mental simulation of various possible courses of action, or the internal evaluation of mental objects with continual reference to the external world, the self, the memory of prior experiences, moral rules, and internalized social conventions. As I said earlier, the neurobiologist's definition is virtually the same as yours!

To illustrate this point, let me mention the recent work of the neuropsychologist Antonio Damasio (whose book *Descartes' Error* I have already cited) and his team. In this book Damasio describes the case of a patient named Elliot—usually referred to by his initials, EVR—whose social behavior deteriorated at the age of thirty-five following the excision of both his ventromedial frontal lobes to remove an invasive tumor. EVR became incapable of planning his actions over the more-or-less long term, even with regard to matters of secondary importance such as ordering from a menu in a restaurant or making a purchase in a store. He was given to interminable comparisons, to continual deliberation over possible options. It was difficult for him to decide what was in his interest and what was not. When he settled on an answer, it was more often than not by chance. He lacked a sense of what was socially appropriate, whereas his intelligence and speech remained intact.

For Damasio, EVR presents a case of defective function at the level of the mechanism governing selection of responses, or evaluation. This deficit is itself the consequence of an alteration of what Damasio calls a *somatic marker;* that is, a sign of an agreeable or disagreeable emotion felt during the internal projection of the consequences anticipated from various possible options. A more systematic study of patients exhibiting the same deficit as EVR has since been carried out by Damasio and his team.[26] These patients were placed in an experimental situation requiring them to select from a deck of playing cards; depending on their selections, they were subject to short-term benefits and long-term punishments of variable degree (figure 5.3). All the patients engaged in immediately gratifying behaviors, even if over the long term this choice exposed them to punishment. In other words, they were no longer able to defer satisfaction of a desire—a capacity that from Epicurus to Kant has constituted one of the chief conditions of ethical behavior.

Another interesting problem: Damasio and his colleagues succeeded during the course of the experiment in recording the somatic response of the subjects—that is, in measuring skin conductance—without their knowing it. The normal subject rapidly learns to make choices that will be beneficial over the long term, a process reflected by changes in somatic response. At the outset he is not capable of giving a reason for them—the response is nondeclarative, unconscious; it is only later, as the game goes on, that he becomes capable of rationalizing his choices, of giving an explicit, conscious justification for them. Implicit evaluation thus precedes explicit reasoning. One may wonder whether this is not often true as well in the case of decisions of an ethical nature. Patients who do not exhibit a somatic response choose at random for the most part, but they can correctly conceptualize even if they have made the wrong choice!

Ricoeur: If I may interrupt for a moment, let me point out that we know much more through the reflection of moralists, through literature—the novel—than through the neurosciences. And so you would be well advised to draw upon a

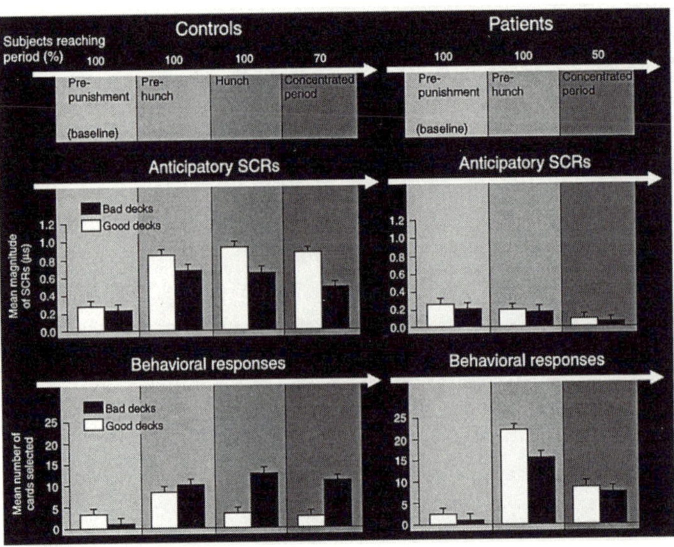

FIGURE 5.3. Evaluation in a brain-damaged subject.

In an experiment devised by C. Bechara and his colleagues, normal control subjects and prefrontal patients are presented with four piles of cards. Each time a card is selected from one of the piles the subject receives money: $100 for cards from piles A and B, $50 from piles C and D. At unpredictable intervals, however, the subject is penalized. In the case of piles A and B, for example, the penalties might total $1250 after ten turns, yielding a net loss of $250; in the case of C and D, even though the subject makes less money after ten turns ($500 instead of $1000), the total penalty is smaller ($250), yielding a net gain of $250. Thus, as the normal subject realizes after a certain number of tries, selecting from piles C and D is advantageous in the long term, even if the immediate payoff is relatively small.

The test is divided into four periods—pre-punishment, pre-hunch, hunch, and conceptual—shown here in terms of average numbers of cards selected from the bad decks (A and B) versus the good decks (C and D), and the mean magnitudes of anticipatory somatic conductivity responses (SCRs) associated with the same cards.

(Top panels) Bars represent means (±SEM) of the mean magnitude of anticipatory SCRs generated before the selection of cards from the bad decks versus the good decks. Anticipatory SCRs are generated during the time the subject ponders which deck to choose from. SCRs

wider field of observation concerning human beings, since within the limits of your field alone one does not know what it means to "evaluate" or "create a norm."

Changeux: If the neurosciences manage only to supplement such definitions, first with regard to possible mechanisms at the level of our brain, in particular concerning what may be considered a conscious choice as opposed to an unconscious, tacit choice—this would incontestably represent a contribution to knowledge.

Ricoeur: We certainly learn a great deal from studying the dysfunctions of moral judgment in its deliberative phase. But dysfunction in relation to what? To interpret the deficit that Damasio describes, a sound analysis of the formation of moral judgment is required. Where in the brain are we to locate operations that come under the head of "internal evaluation of mental objects"? I don't say that we learn nothing about deci-

---

associated with choosing from good and bad decks were not significantly different during the pre-punishment (baseline) period for normal controls and patients. However, there was a significant increase in the magnitude of these responses during the pre-hunch period, but only for normal controls. During the next two periods, SCR activity in normal subjects was sustained in the case of the bad decks, but it began to subside in the case of the good decks (8).

(Bottom panels) Bars in the "Behavioral responses" plots represent means (±SEM) of the mean number of cards selected from the bad decks versus those selected from the good decks. Normal controls selected more cards from the good decks during the pre-hunch, hunch, and conceptual periods. In contrast, prefrontal patients selected more cards from the bad decks during these periods (9).

From C. Bechara, H. Damsio, D. Tranel, and A. R. Damasio, "Deciding advantageously before knowing the advantageous strategy," *Science* 275 (1997): 1293–1295.

sion-making from pathological cases. Here we cross paths with an old debate, masterfully analyzed by Georges Canguilhem in *La Connaissance de la vie,* concerning the relationship between the normal and the pathological. Canguilhem argued that the pathological must not be defined in terms of deficits, but instead as the construction of another sustainable level of relationships with the living world. This changes the nature of the reciprocal conclusions that can be drawn from the two sources of information constituted by what are called "normal" and "pathological." Damasio's observations concerning defective function at the level of evaluation may perhaps be reinterpreted to illuminate Canguilhem's thesis. As for the notion of "somatic marker," it is a typical example of what in an earlier conversation I called a mixed or hybrid vocabulary, where the term signifying interiority refers either to reflexivity (mental interiority) or to cerebral inscription (neuronal interiority). Making allowance for this ambiguity, I certainly learn something about the selection mechanisms of evaluation. But to understand what is really meant by deferring the satisfaction of a desire, which you rightly observe to be one of the dominant themes of writers on ethical conduct from Epicurus to Kant, I have no need to know anything about the brain. Now, must we know our brain better in order to better behave? This is an open question.

Changeux: Given the present state of our knowledge, the contribution of the neurosciences to a humanistic and secular morality remains modest. But perhaps it will make a larger contribution in the future. Scientists can't be asked to predict the future. We know that unforeseen discoveries will revolutionize our thinking! The reference to biological evolution is in any case important, for it eliminates all traces of finality and anthropomorphism. We have both mentioned Spinoza—for me, an essential point of reference. Let's work together to develop a system of ethics that makes no appeal to metaphysics. Let's rewrite Spinoza's *Ethics* for the year 2500!

Ricoeur: But it is necessary to read Spinoza all the way through. Before reaching Part V of the *Ethics,* which deals with Beatitude (and the consciousness of eternity that allowed him to write Part I), we should pause to consider the "Propositions" of Part IV, where Spinoza draws the portrait of the free man: "A free man thinks of death least of all things [this contra Heidegger!], and his wisdom is a meditation of life, not of death."[27] Consider, too, the propositions that follow, concluding with this one: "The man who is guided by reason is more free in a state where he lives under a system of law than in solitude where he obeys only himself."[28] Doesn't this picture supply an alternative to a finality that cannot be found in organic nature?

Changeux: Yes, but only so long as three other propositions of the *Ethics* are not forgotten: "Men's judgment is a function of the disposition of the brain";[29] "We judge a thing to be good because we endeavor, will, seek after and desire it";[30] and "To act in absolute conformity with virtue is nothing else in us but to act, to live, to preserve one's own being (these three mean the same) under the guidance of reason, on the basis of seeking one's own advantage"—independently of any "undiscoverable finality of nature."[31]

Ricoeur: The discussion of the brain is continued in Part II, which concerns the control of the passions. The conversion of passions into reason constitutes the highlight of the *Ethics.* From this emerges the picture of the free man—who, it is true, does without finality altogether.

From Biological History to Cultural History: Valuing the Individual

Ricoeur: I would like us now to turn our attention to what seems to me to constitute the central problem of morality. It is true that our discussion so far seems to have privileged the idea of the normative. But for us as human beings, this idea is inseparable from that of a subject who is capable of affirming himself, of positing himself. This is one of the two components of the key idea of autonomy: oneself in relation to a norm. In this regard Kant is the obligatory reference: he sees liberty as the existential condition of the norm, and the norm as the condition of intelligibility of liberty. It is a matter, therefore, of simultaneously and reciprocally creating the self and the norm. Kant takes this act of joint creation to be a given of moral life; he calls it a "fact of reason." If we adopt his way of posing the problem, the question of the self, of oneself, can be seen to be as important as that of the norm. And so my argument—that it is on the basis of an admitted moral position that we set off in search of our biological antecedents—needs to be extended in a new direction. Another retrospective reading of human descent is required that will retrace the ancestry of the self's autonomy. Another sorting out of the immense diversity of living things, to quote Gould again, needs to be attempted. No doubt the same lines of descent would be privileged, and arranged in the same series, but this time for the purpose of discerning in them other sources of the emergence of humanity. In the Darwinian conception, it is not so much capacities of individuation that are exaggerated as aptitudes favoring the survival of the species. This emphasis seems to me reinforced by Gould, who deliberately takes random variation as his central theme—whence an approach that you yourself call "populationist." This is just the problem: the population is taken as the unit of analysis. The range of "living things" is interpreted as a range internal to a population.

But what are we to say about individuation? It seems to me that another reading of evolution can be combined with the populationist view. I think first of the reading proposed by Hans Jonas in *The Phenomenon of Life* (in German, *Organismus und Freiheit;* in French, *Biologie philosophique*). As the German title makes clear, it is expressly a question of the genesis—with all the reservations that I attach to this word—of the famous responsibility principle. How is it possible that a responsible subject, a free self, should have come into existence? Biology suggests it is due to the phenomenon of organization, which I venture to juxtapose with that of variation. If the latter is populationist, the former is individualist, by which I mean that it concerns the resistance to death of individuals of a species, taken one by one (here obviously I have in mind Bichat's famous remark that life is the set of forces that resist death). It is not surprising, then, that the phenomenon chiefly emphasized by biology is metabolism, involving an organism that continually exchanges chemical substances with its environment and, by means of this exchange between the inner and the outer, maintains its structural identity. This contrast between the continuity of form and the mutability of matter Jonas sees as the first anticipation of what in man was to be called "liberty." This process of autointegration gave meaning for the first time to the notion of an individual—as an entity distinct, I would argue, from the population: a self announces itself before a world. The task of philosophical biology, then, is to follow the development of this germinal form of liberty through the levels of biological evolution. I will mention here only the role assigned to perception, to emotion, at the level of an animality exposed to scarcity and danger: the price of individuation, then, is the growing otherness of the world and the growing solitude of the self. Henceforth the possibility of non-being accompanies the integration of "being-for-life," as though it were its shadow, and makes of life an improbable and revocable adventure.

Jonas is not alone in holding this view. Before him, Kurt Goldstein and Jacob von Uexküll, cited by Canguilhem in *La Connaissance de la vie,* had stressed the initiative of living beings in configuring their surroundings: "The peculiar characteristic of living beings," Canguilhem insisted, "is that they make a milieu for themselves."[32] Here I recall that each of us has mentioned the role of anticipation in the behavior of living beings toward their surroundings. Credit for this observation now needs to be given to the constitution of the biological self. In this connection Canguilhem writes that just as the environment (for which he uses the German term *Umwelt*) of man is "centered, ordered by a human subject," so that of the animal "is nothing other than a milieu centered in relation to the [animal] subject [embodying that] vital value in which living beings essentially consist."[33] "We must," he says, "conceive at the root of this organization of the animal *Umwelt* a subjectivity analogous to the one we are required to consider [as being] at the root of the human *Umwelt*."[34] Accordingly, "biology must therefore first consider the living being as a meaningful object, and individuality, not as an object, but as a [characteristic value]. To live is to spread outward, to organize the milieu from a center of reference that itself cannot be referred to without losing its original significance."[35]

In this passage one sees that the thought of the philosopher-biologist, in both versions of evolution, proceeds backward from the question that he poses concerning the humanity of man in order then to undertake biological observation. It seems to me that it is necessary to include in our discussion of a predisposition to ethical judgment, from the outset, the position of an ethical subject who posits himself; that is, the assertion of a self by itself. And this addition to the idea of a norm is not trivial: what needs to be justified is not only the rationality of a principle of morality, but also the wish that human existence should continue in a way that is worthy of it.

If you will agree to this shift of emphasis, or rather this recentering of the moral problem, I would like then to ask you if evidence can be found of an ethical disposition to the positing of a self.

Changeux: This is a question for the neurobiologist to ask the philosopher—but also one for the neurobiologist to ask himself! You will grant, I hope, that as a member of the species *Homo sapiens* I possess a "self" and that I may examine—in the light of subjective experience, of course—its position with respect to the world and to the creation of moral norms.

First, I wish to come back to the question you raise once again of a retrospective search for biological antecedents, departing from an accepted moral function, and to finish describing my "evolutionist" point of view. My personal experience as chairman of the National Advisory Committee on Bioethics has confirmed my belief in the validity of the approach we are contemplating. Committees of this kind examine ethical problems posed by a particular scientific question on the basis of specific factual documentation. They encourage debate that will be, as far as possible, free from prejudice and unencumbered by a priori moral positions. Experience shows that men and women gathered around a table manage to understand each other in spite of differing philosophies or religious attachments. This approach may be compared with that of science itself, although its aim is different; personally, I cannot imagine proceeding otherwise. Within such a framework, devising rules of conduct for a given field—which therefore involves a normative approach—amounts to jointly constructing ready-to-use maxims, as it were, social representations that frame possible forms of behavior. In the course of conversation, arguments are constructed in the brains of individual committee members: new thought-tools are forged by trial and error, by internal repetitions, and also by reference to written documents or memoirs of prior experience. Gradually an evolutionary dynamic develops, moving from the retrospective to the prospective.

One thing is evident, however. Very few philosophers have inquired into the question of the origins of morality on the basis of the scientific data actually available to them. You do not seem to mention it in your own work; in effect, then, you do not choose between biblical mythology and our knowledge of evolution.

Your remarks on Darwin a moment ago lead me once again to insist that our discussion certainly does concern the survival of the species, through the intermediary of the social group. This brings me to Hans Jonas. He has the courage to pose the question of origins—but in what terms! *The Imperative of Responsibility* begins with a thoroughgoing attack on the biological sciences. In a style not unlike that of an Old Testament prophet who calls down curses, Jonas writes: "The biologist investigating elementary life processes, for example on the molecular plane, proceeds *as if* he didn't know that there was a whole organism in which they were occurring; investigating lower organisms, as if he didn't know that there were higher ones; investigating the higher [ones] as if he did not know that they possessed subjectivity; investigating the highest (and his brain) as if he did not know that thinking determined his being. . . . And [this suits] human science."[36] A whole flourishing branch of research thus finds itself stricken by debility. Jonas goes on to assert that the "concept of 'ends' beyond subjectivity [is] compatible with natural science"[37] and that "on the strength of the evidence of life . . . , we say therefore that purpose in general is indigenous to nature."[38] This dramatic reversion to what is most debatable in Aristotle goes together with a confusion regarding levels of explanation and a very doubtful attempt to relate the form and mutability of matter with the liberty of the self. "I have elsewhere attempted," Jonas says, "to show how already in the 'simplest' *true organism*—existing by way of metabolism, and thereby self-dependent and other-dependent at once—the horizons of selfhood, world and time, under the imperious alternative of being or nonbeing, are silhouetted in a premental form."[39] Other aspects of his philosophy and ethics, on the other hand, merit some attention. He writes, for example: "This sheer fact of feeling, presumably a universal potential of human experience, is thus the cardinal datum of the moral life and, as such, implied in the 'ought' itself."[40] Jonas clearly anchors the moral in the physiological; but the central idea of responsibility can be retained without having to go on chained to the ponderous legacy of romantic idealism and *Naturphilosophie.*

Finally, I would avoid combining Canguilhem's position with that of Jonas. The disposition of living organisms, and above all of human beings, to "organize a milieu" in relation to themselves seems to me altogether real and does not require the invocation of any finality. The survival value of the self-organizing capacities of our brain, like that of the organization of our environment, seems obvious. We will come back to this. The same is true of the ethical disposition to posit a self—a self as another—in the framework of an attribution device that is actualized within the conscious space of the brain.

I hope, and expect, that such devices will be identified before long. First, it ought to be possible to detect somatic markers somewhere in the frontal limbic system. As I've already mentioned, memory traces of faces, animals, and manufactured objects are distinguished at the level of the temporal cortex. Why shouldn't the same be true for the four truths of Buddha, the tablets of the Law, or the concept of liberty? Imaging studies of the geographical distribution of the areas involved in the determination of meaning, in the animal as well as man, are likely to give us access to such knowledge. We have traces that are directly associated with the recognition of an artifact. Why rule out the chance that such a result may be generalizable to the whole set of objects capable of being memorized, in particular rules of moral conduct, along with rules of scientific method and what might be called rules of art? To be sure, the present state of our knowledge does not permit us to draw this conclusion at the moment. But why exclude the possibility?

Ricoeur: I don't exclude it. Let me come back to my point—namely, that the positing of a self that is confronted with a norm in order to inquire into the biological origins of this act presupposes no natural finality or purpose. Quite the opposite: without the emergence of moral questioning, it wouldn't have occurred to us to trace the lines of moral descent. It is by virtue of this fact that the structuring of the environment by living creatures takes on the meaning of a predisposition, of a preparation.

Changeux: Long-term cerebral memories are transmitted from one generation to another by neurobiological mechanisms that constitute an obvious biological constraint on the transmission and the evolution of social and moral norms. The exceptionally long period of neuronal and psychological development in the human child facilitates the imprinting of cultural representations in the brain in the form of impressions that can be reused many times in the course of a person's life. If in cultural evolution certain representations are transmitted with very few modifications from one generation to the next—in particular a certain type of religious, symbolic, and practical representation—others, by contrast, evolve rapidly. Thus arises the problem of the plurality of cultures and of the relativism of morals.[41] Darwin himself, in *The Descent of Man,* had already proposed the analogy between the evolution of species and the evolution of languages. He suggested that "the formation of different languages and of distinct species, and the proofs that both have developed through a gradual process, are curiously parallel."[42] Certain sounds become words. One finds similarities between distinct languages due to common descent, "reduplication of parts," and the presence of "rudiments." Certain languages and dialects become crossed; variants grow up and spread and, as a result, become organized in subordinate groups. "We see variability in every tongue," Darwin remarks, "and new words are continually cropping up; but as there is a limit to the powers of the memory, single words, like whole languages, gradually become extinct."[43] He goes on to say that the "survival or preservation of certain favored words in the struggle for existence is Natural Selection"[44]—an *epigenetic* sort of natural selection, of course. Similarly, our brain should have capacities for *ethical innovation* in the selection and transmission of the norms of moral life. We do not evolve in a system in which imprints are rigidly propagated from one generation to another.

Ricoeur: I particularly like the analogy you draw, following Darwin, between the evolution of species and that of languages. Here we touch on a phenomenon to which we ought return later, that of dispersion, which constitutes an original aspect of the Darwinian idea of variation but which can also serve as a corrective to it. It remains, as we noted earlier, a populationist concept. Now, if the plurality of languages encompasses a distribution of populations, at least in most cases, this plurality is coextensive with a capacity common to the human species—the capacity for language. In other words, individual languages are not a property of the human species; only the ability to speak belongs to the species. This point is of crucial importance in combating racist ideology, which must be cut off at its root by excluding the concept of species from the diversity of languages. What is peculiar to the human species as a whole is the capacity to communicate by verbal signals; and this very capacity is found dispersed—as it is said in the myth of Babel—over the surface of the earth.

It is here that the analogy with the evolution of species breaks down. The plurality of languages, about which von Humboldt reflected,[45] reduplicates the universality of language, as it were. The relation between language and languages is entirely original. This point applies far beyond the case of language. Human plurality, in the sense intended by Hannah Arendt, constitutes a major phenomenon of the cultural situation of humanity. The plurality is not only linguistic but cultural. Humanity, like language, exists only in the plural. The political aspect of the phenomenon is the most telling, above all in the organization of nation-states: the distribution of power between a great many different political entities seems to be an inevitable part of the human condition, which is to say that plurality, and therefore discord, represent inescapable facts of life. Plurality thus proves to be inherent in the question of universality. The universalism for which we argue can only be coextensive with a more or less well-controlled plurality. We will encounter this problem again in the case of religions. But, as our discussion will lead us to insist, the plurality of religions constitutes another aspect of the phenomenon of variation-dispersion that operates within the human species and not between distinct species—which leads Gould to say that cultural history does not constitute an extension of biological history, something he claims ended, from the genetic point of view at least, one hundred thousand years ago. The question that I pose, then, is whether you can incorporate this phenomenon in your neuronal perspective as an aspect of epigenesis, on the basis of what you call cultural imprints.

Changeux: To answer this question, we need to jointly develop a physiology of cultural imprints, which will make it possible to pose the question of individuation and the uniqueness of each human being in a new way.

6 – Desire and Norms

Natural Dispositions to Ethical Systems

Paul Ricoeur: Because it has been our purpose from the beginning to inquire into the universal scope of morality, we made a point in the first part of our conversations of considering the influence of neural organization on our behaviors, including our moral conduct. It is for the same reason that we now turn to the origins of these behaviors in the evolution of species. I maintained, in the earlier part of our discussion, that it was necessary to examine the origins of the categories peculiar to ethical reflection in order to ask whether an equivalent can be found in the neurosciences. I did not contest, in principle, the possibility of finding one. I wished simply to affirm the autonomy of phenomenology in relation to the neurosciences. With respect to the question of the origins of morality in evolution we are in a comparable situation, to the extent that, in your model, epigenetic development gives way to invention. It is the random aspect of this invention that finds itself enlarged on the scale of cosmic time, with the idea of variation and a divergent and teeming process of evolution. A gap is thus opened up between the absence of visible order in the world of living creatures and our need as human beings for harmonious and peaceful relations. Indeed, the discordance between man's assertion of ethical principles and their absence on the plane of evolution is striking.

I would like to insist on an important aspect of this discordance. Darwin did not cease to castigate man for his arrogance in seeing himself as the end and the crown of evolution. Freud echoed him in identifying the three injuries inflicted on man's narcissism as heliocentrism, evolutionism, and—an injury due to Freud himself—psychoanalysis. Very well. But as far as heliocentrism is concerned, wise men have long regarded the sun as being above the earth, and the earth as the place of their roots and of their graves—whence the very term "humility." Evolution has forced us to square the loss of the arrogance denounced by Darwin with the self-esteem we feel as the responsible authors of our actions. Psychoanalysis doesn't ignore this paradox: if it is true that sometimes we are not masters in our own homes, as Freud put it very well, we nonetheless have to carry on with the work of remembering and mourning. I would speak in the same terms of the need to extend the work of mourning to include the arrogance of human beings confronted with the dispersion and profusion of life. But knowledge itself, the act of knowledge by which we become aware of this situation, is sustained by a strong ethical precept, the very one that Kant enunciated thus: *sapere aude!* Dare to know! We thus find ourselves in a great chasm, as it were, between the loss of arrogance and the daring of knowledge.

Jean-Pierre Changeux: The daring of knowledge is limitless. It is one of the most engaging traits of scientific knowledge.

Ricoeur: It is true that we do not altogether lack ways to bridge the gap between biological evolution and the first level of ethical existence, the affirmation of oneself and the norm. The principal transition that occupies us both has to do with disposition. We have already encountered it in the context of our earlier epistemological discussion. At that point I insisted that experience—what I call integral epistemological experience—doesn't include only the idea of representation, which has dominated the analysis of perception, memory, image, and concept, but also that of capacity, whose biological equivalent is the idea of disposition. My way of speaking privileges the notion of capacity, to which I give great scope on the plane of philosophical anthropology in the person of the able man: *What can I do? What can I not do?* I know from direct experience what I can do and what I cannot do. I may, of course, be mistaken about my capacities. But I have no other alternative but to correct, through the detour of objective knowledge, what remains a firm conviction, what I have called an attestation—that is, the confidence that I can do this or that, that I can learn, remember, think, wish. It is this category of capacity, this *I can,* that I set opposite the neurobiological term *disposition,* represented here by the theory of evolution. This is a strong and interesting correlation. I entirely accept that you overlay the discourse of the phenomenologist and moralist with that of the neurologist, exploring the gradual expansion, over the course of evolution, of the conquest of the domain of epigenetic predispositions. What we have here, then, are two parallel discourses, and the search for correlations that has occupied us from the outset is rendered more arduous by the introduction of the evolutionary dimension. To the notion of the *I can* in the discourse of the phenomenologist (now the discourse of the moralist) has come to be added that of evaluation—"strong evaluation" in Charles Taylor's sense, which incorporates the relation between the self and the good. In this regard the notion of normativity extends the notion of evaluation. A gap thus opens up between ethical discourse and a conception of evolution that takes into account the idea of random variation rather than that of centered individuality, as in the work of Goldstein and Canguilhem. This gap is masked by a confusion between two uses of the word *origin,* understood in turn in the sense of antecedence—or descent, to use Darwin's term—and in the sense of justification. Here we have another instance of semantic amalgamation—

Changeux: Of which I am not guilty. "Origin," for me, signifies descent, antecedence, and above all a point of departure. Scientific knowledge needs validation and demonstration rather than justification. Mythic discourse, by contrast, requires an "account of beginnings" as justification of its origins.[1] It is there that the amalgamation occurs. The biblical account of Genesis was, and often still is, taken literally, both in the sense of a material point of departure, the starting point for the ascent of man, and in the sense of a justification of the system of Judeo-Chistian belief. Look at the controversy that this has aroused over the last twenty-five years in the United States,[2] where Protestant creationists actually succeeded in persuading the Louisiana legislature to pass a law that prohibited the teaching of evolution unless it was balanced by instruction in "creation science"!

Ricoeur: Perhaps I don't make myself clear. My position has nothing to do with the creationism of American fundamentalists. The paradox, moreover, is that in the case of the Louisiana law, which later was struck down as unconstitutional by the Supreme Court, these propagandists obtained the support of so-called scientists while the most renowned theologians came to the defense of the theory of evolution! Let us therefore come back to philosophy. The justification of which I speak constitutes the theme of Kant's *Critique of Practical Reason:* what is it that grounds the link between liberty and moral law? From this perspective, "origin" does not mean the same thing as it does in the theory of the evolution of species. The confusion that I wish to dispel here is still more serious in the case of the word *foundation,* which can also mean two things: the foundation of a building, the underlying layer, to which corresponds what I called the "substrate" in the first part of our discussion (just as certain scientists, I believe, speak of the "neural basis" of mental activity), and, on the other hand, legitimation in an ultimate sense.[3] With this second sense we find ourselves faced with a new problem, which is no longer that of evolution—that is, the question of tracing the history of living species, of which ours is one—but the problem of how the human species ought to behave, how it ought to act. The great difference between the human world and the animal world is that the animal world has norms created for it by its genetic, and possibly epigenetic, endowment. This is not the case in the human world. Here I would like once again to refer to Kant, who argues in *Anthropology from a Pragmatic Point of View*[4] that man's natural endowment is incongruent with his moral and political obligations: although nature has left us unfinished with regard to our faculties and dispositions, nonetheless it falls to us to take responsibility for organizing our experience, which we do through a structuring activity that is normative in character. It is plain to see that the notion of "origin" changes meaning here, and I would join Kant in appealing to a normative a priori such as the categorical imperative: Act solely in accordance with the maxim that you would want to become a universal law.

By contrast I part ways with Kant, and rejoin you, when he separates the whole normative domain of duty (which embraces the imperative and associated prohibitions) from the domain of desire. He even says sometimes that desire is pathological. I react then in Aristotelian fashion by saying that desire must be put into a synergistic, or mutually reinforcing, relation with the normative. In this context I am very much interested in your research on fundamental moral sentiments and, in particular, on moral dispositions.

Changeux: When you say that the animal world has norms imposed on it by its genetic and epigenetic endowment, I see a double risk of confusion. On the one hand, you use the word *norm* to define animal behaviors, although we had agreed to reserve it for moral behaviors. And then, more fundamentally, one can't settle the question simply by asserting that things are not the same in the human world, given that the epigenetic aspect of the production and acquisition of moral rules is, as I insist, essential for the human race. Let's not call Kant—a pre-evolutionist philosopher—to the rescue in a discussion of evolution. I am nonetheless in agreement with the idea, which we will come back to, that the "structuring" evolution of norms takes over epigenetically from the natural evolution of species.

With regard to moral sentiments, which figure in so many theories of morality, from Aristotle to Darwin and, along the way, Adam Smith, I would like to mention the recent work done by Roger Blair,[5] a child psychologist, on the inhibition of violence. Blair's research builds on work in animal ethology, in particular that of Konrad Lorenz,[6] who showed, for example, that in the case of violent conflict among dogs, the victim of aggression causes the attack to cease by giving very specific signs. For instance, if the dog being attacked exposes his neck as a sign of submission, the aggressor stops biting. Blair adapted this concept to the child in the form of a developmental model of the moral sense. Between four and seven years, the normal child who attacks another becomes sensitive to his sad facial expression, his tears and crying, and subsequently refrains from acts of violence. What might be called moral emotions now intervene: empathy, sympathy, guilt, remorse. The acting out of violence is inhibited. Whereas autism seems to result from a selective alteration of a child's theory of mind, of the capacity for attribution, Blair suggests that psychopathic children exhibit a selective deficit of the violence inhibitor. Consistent with this view is the fact that the psychopathic child shows no emotional reaction to the distress of others; he is violent and aggressive and, despite the knowledge that he causes others to suffer, feels neither remorse nor guilt, though his theory of mind remains intact.

Various authors have proposed a theory of the development

of morality in the child based on punishment. On this view, fear of punishment for transgressing moral codes conditions the child to behave appropriately. Blair's work tends to limit this hypothesis, favoring instead a model that lays emphasis upon the spontaneous activation of the violence inhibitor and of the moral emotions of empathy and sympathy in the course of development. His research lends support to the thesis that these dispositions are intrinsic and innate properties of the human brain—in other words, to use Jacques Mehler's phrase, properties of "being born human."[7]

Ricoeur: Yes, the violence inhibitor operates together with the various factors of sympathy in such a way that one cannot bear the sight of violence without trying to stop it. This component of predispositions is part of what I would call the naturalistic element in ethics. Thus, at the level of capacities, I adopt your notion of disposition, according to which I am, by my very biological nature, by the very fact I am a living being, disposed to display not only cruelty, but also sympathy, toward others.

I would say that one of the new problems of contemporary ethics, by comparison with ancient ethics, is how to establish a mutually reinforcing relationship between benevolent predispositions and norms. What stands in the way of an overly optimistic view of establishing such an arrangement between the natural and the normative is connected with the problem of evil—namely, the irreducible propensity to violence. We will surely come back to this point. In the meantime, let me summarize my argument so far. I want to call attention, first, to the problem of predisposition; second, to the necessity of introducing the normative; third, to the necessity of coordinating the realm of desire and the realm of the normative.

Changeux: We have already discussed at length the problem of predisposition. The necessity of introducing the normative, which is to say rules that limit the range of possible behaviors (in its negative formulation) or designate a behavior to be followed under definite circumstances (in its positive formulation) can be interpreted quite naturally, I think, in terms of an evolutionary framework that incorporates cultural evolution. The number of possible combinations between neurons and synapses capable of contributing to representations and of organizing behavior is gigantic—astronomical, in fact. We find ourselves faced with a combinatory explosion of accessible behaviors. A first selection involves the hierarchical arrangement of representations. The establishment of intentionality is part of this process. Another part has to do with introducing high-level mental objects that serve as frameworks for individual behavior, limiting choices and, by structuring our experience of the world, working to harmonize individual behavior with the necessities of social life. We have to restrict the scope of randomness introduced by genetic, epigenetic, and cultural evolution—a considerable range of possibilities both on the neurological plane and on the plane of behavior.

Ricoeur: It is therefore necessary to choose between these possibilities, on the basis of ethical impulses and the relationship between the self and the norm.

Changeux: Normativity makes it possible to narrow the range of pertinent choices facing the moral subject in a particular historical, social, or geographical context. Norms orient human behaviors and work to facilitate the life of the social group; they serve as what might be called behavior tools. Logical rules, the Cartesian *regulae,* concern behavior to be followed by those who search for truth—such rules are, in effect, ready-to-follow rules for thinking straight. Artists similarly impose rules upon themselves in their art. "I like the rule that corrects emotion," Braque said. Moral rules, for their part, are schematic instructions for behaving appropriately, stored in the memory of human societies during the course of their history. They prevent individuals from behaving in ways that disturb their own lives as well as the life of the social group, and so constitute obvious "economies" in behavioral cost. How far do the neural and behavioral predispositions that contribute to the elaboration of moral rules have their origins in animal species that preceded humans? That is the question I want to ask.

Ricoeur: You do indeed proceed retrospectively, then, searching for the origins of the human ethical impulse. Let us consider the mix of aggressivity and sympathy—cooperation, in fact—in many animal species. The human ethical impulse rests, then, on a selection carried out among the dispositions inherited from our genetic ancestors. This selection rests in turn on an evaluation, a preference, that involves our deepest conviction about humanity, namely that it is better to be at peace than at war.

Now, to create peace among men, much more than dispositions are required. Another sort of device is needed, so to speak—in particular, institutional devices. In Kant this notion takes the third, and most daring, form of the categorical imperative: Act in such a way that the maxim of your will can always hold at the same time as a principle of universal law. A whole politics is implied by this formula, which leads, via law, to a theory of the state and, finally, of peace.

Changeux: I am very interested in Kant's *Perpetual Peace*.[8] To discuss it we would have to broaden our debate to include politics and institutions. For the moment let us simply note once more the need for feelings of sympathy and the desire for peace to be harnessed with the evaluation of rules that are capable of being extended to the whole of humanity.

Ricoeur: *Perpetual Peace* is a marvelous text, in particular for its treatment of hospitality, the right of the foreigner to be received in my land not as an enemy but as a friend; hospitality thus illustrates on the political plane, in the broad sense of the word, the purely moral idea of a city in which one is both legislator and subject. This synthesis (for Kant, an a priori synthesis), between one's position as subject—obeying rules—and as legislator—producing rules—creates a link within each of us between the servant and the producer of rules. It represents a very, very high degree of normativity.

Changeux: Isn't this the very definition of democracy on which we act as citizens, with our brains—that we produce rules and at the same time follow them? What interests me is trying to understand how normativity gradually emerges on the basis of the predispositions of the human brain and of human history.

Ricoeur: It isn't sustained by some sort of progress inherent in nature, as Gould, following Darwin in ruling out any notion of "superiority" or "inferiority" among the various species, emphasizes again and again. For normativity to emerge, it must presuppose itself; that is, become a self-referential notion.

Changeux: No, it doesn't presuppose itself; it constructs itself in a historical perspective by means of human brains capable of exactly such self-reference. But I would rather that we come back to the third point of your argument, about the creation of synergy—an excellent term—between benevolent predispositions and norms. How is agreement to be found between the realm of desire and the realm of the normative? The evolutionary framework considerably facilitates the definition of levels of complexity, or rather of organization, that interlock with each other like Russian dolls, to use François Jacob's metaphor.[9] Henri Atlan has distinguished several levels of ethical requirement and moral judgment.[10] I myself have also thought about the matter in this way, though perhaps from a more deliberately evolutionary and neurobiological perspective.

The Biological Bases of Rules of Conduct

Survival of the Species

Changeux: The most elementary level, whether one likes it or not, is that of the survival of the individual and the species. This desire to live, this thrust toward life resulting from the aggregate activity of neurons that Panskepp, in his theory of emotions (figure 6.1), calls motivation,[11] is peculiar to higher living things and to the human species in particular. Additionally, of course, there are systems of neurons engaged in the major vital functions of eating, drinking, and reproducing.[12]

Philosophers agree with biologists on this foundational principle, despite the difference in context in which it is presented. For Spinoza, "The [effort] to preserve oneself is the primary and sole basis of virtue."[13] For Hans Jonas, "the imperative that there be a humanity is the first one,"[14] supplemented by the injunction that this humanity propagate itself permanently in the future. If our first human ancestors had advocated self-destruction—generalized homicide—as the principal moral value, we would not be here today to talk about it.

Natural—what might be called experimental—situations in this domain are provided by human populations subject to extreme conditions that cause them to adopt surprising moral rules of survival. The case of a group of tourists accidentally stranded in the Andes Cordillera who became cannibals attracted everyone's attention a few years ago. In an entirely different vein, Marcel Mauss described how moral rules and re-

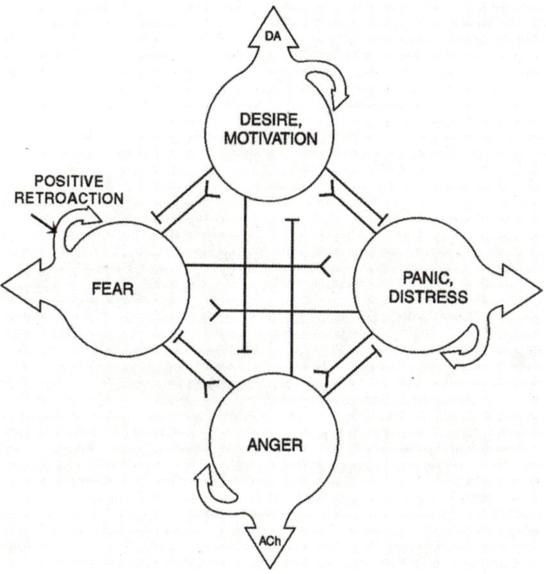

FIGURE 6.1. Panskepp's theory of the emotions.

Jaak Panskepp, inspired chiefly by work carried out in animals (the rat and monkey), proposes that the emotions arise from the activity of innate cerebral curcuits, which play an organizing role in behavior by lastingly activating or inhibiting certain classes of actions. The activity of these circuits can be subjected to the conditional control of a stimulus from the environment that at the outset is emotionally neutral; it contributes to the selection of high-level conduits, which is to say to the evaluation of representations oriented toward action. Panskepp distinguishes four large circuits that are mutually inhibited and that exploit the midbrain, the limbic system, and the basal ganglia in different ways. *Desire* (or motivation) brings into play circuits involved in electric and chemical self-stimulation as well as in pathways of exploration and intake/consumption; dopamine neurons figure in these circuits. *Anger* (or rage) exploits the neurons of the hypothalamus and mobilizes, in particular, acetylcholine. *Fear* engages different circuits, in particular the nuclei of the amygdala. Fourth and finally, *distress* (or panic) is manifested during the rupture of social cohesion; the cries emitted by the guinea-pig on being taken away from its mother can be very selectively reduced by morphine. From J. Panskepp, "Towards a general psychological theory of emotions," *Behavioral and Brain Sciences* 5 (1982): 407–467.

ligious practices change among the Eskimos between summer and winter.[15] During the polar winter the Eskimos gather in their igloos and, living in a state of continual religious elation, abandon themselves to a generalized sexual communism; with the arrival of summer, the patriarchal family is reformed. The Inuits, as we know, practice euthanasia upon their elderly when it becomes too difficult to go on living. The Iks of East Africa suffer from hunger to the point, as Colin Turnbull has reported,[16] that they flee their homes to avoid having to share the small amount of food they have, and forcibly open the mouths of the elderly to rob them of whatever food hasn't yet been swallowed. The Iks actually laugh at the misfortune of others.

More tragic still is the account of those, such as Primo Levi, who survived the Nazi death camps. "Under the hallucinatory pressure of physical need and suffering, many social habits and instincts disappear," he writes. "Here the struggle for life is without respite, because everyone is desperately and ferociously alone. . . . The simplest thing is to succumb."[17] But most struggled to survive to the best of their strength. "One has to fight against the current; to battle every day and every hour against exhaustion, hunger, cold and the resulting inertia; to resist enemies and have no pity for rivals; to sharpen one's wits, build up one's patience, strengthen one's willpower. Or else, to throttle all dignity and kill all conscience, to climb down into the arena as a beast against other beasts, to let oneself be guided by those unsuspected subterranean forces which sustain families and individuals in cruel times."[18] He goes on to add: "I feel grateful towards my brain: I have not paid much attention to it, but it still serves me well."[19]

This level of survival, not mentioned by Atlan, seems to me essential. Who can deny the importance of this unquenchable thirst for life that man owes to his brain, even under the most difficult conditions?

Ricoeur: I would like to come back to the notion of survival that you put on the most elementary level of your evolutionary and neurobiological schema. You speak of the survival of the individual and the species. And indeed the personal desire for survival is shared by every member of the species. The relation between the self and the norm implies something more and different, namely the irreplaceable—or, better, unsubstitutable—character of each individual. The various forms of social Darwinism proceed from a disregard for this difference. The same thing is true of the classical versions of utilitarianism, where the happiness of the greatest number may entail the sacrifice of a minority. Jean-Pierre Dupuy, in his studies of Rawls,[20] has insisted on the sacrificial aspect of utilitarianism. Speaking of the singularity of human beings, I think that the testimony of the thinkers you cite, from Spinoza to Jonas, points in the same direction: the *conatus* of Spinoza is that of a singular mode, to the exclusion of all generalities, and Jonas's imperative of responsibility supposes that the concern for human survival is supported by rules of prudence that the author groups under a "heuristics of fear," which is to say a reckoning by each person of dangers and causes of harm. Survival therefore becomes a moral and political imperative. One may certainly speak, as you do, of moral rules of survival. But this is precisely what they are—rules—even if their content changes, as the examples that you give show. Their formal status as rules is, however, distinct from a simple desire for survival where the fate of the individual and that of the species are still poorly distinguished. Except for this reservation, which is not a negligible one, I agree with your first level.

The Pleasure Principle

Changeux: In addition to survival, there is the struggle against suffering and the search for pleasure. For Epicurus, to attain happiness through individual pleasure is the "principal and innate good," "the beginning and the end of human life." But not every pleasure is to be sought. Epicurus establishes a hierarchy of desires: desires that are natural and necessary—the drink that quenches thirst, the relief of pain, and so on; and desires that are neither natural nor necessary—honors, glory, riches, women (or men), which must be eliminated. Pleasure is characterized by the absence of bodily suffering and "troubles of the soul." To the extent that survival has been assured, the individual will tend to lessen his pain and suffering. Here one meets the Four Noble Truths of Buddha's teaching, which amount to an authentic physiology concerning the universality of pain, its origin, its suppression, and the eightfold path that leads to this suppression.

Ricoeur: I am delighted that you mention the struggle against suffering, and the search for pleasure, in addition to survival. The example of Epicurus leads, as you say, to a stress being placed on a hierarchy among desires. This concern is common to Epicurus and all those who might be called Socratics, as well as to the Stoics with their famous ideal of ataraxia. Epicurus certainly occupies a special place. And the comparison with Buddha is sound. But the Four Noble Truths of Buddha's teaching bring into play a whole wisdom of illumination containing the very elevated and difficult idea of "extinction," as specialists translate the well-known term *nirvana,* which involves a very demanding asceticism that too many Westerners imitate the easy way. The extinction of desire proposed by Buddha appears to go well beyond even what Epicurus advocates. Here I would like to indicate my own position with regard to these propositions that I associate with wisdom. I feel myself still very close to Kant—not the Kant of the *Groundwork* or of the *Critique of Practical Reason,* but the Kant of *Religion within the Limits of Reason Alone.* Along the same lines I would say that the ultimate aim of moral life, which according to Kant is bound up with religion, is to liberate in each of us what might be called our basic goodness. But this basic goodness is obscured, covered over, denied by what Kant calls the propensity toward, or penchant for, evil. Goodness needs to be freed—it is held captive by a free choice, indeed an absurd one, which found its supreme expression at Auschwitz: that of choosing evil for the sake of evil. But we will certainly come back later to this historical propensity, which, unlike the inclination to goodness, is not an original disposition.

Changeux: Unlike, too, the enlargement of sympathy, to use Darwin's phrase. At a higher level, I would introduce the notion of harmony or affective equilibrium—the "welfare" of the English utilitarians, which runs from the hedonism of Bentham to Mill's immediate happiness and even to ideal, selfless happiness. The neural definition of this state becomes more difficult than those of pain and pleasure, whose specialized circuits we have already both mentioned. Happiness is something more encompassing that links the cognitive with the affective, the prefrontal with the limbic. At this juncture I would venture to connect it with what you call the good life, those ideal plans for life and dreams of accomplishment at which our actions aim. I am aware that I am enlarging the sense of the word *life* here. This attempt to live well requires, if only on the plane of intentions, as large an access as possible to the representations that suddenly appear in the conscious space of each person's brain. To conceive oneself as being free is also Spinoza's "joyous affirmation of the power to be."

Ricoeur: A certain ambiguity seems to attach to the word *life* that I would like to dispel. On the one hand, it designates the basic referent of biology as a science. It signifies simply that all the models submitted to the test of verification or refutation refer to it in the last analysis, albeit within the limits of competence of the science in question. Life, in this sense, is what one speaks of in biology. The use of the word by a moralist such as Aristotle who speaks of living well is something different. Here it is used in its usual sense, as when we speak of the life we lead, of the manner in which we conduct our life. This use became a philosophical one with the attempt to rank kinds of life in a hierarchy, as with the Socratics and with Epicurus himself. A factor of preference, of evaluation, of greater or less value now comes into play that is not contained in the scientific usage of the word. Here "life" has another meaning than that of being an object of knowledge—the knowledge of life, as Canguilhem titled his book.

Changeux: This is the sense of living well.

Ricoeur: Unless, once more looking back in the way I described a moment ago, we include among the performances of life, in the biological sense, those that could be considered as anticipations of—and therefore predispositions to—the good life. Here I would like to venture a hypothesis, a risky one to the extent that it oversteps the boundary between epistemology and ontology. For Hans Jonas, life as resistance to death, as expansion, as a joyous affirmation of the power to be, to paraphrase Spinoza once more—life has already chosen, as it were; it has preferred itself to nothingness. Jonas does not hesitate to recall the question posed by Leibniz: "Why is there something rather than nothing?" Well, Jonas says, the answer is to be found in the affirmation of life, which unites "is" and "ought." Life prefers itself to nothing; life thinks highly of itself; life approves of itself. If we do not see this, or no longer see it, this is because the Copernican and Newtonian reading of the world is that of a dead universe, unentitled to life, as it were. It is with great caution that I cite this argument, which occupies a prominent place in Jonas's work between the ancient Gnostic denial of the world, his primary subject of interest, and his reformulation of the Kantian imperative in the sense of a responsibility toward life in generations to come. This interpretation echoes certain aspects of the philosophy of Leibniz, and even that of Spinoza, to the extent that Spinoza's philosophy, as my late friend Sylvain Zak argued,[21] is through and through a philosophy of life—witness the central place in it of *conatus,* the effort to persevere in being. No matter what one may think of Jonas's interpretation, it is to be classed among those retrospective readings that, inspired by a problem of moral philosophy, look for support back beyond the human. From this point of view, to be alive, to wish to live, to prefer life to death—these are all the same thing.

Changeux: They amount to a will to live—the effort to live.

Ricoeur: The effort to live—the desire to exist.

Changeux: Yes, the desire to exist oneself and with others. We are in perfect agreement. In joining you in speaking of oneself as another, I come now to the level of interpersonal relations.

Sociability

Changeux: The human brain's capacity to judge not only makes conscious (or unconscious) reference to individual values of survival, affective harmony, and the good life. The human species is just as much a social species, and I have already mentioned among the predispositions to a social bond—attribution, inhibition of violence, empathy, and sympathy—what, on the evolutionary plane, singularizes the human species and

FIGURE 6.2. Prince Peter Alekseevich Kropotkin (1842–1921).

Geographer, naturalist, and evolutionary theorist, Kropotkin played an important part in the elaboration of anarchist doctrines in addition to proposing an evolutionary ethics founded on reciprocity and cooperative behaviors. His book *Mutual Aid: A Factor of Evolution* (1902) went through several editions in his lifetime and led to novel developments in evolutionary theory that placed emphasis on cooperation as well as competition.

in particular this disposition to cooperation, which after Darwin was noted by Kropotkin (figure 6.2) in his book *Mutual Aid: A Factor of Evolution,* based on his own observations of nature in Siberia.

Kropotkin noted that in very difficult climatic conditions species survive to the extent that individuals gather together and help each other: "The more individuals keep together, the more they mutually support each other, the more are the chances of the species for surviving as well as for making further progress in its intellectual development."[22] According to him, "among the carnivorous beasts there is one general rule . . . [i.e.,] they never kill one another"[23]; for the "lesson of nature was thus, that even the strongest beasts are bound to combine."[24] Kropotkin considered the instinctive practice of "mutual sympathy" as the point of departure for all the "higher feelings"—justice, equity, equality, self-sacrifice—which jointly lead to moral progress.[25] This feeling of moral obligation, of which man is conscious, is not divine in origin, but is found in nature with, on the one hand, the animal sociability we already mentioned and, on the other, the imitation of what primitive man observes in nature.

Nonetheless, taking into account the desires of others and their suffering does not, even where there is sympathy, systematically produce an action aimed at easing such suffering. Intentional cruelty is, in fact, possible. Violence can assert itself and, by gradually destabilizing the social group, put the survival of individuals and their affective equilibrium in peril. Generally speaking, as Henri Atlan has argued, the immediate search for pleasure or the too rapid elimination of suffering can lead to violence; in the interest of the common good, they should be deferred. Devising norms of collective life thus becomes indispensable. It is, in effect, the price to be paid for reconciling the representational capacities of the human brain, its capacity for judgment, and the material conditions of social life. This production of norms is a response to the creation of a synergistic relation between individual desires and the social group. In effect, the selection of systems of moral values supplies natural predispositions that are specific to *Homo sapiens,*[26] at a given state of the cultural evolution of the social group; such a normative synthesis would harmonize, in a provisional and revisable way, the three histories that take shape in the brain of each person: the evolution of the species, the individual's personal history, and finally the social and cultural history of the community to which the individual belongs. It can readily be seen—and this is the key step of my argument—that the norms invented by humanity in the course of its history naturally exploit sympathy and the inhibition of violence in the context of a permanent process of cultural evolution. It may be, then, that the enlargement of sympathy and the suppression of violence constitute the raw material for a universal and fundamental normativity of human morals.

In Chinese tradition, this normativity is presented in both a negative form, with Confucius ("Do not do to others what you do not wish done to you") and a positive form, with Mo Tzû ("He who loves others will be loved in his turn; he who causes others to profit will profit in his turn"). In the West, the negative form was set down by the Jewish scholar Hillel, St. Paul's teacher, in the Babylonian Talmud ("What is hateful to you, do not do to your neighbor"); the positive form is found in the Christian gospel ("Do unto others as you would have them do unto you" [Matthew 7:12]). It expresses a norm of reciprocity in the social group founded upon an understanding of oneself in relation to others.

In various cultural and historical contexts of recent human evolution, a common normativity developed that was not simply ethical in nature but was typically associated with the symbolic systems of representation of particular religions and philosophies. Christianity in Western Europe and Buddhism in the Far East offer examples of this common normativity within a particular cultural group, whose harmony depended on reconciling spontaneous dispositions toward sympathy, enlargement of sympathies, and consideration of others within the framework of the history of the social group and its conditions of life.

Ricoeur: You are quite right to introduce at once the relationship to others, at the level of interpersonal relations. At the most fundamental level of ethics, prior to any strictly universalist requirement of normality, it is necessary to extend what, with Aristotle, I call the desire to live well so to include the desire to live well with others—under, I hasten to add, just institutions. You are right, too, to mention the golden rule in a variety of formulations across cultures. With this formula a certain threshold of humanity is crossed. But your main argument, that the norms invented by human beings in the course of their history naturally exploit sympathy and the inhibition of violence, must in my view be reinterpreted in the sense of a subsequent search for a fulcrum in evolution. Propositions concerning aggressivity need to be sorted out from ones concerning sympathy and the struggle against violence. In this sense I agree with the idea of an enlargement of the dispositions to morality present in other living beings. But the golden rule, it seems to me, is a point of arrival in evolution because it is a point of departure in moral reflection. It is a point of departure to the extent that the idea of another must be formed with the full force of an otherness that enjoins me to responsibility, as Levinas puts it.

Changeux: I would be more cautious. I would avoid saying "because," replacing it instead by "and." In fact, I consider the golden rule neither as a point of arrival nor as a point of departure, but as a stage in the neurocultural and historical development of moral normativity. There is the problem, next, of generalizing this discourse that I've borrowed from you—

Ricoeur: I've borrowed it myself: I am a disciple of Aristotle, Kant, Hegel, and perhaps to some degree the Nietzsche of the *Genealogy of Morals* and *Beyond Good and Evil*—but with reservations.

The Level of Humanity

Changeux: Now we come to the level of humanity. We witness today a sort of universalization of communication, despite great cultural differences whose symbolic systems, as I have mentioned and as you yourself recognize, are transmitted in an epigenetic but nonetheless faithful manner from one generation to another within a given social group. Under these conditions, we see a conflict arise between the symbolic power of religious and philosophical conventions, on the one hand, and fundamental ethical obligations on the other. There is conflict, but above all confusion, between these ethical obligations and trivial social conventions, such as the wearing of beards or veils or hats, dietary habits, rituals and signs (crossing oneself or prostrating oneself, for example), going to church or to temple or not going, and so on.

The American psychologist Elliott Turiel has carried out a fascinating series of experiments on the moral and social reasoning of children and adolescents, which demonstrates that they unambiguously distinguish judgments of moral necessity, which are obligatory and noncontingent, from judgments referring to social conventions, which by contrast are optional and contingent.[27] He inquired into the beliefs of children belonging to two distinct fundamentalist religious communities: Amish Mennonites and Orthodox Jews. He asked them very specific questions about rules of conduct concerning, on the one hand, the day of worship, baptism, the obligation of women (or of men) to cover their heads, and the observance of dietary rites. A large majority of children in both communities broadly accepted that children of other religions did not respect their religious practices; they even admitted that their own rules of prayer and diet could not be followed if such rules had not previously been "given by God." All this the children saw as belonging to their "private life." By contrast, the idea that they or children of other communities might disobey moral rules proper—rules prohibiting theft, slander, damage to property—seemed to them unacceptable, even though these rules were not of divine origin.

Children therefore unambiguously—and from the age of thirty-nine months—distinguish moral rules judged to be obligatory, bearing upon the concepts of happiness, justice, and law, and founded on honesty and the idea of avoiding doing harm, from conventional rules judged to be contingent and nongeneralizable, even if they are supposed to issue from the word of God. Children make an essential distinction that in practice adults very largely lose. This loss is apt to give rise to very serious generational conflicts. Isn't the deep sense of incomprehension, often accompanied by hatred and violence, felt by many young people today the result of confusing these two types of rules?

Such systems of symbolic representation, principally religious, are at the root of very serious conflicts in a great many situations past and present. Too often, circumstantial social conventions prevail over fundamental moral obligations—obligations that I do not hesitate to characterize as natural and universal.

Ricoeur: The passage from interpersonal relations to the level of humanity takes us to a new and higher threshold. In this regard, you are in the same situation as I am, searching for a fulcrum for the rule of universalization. Universalization is an a priori rule. I don't see how it can be deduced from the fact of being alive, desiring, and so on. One may certainly find support for it in favorable predispositions. But the naturalist derivation seems to me more difficult in this case, owing to certain peculiar aspects of human violence. Here one is confronted with the formidable problem of evil. Without yet inquiring into its origins, let us limit ourselves to the enigma of its appearance. No matter what we may be able to say in this regard, I insist on remarking for the moment that the fundamental aim of ethics is to liberate goodness. Liberate it from what? This is what we shall have to decide.

Changeux: Quite so. In this attempt at universalization, the fundamental predisposition of the human brain to represent itself as another is obscured, indeed opposed, by the often constraining conventions that accompany rules of discrimination and exclusion, if only with regard to the institution of marriage. Surprisingly, as a result of the "authoritarian" epigenetic impregnation of the child's brain by the conventions of the cultural community in which he or she lives, initially through the family, the feeling of cultural belonging is extremely keen and stable at an early age. In the absence of rational choice, the emotions associated with this feeling are very strong and subject to violent reactions.

Those who aspire to a humanist and pacifist conception of citizenship, as I do, may hope at this juncture that the progress of knowledge, particularly in the human and social sciences, will help raise the level of debate above any hegemonic attempt to impose one system of beliefs to the exclusion of others. Certain studies ought to permit us to objectively distinguish the imaginary, the mythical, and the contingent, which in varying proportions are present in every cultural tradition, from the body of moral sentiments peculiar to the human species. Why disallow science the chance to help us understand which ethical arrangements are fundamental, which ones ought to be universalized? This measure of objectivity allows us to join authors such as John Rawls and Jürgen Habermas in conceiving of ethics not in terms of a particular cultural community, but in terms of a theory of society that concerns the entire human species, cultural attachments and schools of thought aside. Indeed, for Habermas, "a theory of argumentation must take the form of an 'informal logic,' because it is impossible to *force* agreement on theoretical and practical-moral issues either by means of deduction or on the basis of empirical evidence."[28] What is needed instead is an extensive process of communication, made up of individual deliberations, by which participants of distinct cultural origins manage to reach agreement about a *reasonable* project of action.

Rawls, following Kant, distinguishes "reasonable" from "rational," arguing that rational persons will act in an intelligent manner but that reasonable persons will do more than this. They will take into account the effect of their actions on the well-being of others. They will supplement the notion of equal justice for all with that of social cooperation that is equitable and acceptable for the whole of society and that provides a guarantee of peace.

This collective appeal to the reasonable enlarges ethical debate beyond cultural barriers and social conventions. Rawls puts it this way: "Insofar as we are reasonable, we are ready to work out the framework for the public social world, a framework it is reasonable to expect everyone to endorse and act on, provided others can be relied on to do the same."[29] By submitting specific and limited projects to the continual test of a universalization of the reasonable, ethical debate over the selection of moral norms opens up limitlessly in time and space. As an evolutionary phenomenon, it allows the natural dispositions of the species to be realized in complete spontaneity, now not merely at the level of the cultural community but on the scale of humanity as a whole.

Ricoeur: I would like to comment on the contrast on which you so insist between obligation and convention. Specifically you distinguish between "fundamental ethical obligations" and "social conventions," chiefly ones having a religious coloring. One encounters the same opposition in Kohlberg, subsequently adopted by Habermas. It seems to me overdrawn. First, it makes the attempt to naturally derive morality more difficult to the extent that you deprive yourself of a grounding in morals, customs, practices. You condemn yourself to a formalism still more disembodied than the one that I assume in treating the rule of universalization as an a priori. Nonetheless it is necessary that this rule have a hold over something, that it apply to maxims that are the product of daily practice. Here we touch on the difficult connection between the universal and the historical. And we encounter once more a problem that we met with earlier, having to do with the dispersion of humanity, not only with respect to languages but also to customs and morals. The enormous question of human plurality cannot be settled in a single stroke by opposing obligation to convention. You yourself speak of cultural community, cultural attachment. In this regard, I feel myself closer to Rawls than to Habermas. The theory of justice, Rawls says, demands that the principle of fairness rely on "considered judgments," and therefore on various designs of the good that may differ from each other, indeed may be quite divergent, but that admit of being put into synergistic relation with each other. I would propose therefore replacing the term *convention* in our vocabulary by *conviction,* on the condition that such convictions have been submitted to critical test and, by virtue of this, qualify as considered judgments. That said, I can only join with you in wishing that the sciences, and in particular the human sciences, will contribute to the incorporation of ethics, and ethical behavior, in our daily activities. Insofar as science is also an ethical project, constituting one practice among others, this hope is perfectly reasonable.

Changeux: Science is a practice that aims at universalization. But I want to keep the distinction between convention and conviction. Convention, in my view, does not include authentic moral judgments—what Rawls calls "considered judgments." It doesn't seem to me that dietary or clothing prohibitions, for example, ought to figure among such convictions. By contrast, conventions may pose problems with regard to the acceptability of rules of conduct even if such rules qualify as considered judgments.

Ricoeur: We can agree on this—that a practice that aims at universalization joins together the theoretical and the practical by aiming at the true and at the good, which is to say fairness.

Passage to the Norm

Changeux: To summarize my position at this stage of our discussion, I would say once more that the adult human brain may be considered as the result of at least four interlocking evolutions, each one subject to random variability: the evolution of species in paleontological time, together with its consequences for the genetic constitution of human beings; individual evolution, through the epigenesis of neural connections, which occurs throughout the individual's development; cultural evolution, likewise epigenetic but extracerebral, which spans not only psychological time but also age-old memories; and finally the evolution of personal thought, which occurs in psychological time and draws upon individual and cultural memories that are both cognitive and emotional.

The fundamental idea is that each of these evolutions is embedded in the others and proceeds in accordance with a general schema of variation-selection-amplification. This is the schema that Darwin used to account for the evolution of species. The hypothesis that I propose along with many others—Popper, Edelman, Tooby and Cossmides, Boyd and Richerson—is that this schema remains valid within the framework of epigenetic evolution, on the condition once more that one can define the level of organization at which a pertinent relationship is established between neural organization and "psychological" function (understood as consisting in processes of stabilization and selection). I have also mentioned the projective style of the functioning of our brain. In this mode the brain produces representations that precede or anticipate action upon the world; that determine a plan that may be described as deliberate and voluntary. At bottom, we are always in a state of mutual anticipation, of wait-and-see. We exchange looks, I anticipate (or not) your response and, in any case, I try, perhaps not to convince you but, at least to make you understand what I am thinking.

This projective style is completed by a disposition, once again exceptionally developed in humans and, to my mind, of great importance—creativity. Neurobiological models are often criticized for their inability to account for the capacity to create. One hears it said that neuronal man is "a fly trapped in a bottle," a rigid and cold automaton without emotion or the capacity to learn—in short, a robot lacking any of the attributes of humanity, specifically creative power. The current state of knowledge certainly does not permit us to propose a rigorous scientific model of creation; but, if we look to discoveries that are likely soon to be made in the neurosciences, it seems reasonable to suppose that creativity results from epigenetic combination at the level of the evolution of individual thought, involving the highest cognitive and/or affective representations. It may be that spontaneous combinatorial variations are the source of new ideas. This hypothesis, which I have developed using the example of painting and artistic creation,[30] can be extended to the domain of ethical normativity. As chairman of the National Advisory Committee on Bioethics from 1992 to 1998, I came to appreciate the essential role that innovation plays in questions of applied ethics, for it very frequently yields new solutions to apparently insoluble moral dilemmas. Creativity is quite characteristic of the human species. Perhaps this disposition builds upon what might be called an exploratory behavior that is already found in animal species.

Ricoeur: I am struck by two things in your presentation. First, I wonder if it isn't at the prompting of our common experience that we take into account these two phenomena of projection and creativity, without their corresponding to any kind of neurological knowledge. Out of this shared experience comes your desire to extend the scope of the neurosciences to take in the projective and creative aspects of mental activity. Creativity covers vast domains that include the arts, sciences, ethics, and politics. I wonder, then, if our ordinary experience, the experience we all share as persons—the structures of which are only articulated conceptually by philosophers—isn't ahead of your science. It is this experience that makes dialogue between us possible. In other words, you mustn't lose sight of the field of human experience whose most inventive aspects you seek to capture, thanks to the element of randomness present in the structures that are the object of your research.

Changeux: This I do not at all dispute.

Ricoeur: At the same time such experience offers the possibility of seeing how the two discourses fit together. We have to be clear that they have different origins. The experience of which I am speaking is not the province of the neurosciences. It is common experience.

Changeux: Here I share your point of view entirely.

Ricoeur: What I would challenge, however, is your ambition to take over neighboring sciences, little by little, and ultimately common experience as well.

Changeux: That isn't necessarily the scientist's dream. To the contrary, many neurobiologists, out of a concern for experimental and conceptual rigor, refuse to permit themselves this type of ambition, feeling that it goes beyond what their own discipline allows them to assert. As a neurobiologist I take the risk of going beyond current knowledge—while trying to remain cautious and critical.

Ricoeur: This is why I would speak instead of trying to fit a developing science together with a realm of experience that is far in advance of this science.

Changeux: This approach is not new. It is found in Comte, Marx, and Wittgenstein, as well as Carnap and the members of the Vienna Circle, together with the idea that science has no limits, that there is nothing unknowable, only the unknown.

Ricoeur: The related idea of the unity of science is problematic, however.

Changeux: I myself am much attached to it. It is not a question of proposing a mythical grand synthesis of all human knowledge, but of preventing knowledge from being partitioned into incongruent and irreducible spheres, sealed off from each other without any possibility of communication. Talk of irremediable "epistemological ruptures" is unsupported by the evidence. Differences between disciplines with respect to methods, instruments, and theoretical discourse do, of course, exist; but the continuity of knowledge is real, from the atom to the molecule, from the molecule to the cell, and so on.

As Carnap said, science has no boundaries in either time or logical space.[31] There is constant progress in scientific knowledge, a permanent and ongoing boom in the direction of greater scientificity. "Science," as Comte wrote in the *Discours*

argument likewise departs from a presumed end, a horizon of meaning, that he calls *Geist* (a word that, like the French *esprit,* may be translated either as "mind" or "spirit"). And it is under the name of phenomenology—a term that in Hegel means something different than it does in Husserl—that he undertakes to examine the sensible history of mind. This history, attracted by its end, is presented as a progression that moves from threshold to threshold through an increase of meaning: there is more meaning in perception than in sensation, more in the concept than in perception, more in theoretical reason than in the concept, more in communal experience than in individual consciousness, and so on. This model is extremely important for a properly ethical approach: the notion of thresholds and creative progressivity is clearly an improvement on the narrowly biological picture of life as something pushing from behind. Thus, thanks to this brief detour via Hegel, we meet up again with our earlier discussion of the use of the term *life.* When I employ this term in philosophical discourse, I speak of life as a level of experience. This is the level of desire, of fear, which already contains a tacit evaluation—what Canguilhem has in mind when he speaks of "vital values." The question is whether one can pass from this type of evaluation, through pleasure and pain, the agreeable and the useful, to a strictly moral evaluation that introduces something more, something that is implicit in the wish to live well, namely validity, legitimacy.

It seems to me that here we have an altogether fundamental discontinuity. It is by virtue of this discontinuity that one may turn around and ask if, along the route traveled, some trait did not anticipate the passage to the norm. On this point I am very close to your view: the discontinuity of the norm does not abolish the continuity of dispositions; it is superimposed on it, and the problem becomes how to connect the two points of view correctly. Here too we touch on the point

sur l'esprit positif (1844), "may be likened to a simple methodical extension of universal wisdom."[32] Earlier, in the *Cours de philosophie positive,* he had asserted, "There is no reason to think that the most complex phenomena of living bodies—social phenomena—are different in kind than the simplest phenomena of natural bodies."[33] This led Durkheim, Comte's successor, to "apply the principle of causality" to social facts within the framework of a unifying model of objective knowledge.[34] The excesses to which positivism has led are well known, and care must be taken not to repeat them; even so, I find the attempt at least to unify objective knowledge appealing.

Ricoeur: But in science there isn't any methodological unity. There is perhaps a unity of aim, of wanting to know—a shared objective. But there is a plurality of referents, in the sense of the ultimate objects *on which* each science bears.

Changeux: I don't want to be thought of as a sort of Laplace of the human sciences—someone who seeks to reduce ethical normativity, past and present, to a set of equations on the basis of our knowledge of the brain, the history of humanity, and the evolution of our cultures and civilizations. Nonetheless, as a theoretical matter, the ideal of a normative science integrated with a general philosophy positing the unity of science seems to me a worthy ambition. It is obvious that, for the moment, this project is not realizable either in substance or in detail. That shouldn't prevent us from thinking about it, from engaging in reflection that places itself as near as possible to objective knowledge in the "order of truth," as Habermas recommends, and encourages us, in Lucien Sève's phrase, "to invent, and implant in life, individual and social practices that are both civilized and civilizing."[35] Even if the aim of a scientific ethics appears to many a utopian one, and a cold and dangerous utopia at that, we must try continually to construct, step by step, a provisional morality—here again the echo of Descartes—that will help us to resolve day-to-day questions of ethics.

Ricoeur: With regard to the project of the unity of science, I would say that one may speak of science from two different points of view. On the one hand, from an epistemological point of view, with reference to various types of modeling. The fact that modeling is not the same in chemistry as in biology, or in biology as in physics, entails a pluralism of scientific disciplines. On the other hand, one may see science as a unity, but a unity of aim rather than of methodology. By "aim" I mean the impulse of curiosity—the urge to understand what it is to be a person living in the world.

Changeux: I think we share the same aim.

Ricoeur: Science, because it is a theoretical practice, has a history, as do morality, the arts, and politics, with the same hazards and conflicts; its teams of researchers, like all teams, have complex social relationships exhibiting varying degrees of competition and collaboration. Science has a history, and an unknown horizon, because it maps out its course as it goes along. The idea of unity is part of its aim, but this cannot be accomplished simply by totaling up types of modeling and types of explanation.

Changeux: Nonetheless the idea of unity remains a common aim—

Ricoeur: I share this openness of the scientific spirit, to the extent that it is a matter of determining how far a scientist will be able to explain, in terms of his own system of modeling,

the results not only of sciences other than his own but also what has happened throughout cultural history.

The second thing that strikes me about your presentation of a naturalistic, evolutionary approach to ethics, is the emphasis you place on continuity—as though life were pushing from behind. I said earlier that it is by looking backward from the position of the self and the norm that the scientist can consider the course traveled by science in the light of morality. Consequently, despite the dispersion effect that is characteristic of the diversity of living things, he may privilege one route leading to man rather than another—whence the appearance of progress or, as I just put it, of life pushing from behind. At the same time, the norm now appears to constitute a fact, a datum falling under the head of empirical description. Hume's distinction between "is" and "ought" seems to have been done away with. Nonetheless, the phenomenological interpretation that I propose contains, in its strictly ethical phase, a recognition that there is a difference between description and evaluation. Now this evaluative dimension causes thresholds to appear, and it is in this connection that I would argue for much more of a discontinuist view of evolution than yours, an evolution stripped of its anthropomorphic character of progress.

Changeux: You know how hostile I am to any suggestion of anthropomorphism with regard to biological evolution. I have *never* used the term "progress" to describe biological evolution. I have used, and will continue to use, the more objective and neutral term "increase in complexity," particularly in the case of the evolution of the brain.

Ricoeur: I have in mind another model than the ones we have discussed until now, if one may use this term to refer to something other than the kind of modeling done by scientists: the model proposed by Hegel in *The Phenomenology of Mind*. His

where I am furthest removed from the Kantian tradition, which holds that the a priori character of moral obligation has no root in the living world. A better approach to the problem of connecting norms and dispositions is offered by the moral philosophy of the post-Kantians, specifically Hegel, whose analysis I have just sketched. This is why I like to describe myself, as did Éric Weil, as a post-Hegelian Kantian. What Hegel makes us reflect upon is this feeling of degrees—not only of complexity but also of evaluation, through the augmentation of meaning. For me, one of the fundamental problems of ethics is to correctly match up the level of validity with the level of desirability. I wonder whether this can be done by appealing exclusively to the influence of so-called naturalistic factors, such as altruistic sentiments, which I see as a source of inspiration for the ideal of justice and goodness, but not a justification. In other words, justification may not always coincide with motivation.

Changeux: This Hegelian expansion from threshold to threshold, by successive degrees, with an increase in meaning from sensation to perception, from perception to concept and so on, corresponds in my thinking to the notion of levels of organization that, at each level, incorporate variation and evaluation. Not only have I mentioned these levels of organization in connection with the body—from cell to tissue, from tissue to organ, from organ to organism—but I have also much insisted upon the cleavage between levels of organization of the nervous system, which it seems legitimate to see as corresponding to levels of mental representation that become more and more integrated the higher one rises in the hierarchy. This idea can obviously be applied to the cultural world, to the social world—

Ricoeur: Which we know in a different way.

Changeux: Which we know in a different way. As you were saying, the connection with what we know of our brain remains to be established for the most part. For my part, however, I see no fundamental obstacle to establishing the connection. You speak of passing from threshold to threshold. Clearly this aspect is not inconsistent with what is classically accepted regarding the continuity of evolution. Various elementary, discrete, and apparently discontinuous stages intervene in the course of biological evolution. That is one thing. On the other hand, by contrast with the living creatures found on Earth today, the intermediate species that lived in paleontological epochs are often not well known. This is true in the case of human beings as well. There appears to be a discrete jump between the states of consciousness of a chimpanzee and those of a human being. Similarly, the transition may seem sudden between the undoubtedly organized cries produced by Old World monkeys, or by chimpanzees, and human language. This apparently discontinuous characteristic cannot be used, however, as an argument against the idea of evolution.

I would even say that recent theories of evolution—like Gould and Eldredge's theory of punctuated equilibria[36]—call attention to remarkable differences in the pace of evolution of species that could be taken for authentic discontinuities. According to Gould, the majority of species remain in prolonged "stases," the logical expression of the successful adaptation of large populations. This is the case, for example, with a certain brachiopod, Lingula, a marine invertebrate that has scarcely changed since the Cambrian, which is to say for more than five hundred million years. By contrast, rare and complex events may occur that shatter this stability and generate very rapid evolutions—punctuations that, on the scale of paleontological time, give the impression of discontinuity. This is the case with elephants during the Tertiary, and with mankind, which arose in less than four million years from *Australopithecus* or from one of its relatives.

To a certain extent, the evolution of mankind's ancestors corresponds to what you have just described in terms of successive thresholds and growth in performance within the framework of a projective style accompanied by a greater complexity in evaluation systems and, by means of these, an increase in meaning. Meaning corresponds to the capacity of the organism to explore the external world and to know itself, to produce increasingly higher-order representations within increasingly elaborate evaluation systems, without there being any need to assume a rupture or postulate some teleological process of "attraction." Indeed, one of the major topics of research in the neurosciences today concerns the various processes of evaluation that, at each level of organization, intervene in the selection of behaviors.

In short, the capacity to reason, to analyze one's own behavior, and to evaluate possible courses of action by the criterion of universality—as Kant urged, following the Stoics—is unquestionably one of the systems specific to the human brain that act in synergy—I use your term—with those that define desire, no less than the moral sentiments of empathy and sympathy.

In this connection, I wish to come back to what you call the principle of justification, or of legitimacy, in moral evaluation. On your view, a fundamental discontinuity obtains between dispositions and justification, which may not always coincide with motivation. I quite agree. To justify is to produce a proof, to demonstrate the soundness of a judgment. In an evolutionary conception of normativity, this soundness is not established by reference to any a priori principle, but only a posteriori. It results from a convergence among conceptions that occurs through the opening of cultures and sensibilities to each other, in the course of reasoned debate that does not exclude appeal to common—indeed universal—rules of procedure. Instead of seeking some justification that accords with an imaginary horizon of meaning that Hegel calls "mind" or "spirit," it seems to me more appropriate to reason concretely. Myself, I would replace the principle of justification by that of the *most sensible plan of action*—what Russell called the "most fortunate act." Instead of thinking of justification from the Hegelian perspective as a form of traction by which human beings are pulled forward toward the good, it seems to me more appropriate, even if more prosaic, to examine what the actual consequences of a norm of action might be in everyday practice. Russell suggests that "the objectively right act is that one which, of all that are possible, will probably have the best consequences."[37] Again we encounter Spinoza's "adequate" action, with reasoned debate—the "normative synthesis"—making appeal to the natural dispositions of the species, expressed as fortunate acts on a universal scale.

Finally, from the perspective of the successive levels of ethics—individual survival, affective harmony (or the good life), the social group, and, finally, the level of humanity—a single discourse of justification seems to me very dangerous. We are dealing with an embedding of multiple choices that depend on the *urgency* of a particular situation. Individual survival will prevail over affective harmony in the case of famine. A concern for universality will be privileged in more favorable situations. There will never be an ideally justified sovereign good, only common projects to be carried out step by step.

Philip Johnson-Laird has posed the theoretical question of whether an automaton endowed with consciousness (understood as the property of a particular class of algorithms) can be constructed within a hierarchical framework.[38] To do this, he imagines a "phylogenesis of automata"—an evolution analogous to biological evolution, in three stages that correspond to increasingly elaborate *architectures*. The first level is that of a Cartesian-style machine that makes no use of symbolism. The second corresponds to a machine that constructs symbolic models of the world in real time and possesses a rudimentary consciousness—awareness—like that possessed by higher animals and small children. Finally, the third type of automaton consists of models of systems that have the capacity to include models of models, with interlocking hierarchies, and possess the property of being self-reflecting and, above all, of acting and communicating in an intentional way. This type of automaton has not yet been constructed; but it is not, in principle, unrealistic. Henri Atlan has discussed models of self-organizing automata that exhibit, in his phrase, an "infinite sophistication."[39] More prosaically, the formal organism model I mentioned earlier, the one that passed the Tower of London test (figure 4.3), is a very partial implementation of certain features (hierarchically interlocking and self-evaluating levels) of Johnson-Laird's third type of automaton without, however, having the capacity to communicate. One may even attempt to model, in neuronal terms, the global workspace we mobilize when making a conscious mental effort.[40]

The realization of such dispositions assumes a conceptual continuity among them. Why, then, postulate a priori an abrupt discontinuity in the genesis of moral norms? To be sure, the growing complexity of the organism, whether artificial or natural, gives access to new representations, practices, and evaluations. This needn't imply the dramatic qualitative change you suppose in passing to the stage of normative behavior; it simply attests to the considerable enrichment of human faculties made possible by access to cultural memory and intentional intercommunication. I would say, to the contrary, that the continuity of animal and human dispositions overrides whatever discontinuity may seem to attach to the invention of moral norms.

Moreover, the distinction you make between life as a force that pushes from behind, as it were, and a creative progressivity that pulls human beings forward seems to me a mere word game—as though there were a radical difference in the engine of a car because it has front-wheel rather than rear-wheel drive! I would distinguish instead between "blind" biological evolution and an evolution of societies and civilizations in which intentionality, the projective capacity of the human brain to devise plans for itself and for others, intervenes in a vigorous manner.

Under these circumstances, I find it useful to reexamine the actual meaning of the word *progress*. First, let us distinguish between "progress" and "progressive." I might add that, in order to avoid any ambiguity, I prefer either "continual" or "gradual" to "progressive": *Natura non fecit saltum* ("Nature does not make leaps"), as Darwin was fond of saying in his debates with the geologist Sir Charles Lyell. In the seventeenth century, "progress" still had the neutral sense of advance in an action, to which came to be added the idea of advance to better and better conditions, or continuous improvement. The former sense was subsequently displaced, first in the domain of education and scholarship, and then in philosophical writing, under the influence of the nineteenth-century identification of progress with the ameliorative transformation of human societies. In the interval, from Fontenelle to Vico and on through Comte, the progress of human societies was conceived as a succession of *ages*—theocratic, heroic, and civilized for Vico—or *states*—theological (or fictive), metaphysical and positive (or scientific and industrial) for Comte—that corresponded to the deployment of an existing potential, analogous to the mental development of a child.

I agree with Gould in excluding the word *progress* from all discussions of biological evolution, reserving a possible usage of the word for human societies and their productions. Even in this case it is contested by Lévi-Strauss, who prefers a schema that seems to me to be typically evolutionist. In his model, much as in Darwin's, the respective patterns of different cultures merge through a cumulative process of coalition that "sometimes very nearly succeeds, sometimes endangers earlier gains,"[41] and results in either the "collapse of the pattern of one of the groups, or a new combination that consists in the emergence of a third pattern, irreducible to either of the two preceding ones."[42] Lévi-Strauss supplements this model with a critique of the notion of progress that, consciously or otherwise, uses Western societies as a point of reference. He contrasts these with other civilizations that either were several centuries in advance of the Europeans or possessed social organizations better adapted than ours to extreme conditions. He invokes "bounds" that are described as analogous to the "mutations" of biologists, comparing the development of humanity not to "a person climbing stairs" but "to a gambler who has staked his money on several [throws of the] dice and, at each throw, sees them scatter over the cloth, giving a different score each time."[43] Your notion of creative progressivity is readily interpreted within the framework of Lévi-Strauss's model, without the thresholds and leaps associated with such progressivity having any decisive philosophical implications, unless they were to be linked up, as I say, with the punctuated equilibrium model of Gould and Eldredge.

Ricoeur: I must insist on pointing out that you and I do not share the same universe of discourse when we speak of discontinuity: your discourse is that of causality. This is not a reproach—it is a fact. The Hegelian perspective that I mentioned a moment ago, in a provisional way, without any pretension to exclusivity, is very different; it is that of a *Bildung,* of an "education" in the strong sense of the word. Indeed, I would regard all evolutionary models, even ones that incorporate these ideas of threshold, discontinuity, and so on, as being in principle and by hypothesis of the same type. The notion of evaluation, on the other hand, introduces the idea of something being better than something else—the idea, therefore, of being worth more. Moving from this idea, the process of validation proceeds retrospectively, which is to say that each new stage reached makes it possible to understand the previous stage as having been passed. Here we have a phenomenon of a different kind than the biological phenomenon.

Changeux: The word *biological* does indeed give the impression that it is limited to biological evolution. But the analysis I am proposing includes both the neurocognitive and the neurocultural, which in my view are insufficiently appreciated in contemporary research in the human sciences. In fact they lie in an area that molecular biologists do not yet recognize as part of their discipline. Therefore there is more to biology than strict biological evolution: in man, it is extended by cultural evolution and history. This doesn't justify recourse to the notion of a "mind" or "spirit" that somehow "attracts" history. To the contrary, it is a matter quite simply of human beings trying to make better use of their brains in order to live better. Trying to devise plans for living that fit with and for others, realizing that they are tentative and revisable, seems to me less dangerous and more productive than to set off in search of a utopian horizon of meaning. Motivation, patience, and good will[44] are worth more than any ideal justification, which in my view is the source of all fundamentalisms. I have much more interest in constructive research than in a priori justifications.

Ricoeur: I would say there is an ambiguity in the use of the word *biological*. On the one hand, one may use it to refer to a science, leaving its boundaries open. One may then legitimately ask whether all experience can be fitted into this field. By contrast, in a phenomenology of moral experience, the biological is one level among others, what I would call the foundation level—not a foundation in the sense of a source of legitimacy, but in the sense of the bottom level of a building. There has to be a basement in order to be able to build higher, but having an understanding of the basement doesn't give me an understanding of the building. There is, on the one hand, the sense of the biological as inclusive—this is the biological world of the scientists—and, on the other, the biological as a level of moral experience. In the latter sense it is thus a partial level, a basement level that assumes a teleology that always proceeds backward in time. On this interpretation, the sudden appearance of a new level of meaning retrospectively acquires the dual meaning of a going beyond the previous level and a recapturing of it.

Changeux: This ambiguity seems to me profound. As far as I am concerned, the use of the word *biological* is restricted first to the body, to the evolution of species, to the organization of our brain. It is in this sense that it is understood by the general public and philosophers alike. I don't think that each level of neurocultural—I would even say cultural—evolution can be simply reduced to the level beneath it. This is one of the characteristic predictions, from a strictly materialistic perspective, of systems theory. Qualitatively new properties appear at each level of organization, from the simple fact that the constituent elements interact with each other—and this yields a threshold effect. For my part, considering the entire range of human activity—scientific, ethical, aesthetic—I see no need whatever to adopt anything other than the general perspective of the evolution of species and the history of cultures.

Ricoeur: It remains for us to match up our two readings—mine owing more to the Hegelian notion of *Aufhebung* (which means both "canceling" and "preserving") than to your notion of interlocking or embeddedness.

Changeux: The interlocking patterns, or successive relays, of evolution lead us from biological history to human history—keeping in mind that human history corresponds to a much higher level of organization than that which governs evolution from protozoa to vertebrates; and also that it occurs in a quite different biological context since it involves the human brain as well as to the representations that it produces and transmits. Little by little, then, we are led to pose the question of the biological and cultural heritage of moral norms, and therefore of the natural foundations of ethics.

7 — Ethical Universality and Cultural Conflict

The Natural Foundations of an Ethics of Debate

Paul Ricoeur: With the problem of the natural foundations of ethics we enter into a new phase of our discussion. Let me say at once where I stand. I see an ambiguity in the expression *natural foundations,* since the word "foundation," as I pointed out earlier, has two senses: on the one hand, that of a lower level or basement, and therefore of something prior; and on the other, that of legitimation or justification. In a pluralist democratic society such as ours, several sources of legitimacy are in competition. The word *source,* as I indicated previously, I understand in the sense in which it is taken by Charles Taylor in *Sources of the Self,* which is to say as something more radical and more profound than formal rules of debate—say, the public rules of procedure that govern a legally constituted state. It involves conceptions of the good, or, if you like, visions of the world, that constitute the basis of our convictions—hence the importance I attach to conviction, as distinct from convention. It is at this deep level that a delicate relationship between consensus and disagreement is to be found. Given the irremediable pluralism of developed societies, the problem of creating a shared public life is how one gets to the stage where rival traditions must mutually consider themselves to be co-founders if they wish to survive the forces of destruction, both external and internal, that they face.

Changeux: This is exactly why I do not at all share your concern for justification: the very term, including as it does the word *just,* gives the impression that there is a way of making things right once and for all. It opens the door to fundamentalisms and all manner of allegedly divine justice.

Ricoeur: I don't think so. It seems to me that the cultural history of humanity has now reached a point where several systems of ultimate legitimation coexist. The use of the term *justification* signifies that facts are not decisive by themselves—it's a question of deciding "what is better than," of being able to rank value judgments. You yourself have admitted, following Epicurus, that ethics involves creating a hierarchy of desires, from pleasure and pain through the useful and the agreeable until finally one reaches the highest level, at which the uniqueness of human persons is recognized. But then what is it that legitimizes our idea that persons are unsubstitutable, irreplaceable? It is at this level that systems of justification reach down into divergent sources of conviction.

Changeux: I'm pleased that you speak of "systems of justification" in the plural. To begin with, as Gould (and Darwin before him) have shown, the existence of man on earth needs no justification. You have mentioned this point yourself. The conception of man as a cosmic accident has nothing to do with any sort of culmination, either with respect to human nature or to human productions. I insist once more on the fact that epigenesis and learning contribute as much to individual diversity as to the unity of all people. On this point the philosopher ought to feel reassured, it seems to me, that there is no need to appeal to any supplementary justification. As for the phrase "natural foundation," for me it signifies quite simply a unique and sufficient reality that exists by itself and that is understood through itself alone, one that makes no reference to anything occult, supernatural, or magical, only to a material nature.

Finally, I continue to maintain the distinction between convention and conviction. A conviction is weighed, amended; it evolves, particularly in the course of reasoned, open, and informed debate. A religious social convention, for example, such as what one finds written in liturgical texts, is a cultural signature guaranteeing the identity of a community. It may, of course, give rise to casuistry; but more often conventions pose an obstacle to the universalization of ethical debate through what I would call communocentrism. The decentering of debate—I apply Piaget's term to intercommunity relations—seems to me critical, leaving each school of thought, each cultural community wholly free to express itself, on the condition (as I mentioned earlier, citing Rawls) that each expresses itself in terms that all participants have accepted. In this context, I prefer the term *opinion* to *conviction,* which preserves something of its primary sense of proof of culpability, of certitude, indeed of denunciation. I argue for a benevolent and informed mutual understanding in which all opinions may be expressed while remaining free to evolve.

Ricoeur: I give no other sense to "conviction" than that of an acquiescence by the mind in what it holds to be true, good, and just. I also like the term *approbation,* which I find in Jules Lagneau and Alain.

Religion and Violence

Changeux: The problem of devising a natural and universal ethics is extremely difficult in a world in which cultural conflicts reign. These conflicts, political for the most part, are rooted in cultural differences and, in particular, differences of religious opinion. I myself used to be a religious person. On entering the world of scientific research, my daily conversations with Jacques Monod, together with my own personal reflection, forced me to question the gap, commonly found among scientists, between personal beliefs and theoretical practices. A humanist asceticism seemed to me urgent, and more sincere. This moved me away permanently from religion.

Certain positions taken by the Catholic church today are a source of concern to a citizen-scientist who sees himself, as I do, as both tolerant and responsible. One can only be indignant at the curious alliance, even if it may only be temporary, between Rome and Islamic fundamentalists who, by their refusal to encourage chemical contraceptive methods at the Cairo Congress of 1994, fail to confront the global problem of overpopulation and the disasters associated with it. One is astonished to find, in the official statements of the Vatican, not only that no mention is made of condoms but that their use is seen as a transgression of Christian morality—when they are an essential instrument in the struggle against the spread of the AIDS virus. On the other hand, the ban on medical assistance in conception for couples who wish to have children allies obscurantism with inhumanity. Awareness of the latest advances in biological and medical knowledge is a moral duty of the first necessity: science exists to help men and women survive illness and to live better lives. But the positions adopted by the Vatican in the name of moral truth are sometimes contrary to what one would suppose morality to be. Scientific knowledge and religious identity find themselves at odds here, just as certain universal ethical imperatives come into conflict with religious particularisms or to social conventions that vary from one culture to another. Disagreement between scientific knowledge and statements made in the name of morality by certain of the great religions of the world will not soon vanish. And this poses a fundamental challenge to philosophy. Not only must the scientist alert the public to advances in knowledge, keep it informed about what may ease its suffering, help it conquer disease; the secular philosopher, who is concerned with how individuals think, act, and react to ideas and events, has a role in shaping opinion that is every bit as important. In my view, the philosopher must not only accept that certain religions, certain modes of religious thought, stand opposed to principles of universal morality—he ought also say so publicly.

It is dismaying, to take another example, that the Catholic Church refuses to exclude the death penalty from its catechism. Each fresh declaration of repentance, no matter how welcome, whether in connection with the Crusades, the Saint Bartholomew's Day massacre, or the Holocaust, only confirms its complicity in indefensible crimes against humanity or provides evidence of compromises that are universally condemned (figure 7.1). Such violence continues today. Among a thousand instances, it suffices to mention the massacres at Hebron, at the tomb of the patriarchs; or the cruelty of the conflict between Catholics and Protestants in Northern Ireland. Their like is a daily occurrence throughout the world.

Ricoeur: There are several things in what you have just said. Concerning the stance of the Vatican on the issue of sexual morality, contraception, and the condom, I am in complete disagreement with it. A religious—in this case Christian—conception does not deductively imply an unequivocal response so much to problems affecting public health as to the question of how to lead one's private life, personal and familial, in a responsible manner. As I wrote on the occasion of the encyclical *Splendor veritatis,* apart from general principles of ethics relating to respect for persons, compassion, and love, there is a place for individual decision-making in situations of

Le malsacre fait a Tours par la populace au mois de Iuillet. 1562.
A

FIGURE 7.1. Wars of Religion.

A. *Massacres of Protestants at Tours by Catholics,* by Jean Perrissin and Jacques Tortorel, wood engraving. (Print Collection, Bibliothèque Nationale, Paris.)

The engraved print—a plausible (and, in some cases at least, true)

uncertainty, for practical wisdom brought to bear on controversies that public debate must frame with minimal rules of consensus. In other words, what I criticize in such encyclicals is the denial of a place for commonsense judgment, of the responsibility of each person to look into his or her heart and decide. That said, our discussion must now turn to the question of what place the school of thought you represent—for which science, as a theoretical practice, suffices to found a natural and universal ethics—should occupy in a pluralistic society such as ours. The first thing I need to hear from you, given your plea on behalf of the secular orientation you share with Jacques Monod, is some further defense of your view of religions as sources of violence. Naturally I think it is necessary to take into account the political exploitation of denomina-

---

portrait of events as well as a polemical image serving partisan interests—contributed a visual dimension to the *littérature de combat* of the wars of religion in France (1562–1598). Perrissin, an artist from Lyons, was charged in 1569 along with his assistants with engraving forty scenes "concerning the wars, massacres, and troubles [that have] befallen France these last years." These plates, including this scene of the massacre of the Huguenots by wild Catholic crowds, aimed at accumulating precise details regarding the identity of the victims and the circumstances of their death in order to demonstrate the cruel treatment suffered by the faithful.

B. *Massacres of Catholics at Nîmes by Protestants,* by Richard Verstegan, engraving. (Print Collection, Bibliothèque Nationale, Paris.)

Richard Verstegan was a scholar and artist trained at Oxford who took refuge in Paris in 1582 for his part in the publication of Catholic works. *Le Théâtre des Cruautés des hérétiques de notre temps,* first published in Antwerp, depicts the physical abuse perpetrated by the Huguenots: (A) a Huguenot captain wearing a necklace made of the ears of priests; (B) a priest whose ears and nose have been cut off; (C) a priest whose belly has been cut open and his entrails mixed with oats to feed the horses of the Huguenots; and (D) Catholics who were thrown down the wells of the bishop of Nîmes.

tional differences before tackling the real problem, as I am quite willing to do, of the relation between conviction and violence that is characteristic of religion. But first let us note the confusion in many parts of the world between religion, as a cultural phenomenon, and nationalism.

Changeux: At Hebron it was not a case of nationalism. An Israeli soldier took out his machine gun—in a holy precinct.

Ricoeur: The great majority of Israelis are (as they themselves say) "secular" Jews, who too often use their religious heritage for purposes of ideological justification.

Changeux: The visitor to Israel is struck by how much a part of daily life the distinction between Jews and non-Jews (particularly Muslims) actually is. The visitor to Islamic countries sees the application of the *shari'a,* or Islamic law, and everything this implies in the way of inhumanity and all that is against nature: the thief's hand cut off, the adulterous woman stoned to death, criminals hanged in public from a crane. Now that the superpower confrontation between capitalism and communism has come to an end, the majority of conflicts in the world have been religious in origin with religion being invoked, if only indirectly, as an essential element of cultural identity. One has only to think of the massacres that recently left Algeria covered in blood!

Can we hope one day—I pose the question optimistically—to devise an ethics of universal appeal in a world dominated by cultural, and particularly religious, conflicts? Is it possible—my hope is that it will be—to construct a secular ethics that goes beyond cultural differences and is democratically accepted?

Ricoeur: Can the problem of the significance of religions really be resolved on the basis of a true observation of religious sociology, namely that religions create violence? To my mind, there is a deeper question: is it possible to recognize in the religious impulse a foundational concern with bringing about peace and, at the same time, to explain how such a purpose came to be deflected—not only for political reasons but also for reasons internal to the religious impulse itself? I hope to have the chance to come back to this question a bit later. But I feel confident in saying that it does not come under the head of religious sociology. You, on the other hand, ally yourself with the scientific point of view—I mean, for you, the sociologist's observation settles the question: religion produces war.

Changeux: No, I do not say that religion necessarily leads to war. Freud emphasized that "religious intolerance, which was foreign to antiquity . . . , was inevitably born with the belief in one God."[1] Certainly monotheisms are sources of intolerance; in certain cases, as in India, polytheisms can give rise to intolerance as well. What I mean here is that religion ought to possess, as the word itself indicates, the essential social function of bringing people together, gathering them in a group, creating trust, providing comfort in the face of a hostile world and of death, as must have been the case with the earliest human communities when the species first began. For Durkheim, religion is a "system of forces" that involves processes of creative association by which individuals and groups construct representations, ideas, and norms, which together form a collective consciousness. This amounts to a kind of shared memory, where the common long-term memory reemerges in daily life in individual working memories. Religion results from the "fusion of consciousnesses, their communion in a single thought, their cooperation in a single task; from the morally invigorating and stimulating influence that every human community exerts upon its members."[2] Religious life, in one of its two main purposes, is oriented toward thought:

it gave primitive man "explanations" of his origins, as well as of disease and death, and helped him in his struggle against a hostile nature. Durkheim rightly notes that scientific thought gradually came to be substituted for religion in all matters involving intellectual cognitive functions: "[I]n a general way, it brings a spirit of criticism into all its doings, which religion ignores."[3] In its other aspect, religious life is oriented toward action: it is made up of symbolic structures, rituals, that play a crucial role in strengthening social bonds. The cloaking in myth of moral dispositions specific to humanity helps man to live a better life, by denying the contingency of his existence and allowing him to accept the reality of death.

The American anthropologist Ray Rappaport extended Durkheim's approach by proposing a cybernetic interpretation of religion.[4] On this view religion is a system of regulation ensuring homeostasis—the maintenance of the system despite external disturbances—at minimal cost. Rituals and beliefs are elements of communication systems that reduce ambiguity; as "context markers" or "cultural badges" they possess meaning only within the communication system in which they are transmitted. More often than not, their appeal to the supernatural—trans-substantiation, resurrection, reincarnation, to mention only a few of many sacred mysteries—is contradicted by the most obvious facts of observation. The efficacy of such beliefs depends precisely on the fact that they are *not verifiable,* which is to say that they can neither be proved nor disproved. This invulnerability to empirical test is the very source of their power. As articles of faith inculcated from the youngest age in the depths of the developing cerebral network, their emotional impact is considerable, analogous to the mother-child or grandparent-child relationship with which they are mingled.

The essential role of trust in communication, just like the symbolic power of religious conventions, was no doubt useful in order to impose on the whole community respect for fundamental ethical obligations. Consequently they have been perpetuated until the present day, linking moral and religious life for thousands of years. For Rappaport, the emotions associated with rituals were already abundantly present in other animal species—one thinks of the mating displays of birds of paradise or of the various forms of territorial defense. Unlike the social life of insects, social organization in man is to a large extent genetically *underdetermined.* Intelligence is more innate than sociality, and acts as a solvent—beware of philosophers and scientists!—that leads to individual and selfish behaviors. Religious life, with its encouragement of holiness, is a sort of epigenetic intermediary aimed at containing individual self-interest through the establishment of arbitrary social conventions that give rules of moral conduct their force. As a result, Rappaport holds, it is a less costly alternative to the police power of the group or state in ensuring that good prevails over evil and reducing the suffering inflicted on others.

But today, despite the words of peace that they utter, without tangible result, religions divide humanity more than they unite it—thus the price of cultural evolution and history.

Ricoeur: I entirely accept your description of the matter at the level of sociology of religion, and for the most part at the level of cultural anthropology with respect to Rappaport's interpretation. I would like to return for a moment to the role assigned in your account to trust. This goes far beyond the idea of the symbolic power of religious conventions, although the fundamental religious phenomenon comes to be culturally registered at this level. It seems to me that the underlying phenomenon is the trust one has in the word of others. Other people are understood, first of all, as the transmitters of religious messages; behind them stand the founders of religions, who are men of their word—of their acts, really, but these acts are meaningful. Finally, still further back, or higher up, there is recourse to a word that these founders declare to have been received, a fundamental word of last resort. The idea of being preceded in one's capacity for speech by the word of another is for me the point of origin, the point of departure, and, in the last resort, the ultimate source of religious authority.

Changeux: Permit me a brief comment about this "fundamental word." What value does it really have, I wonder, apart from a certain aesthetic? In the case of the Bible, Pierre Gibert has persuasively shown that narratives of origin—such as the one found in Genesis, or the Annunciations to Zachariah and to Mary—contain a number of constant themes: "the exclusive encounter between a human hero and a supernatural hero, the absence of any witness, a task and a mission that is beyond the human hero, the whole guaranteed by a sign."[5] The origin of Christianity, in particular, was accompanied by a proliferation of doctrines and a "nebula" of more or less perceptible and legitimate facts. Gradually a "unique and exclusive truth" comes to be established over time through a simplification of events that retroactively determines the beginning. In this connection Gibert mentions Nouailhat's thesis that a simple and unique beginning was only imagined and defined at the time of the great councils of the fifth century A.D.[6] All of this looks very much like a case of cultural evolution through variation-selection of myths and legends!

On the other hand, the transmission of cultural messages poses the problem, charged with consequence, of forgetting and the reliability of memory. To give meaning by reconstructing memories is also to alter them, to falsify them—all quite innocently, of course. In normal subjects, as I mentioned earlier, the implantation of false memories occurs frequently. Every judge knows that a witness's testimony does not constitute proof. The transmission of the word is not always faithful.

This may also be the case with many foundational myths, held to be true but in fact fabricated by the brains of our ancestors, and then propagated from generation to generation, often in extremely precise detail, spreading by means of a sort of social contagion. In this way confusion arises between mythic discourse, which imposes a fundamental word or truth, ethical discourse, and scientific discourse.

Ricoeur: I argue for the difference and specificity of types and levels of discourse. Beyond this, I agree that it is indeed on the basis of this claim to transmit a fundamental word or truth that one must pose the question—a terrible question for religious persons—of how we are to explain the fact that religion is a source of war. Where is the turning point, the point at which the religious impulse is perverted?

I do not believe it is uniquely located outside religion. Let me suggest one possible interpretation: every religion claims to give a human answer to a questioning that comes from above, from a level higher than the human—what I call, for lack of a better name, the *fundamental.* Confronted with an overflow from above, as it were, it tries to accommodate this excess by closing up the sides—laterally, horizontally. This amounts to trying to contain—in both senses of the word—what exceeds all containing. The lateral closing offsets the vertical opening. The Christian *ecclesia,* like other denominational institutions, pursued a strategy of horizontal closure. I associate this phenomenon with the condition of finitude, by which the able man, for whom religion is intended, imposes his limited capacity on the unlimited one that visits him. I am therefore quite prepared to admit what one contemporary author, René Girard, seeking a way out of this impasse in a certain version of Christianity, calls "the violence of the religious."[7] Here I think one may speak of a religious paradox—in the sense in which I have spoken elsewhere of a political paradox—that links force with meaning and violence with reason. These two paradoxes may enjoy a certain affinity, to the extent that each in its own way aims at both loftiness and inclusion. This central enigma of religion means that it can nowhere be universal. To clarify what such a paradox involves, I would compare it with what happens in language.

Changeux: Ah, why?

Ricoeur: My problem is this. To belong to a religious tradition is to belong to a language, and to accept both that this language is my language and that, to begin with at least, I have no other access to language than through this particular tongue. If I don't know other languages, my language is the limit of my world; but my religion is also the limit of my experience of the religious sphere. It is thus a sign, I would say, of great religious culture and of great religious modesty to understand that my access to religion, fundamental though it may be, is a partial access, and that others have access to this knowledge by other routes. Let me propose to you a comparison I am fond of making. I am standing on the surface of a fragmented sphere at a point that lies between different religious areas: if I try to run along this surface—if I try to be eclectic—I will never reach a universal religion through syncretism; but if I go deeply enough into my own tradition, I will go beyond the limits of my language. In moving toward what I call the fundamental—what others reach by other routes—I shorten the distance between myself and others along the dimension of depth. On the surface, the distance separating us is immense; but if I dig down, I draw nearer to the other, who travels the same path.

Changeux: And if you were to travel the same path without religion? I think that this would be much more effective.

Ricoeur: Fine, I've got nothing against it. I'm trying to explain to you what a religious man may say and do in response to your arguments. But I am not an apologist—I'm trying to express my difficulties, my questions, in religious terms. I am not a Catholic, and I have my own difficulties with certain traditional teachings, not only those of the Protestant Reformation but those of the Christian Church in general. In particular, I feel very close to Hans Jonas's view of the concept of God after Auschwitz.[8] Like him, but also along with a still minority current of theologians belonging to various Christian denominations, I think that if there is a category to be abandoned it is that of the Almighty, to the extent that it is not a purely religious category but, I would say, a theological-political category. On the one hand, the idea of the source of the word has been modeled on that of absolute political power; in turn, the image of divinity has been used to justify political power. Religion thus serves as a way of frightening people. At the bottom of this threat is the idea of hell. It is necessary to renounce altogether both this idea and that of the Almighty, even if it means having to seek another idea of power—that of the word—and to link it to the all-weakness of a love that surrenders to death.

I therefore ask you to leave the critique of religion to me, in the name of a religious fundamental to which I have access only through a language of religion.

Changeux: Excuse me—I cannot remain deaf, dumb, and blind before a dramatic reality whose consequences for modern society are devastating. There is nothing impenetrable about the language of religion, even if it touches upon an emotional sphere that is very deeply anchored in the personality of the believer. I have known this sphere—I freed myself from it, and I'm happy I did. You ask me to abandon the critical examination of religion. Why should I? Rigorous analysis in this domain may be very useful, if only through the study of how discourses of justification are put into practice. Owen Flanagan[9] reports one example, a rather curious experiment conducted at the Princeton Theological Seminary.[10] Students were selected at random to give a talk, either on the parable of the Good Samaritan or on the type of job a graduate of the Seminary could apply for. Once the students had finished preparing, they were asked to go to another building, where they were to give their talk. Half the students in each group were informed that they were late and were asked to hurry along. Along the way they came upon a fellow student, slumped over, apparently in great pain (unbeknownst to them, he was acting in cooperation with the experimenters). Did many of these theology students stop to help, like the Samaritan? The answer is no. Of those who did stop, was their concern related to the theme of the talk they had just prepared? Again, the answer is no. The only significant variable was the chance of being late to give their talk. In other words, the pious sentiments associated with compassion and charity had no effect on the behavior of the seminarians. Only the need to be on time modified their behavior. Religious devotion had no impact on their willingness to help. All this deserves to be critically examined—an examination that must not be reserved for the religious alone, but that must be open to all.

Paths of Tolerance

Ricoeur: This brings us to the question of universality. It seems to me that here we must distinguish two levels: one that is strictly ethical, the Kantian level with its contemporary ramifications; and the other religious, that of the claim of religions to decide what is fundamental for the whole world.

What are the implications of the Kantian level with regard

to the public sphere? At most we can expect a universal set of rules, such as those proposed by Habermas, that together constitute a *Diskursethik* or ethics of debate. But that doesn't settle the problem of what topics are to be discussed—there has to be something to debate. Here we find ourselves faced once more with the question of convictions, which does not reduce to a matter of conventions. I do not at all believe that humanity will near agreement about its innermost convictions anytime soon. Here, more than elsewhere, one must make do with plurality. The problem therefore remains how to achieve peace, if not actually mutual assistance, among differing convictions.

And so I come to the other problem of universality—the universality claimed by particular religions—which involves precisely this question of religious peace, to use the term recently employed to characterize attempts to find a way out from the wars of religion at the end of the Renaissance, in the late sixteenth and early seventeenth century.[11] I see this generalized peace among religions as potentially a mutual recognition of the best aspects of Christianity and Judaism, the best aspects of Islam, the best aspects of Buddhism, and so on, along the lines that I suggested a moment ago, in connection with the aphorism that truth resides in depth. My hope is that each religion might renounce any claim to possess the truth and express instead its wish to be a part of the truth—in this way recognizing that outside of itself exists another part of the truth and accepting the following very difficult dialectic: namely, that what is fundamental passes through other languages as well, only I do not know those routes—they are the routes of others. Only in this way can a joint acknowledgment of the different languages of religion lead to the recognition of a fundamental beyond these various languages. The impact of religion on morality thus appears to me to be situated at the level of what I call that of the *sources* of the self and the norm. It is at this level that an answer is proposed—and not imposed—with respect to questions such as what makes us believe that persons are unsubstitutable, why human genes mustn't be manipulated, and the like.

Each of us contributes to the strengthening of this conviction in the unique character of each person, of each person's unsubstitutable character. We can do this through religion, we can do it through reason, and we can do it through art.

Changeux: For my part, I would limit this process to reason and art while adding to these objective knowledge, whose goal is to move forward in the direction of greater truth and wisdom. Why should one pass through religion rather than through the knowledge that we possess of ourselves, as Spinoza suggested, as the Stoics suggested—the knowledge of ourselves that permits us to go not only where religion may lead some, but beyond, and that permits us even to explain religion itself.

Ricoeur: I would not want the pragmatic dimension of knowledge to be forgotten: knowledge intersects the ethical plane in the form of an ability to know. Now, the ability to know is a power. Science is an extension of this power, but it does not exhaust all of the ways of speaking about our relations with the world, among which must be included religion.

Changeux: It is an interesting experience, conversing in different languages, as we have been doing, trying to discover what they have in common—considering religion as a natural phenomenon, as it were, while at the same time recognizing its singularity and its function in the earliest stages of human society.

Ricoeur: It is not by chance that I adopt the metaphor of language, which depends on the parallelism that I propose between the plurality of languages and the plurality of religions. These two pluralities often overlap, in fact, at the cultural level.

Such a parallelism is useful in analyzing what I have called peace among religions. Indeed one finds, at the level of language, a strange paradox connected with the phenomenon of translation, which is our sole means of transferring meaning from one language to another. All translation presupposes a native language distinct from foreign languages. To a certain degree, translation can correct this asymmetry. A paradox remains, however, which is the following: how do we know that two sentences, one spoken in English and the other in French, say the same thing? What does sameness mean in this case? And how can we assure ourselves of it, if not by means of translation itself?

Changeux: An individual brain can establish the correspondence. We hope one day to be able to distinguish in the brain the perceived signifier from the signified that is understood. Objective knowledge, in helping us answer the great questions of humanity, may now be well on the way to finding this common language and thus to granting access to ethics without the aid of religion. There are fewer and fewer believers in modern industrial societies. Now that ethical demands become more pressing by the day, why leave nonbelievers without help?

Ricoeur: I have no absolute point of view that could resolve this question—I am not myself directly in contact with the fundamental. If I did enjoy such a relationship, then everything would be clear. But I remain caught up in fragmentation, in the multiplicity of discourses, in the multiplicity of religions.

Changeux: I think that an authentic secular ecumenicism cannot be limited to the religious but must include all the very many persons who have no religion. An important unifying factor—one that moreover in my view is one of the foundations of tolerance, by comparison with the religious approach—consists in trying to understand why religions have existed, why they have developed as they have, to what questions they have provided answers in the past, and continue now for a certain fraction of the population to provide answers.

The ethical naturalist knows that the internalization of religious beliefs involves epigenetic traces that may vary in incidental ways from one person to another. Because he is aware of the stability of these traces and their strong emotional component, he will not have the intention of convincing believers to *abandon* their faith, but rather of asking them to *understand* the difficulties to which such stability leads. As a result he will be led to develop a great deal of patience, good will, and tolerance. He will also note that religions "have preserved, alongside or within the treasury of their sacred texts, a thousand proverbs, fables, stories, and parables, collected with respect and affection in the daily life of peoples,"[12] and that they bring together personal experiences that form a particularly precious heritage for human memory.

In view of the conflicts that cultural differences are apt to generate today, we ought to try to reflect upon the foundations of an ethics that addresses itself to all of humanity, and not only believers, with the aim of determining the actual location of what you call the fundamental.

Ricoeur: Of course, but it should perhaps not be hoped that conflicts will cease altogether. I do not go so far as to praise difference for the sake of difference, as do some who call themselves postmodernists. I would say rather that humanity will always be more or less both consensual and conflictual—that is necessary to live with that. Having said this, I would like to come back to the connection between the religious and the moral. I have insisted on the difference of their aims. But something happens at the point where they intersect. A moment ago I described love as the weakest form of power. For a contest is played out between love and justice. Love demands of justice that it be ever more just. I therefore do not see in love a substitute for justice—to the contrary. Love says, first, to those who claim to represent justice: you claim to embody the universal, but in fact you are limited by your culture; your claim to be universal falls short of genuine universality—be more universal than you are. Love says again to the upholders of justice: respect not only universality, but also singularity! You do not respect singularity; you respect types, categories. Love says again: you say that you are motivated by the common good—then push the critique of interest, of the world of money, as far as it will go. I see the essential aspect of religion, then, in this hymn to love and in the pressure that love exerts on justice.

Changeux: Freud's analysis of the painful consequences for humanity of this hymn to love is pertinent here. "To the Romans," he observed, "who had not founded their communal life as a State upon love, religious intolerance was something foreign, although with them religion was a concern of the State and the State was permeated by religion."[13] The extreme intolerance of the Christian doctrine of universal love opened the way to anti-Semitism. Whether or not one shares Freud's analysis, the historical reality cannot be forgotten.

On the level of personal life, the Judeo-Christian tradition has subjected a sizable fraction of humanity to an unprecedented sexual repression, which contrasts with many other religious traditions. Religions of "love" did not break the chains of slavery, defend the equality of rights, and offer liberty to mankind—the revolutionaries of 1789 did, *against the opposition* of the Church. It was the philosophers of the Enlightenment, from Diderot to Cordorcet and Voltaire to d'Holbach, who brought about this radical change from an illusory ideal of universal love to the much stronger conception of universal brotherhood. I recognize that the philosophy of the Enlightenment is rooted in the Western Christian tradition. But what an advance! The Declaration of the Rights of Man remains one of the greatest monuments in the history of humanity, even if it was necessary to wait years for slavery to be abolished, for women to attain genuine equality of rights, and for the death penalty to be repealed—not yet, by the way, an accomplished fact in the United States.

Ricoeur: Of course, but you ought also take into account the Terror and the intolerance of a violently anti-religious discourse. With regard to the relations among religions and between religion and non-religion, I think that a dialogue between religions and non-religions is only just beginning. This situation commands us to use the word *tolerance*. Tolerance passes through several thresholds: at the first threshold it consists in supporting what cannot be prevented. But one must pass through this forced tolerance before reaching one that is freely chosen and accepted. It is through my relation to the fundamental—from within this relation, as it were—that I understand there are other convictions than mine. As a result, tolerance is not introduced by third parties who impose a constraint upon me from outside, who say to me: stay within your limits, don't go further. It is from the inside that I recognize there are others besides myself, who think otherwise than I do. If this is indeed the case, the problem of tolerance spills over beyond the relationship between science and religion and involves all convictions. It is not science alone that holds the key to the problem of violence between men.

Changeux: It may at least help solve this problem. Perhaps I am too optimistic, but I think that if we have a better knowledge of the sources and causes of violence we may be able to control its outbreak and, above all, its consequences by foreseeing its occurrence.

Ricoeur: Still one has to *want* to control violence. What makes the malicious man want to commit a malicious act? This is part of what I would regard as the problem of evil: men make other men suffer. This is an absolutely fundamental fact. I think about it a great deal because I am very close to the position described by Éric Weil in his famous treatise *Logique de la philosophie.*[14] This opens with a grand introduction entitled "Violence and Discourse," arguing that to enter into dialogue is to exit from violence. Of course—but one still has to wish to enter into dialogue. Everyone is better off when discourse—argumentation and discussion—is chosen rather than violence. What makes us want to enter into dialogue with others rather than to remain in violence? Does science suffice to answer this question?

The Scandal of Evil

Changeux: The critical method of science, with its concern for objectivity, allows an equilibrium of *reasonable* norms to develop that goes beyond Rawls's notion of reflective equilibrium and his emphasis on the rational.[15] I think we ought not let ourselves be trapped in the rather Calvinist conception that man is predestined to make other men suffer, that he is condemned to malice by original sin. You yourself have remarked: "If you suffer, this is because you have sinned." This assumes the inevitability of a divine plan. There is nothing we can say to others about their suffering; and faced with our own suffering, we can say only: "So be it."

Ricoeur: But this is exactly the position to which I object! "You suffer because you have sinned"—that is the position taken by Job's friends. It is because Job challenges them that God says, "Ye have not spoken of me the thing that is right, as my servant Job hath." I totally object to such an explanatory view.

Changeux: It is the view that many religious persons have held for centuries and one that is still held today in connection with the origin of AIDS, considered as a divine punishment.

Ricoeur: You must have noticed that no official of a Christian church has ever held this view.

Changeux: This view has existed.

Ricoeur: It has existed.

Changeux: And in a culture that claims to be Christian.

Ricoeur: I do not endorse this kind of argument from punishment.

Changeux: I do not say you do, but it is a view that derives from Christianity, that has been held and that continues to be held—even if less commonly than in the past—in a good many hospitals and clinics that refuse morphine to drug addicts, women undergoing abortions, and terminal cancer patients.

Ricoeur: I am responsible for my views, not for those to which I object—not for those of Job's friends! For me, evil is the capacity to challenge the value of life.

Changeux: The theologian Eugen Drewerman has described evil as any force destructive of the community, including sadness, anguish, and despair.[16] The existence of evil is a challenge to the instinct of life that is in us; to social bonds and the capacity to understand others, to represent their mental states to ourselves, to grant them our sympathy, our friendship, and perhaps our love. I wonder if we do not judge as bad, or evil, what runs counter to a harmonious life in society, to the common good and the joy of living, to the survival of the individual.

Ricoeur: And especially to the survival of others. The word *survival* is very selfish.

Changeux: It seems to me desirable to avoid setting evil in an existentialist perspective, as a purely human avatar of a divine good. It is more appropriate to give concrete definitions of evil, while acknowledging—as we saw earlier with Primo Levi—that under extreme conditions of the most total destitution the golden rule may not apply. From the perspective of a multi-leveled evolutionary ethics, there cannot be a unique and exclusive definition of the Good. One would even expect there to be contradictory definitions between interlocking hierarchical levels. Evil, for example, is played out at the level of sociality, determining how much of my own survival or of my own quality of life I stand to give up (or gain) to the benefit (or detriment) of others in the social group. Evil is that which opposes survival and society. For this reason it may be supposed that the abolition of all forms of violence destructive of social life, assuming an interest in eliminating violence were one day to become a rather general normative orientation, would work to enlarge sympathies. We have discussed this point in some detail.

As for fear, it is one of the four fundamental emotions in Panskepp's model. It comes under the direct control of a particular structure in the brain called the amygdala. Fear permits us, of course, to avoid danger (figure 7.2). It contributes to sur-

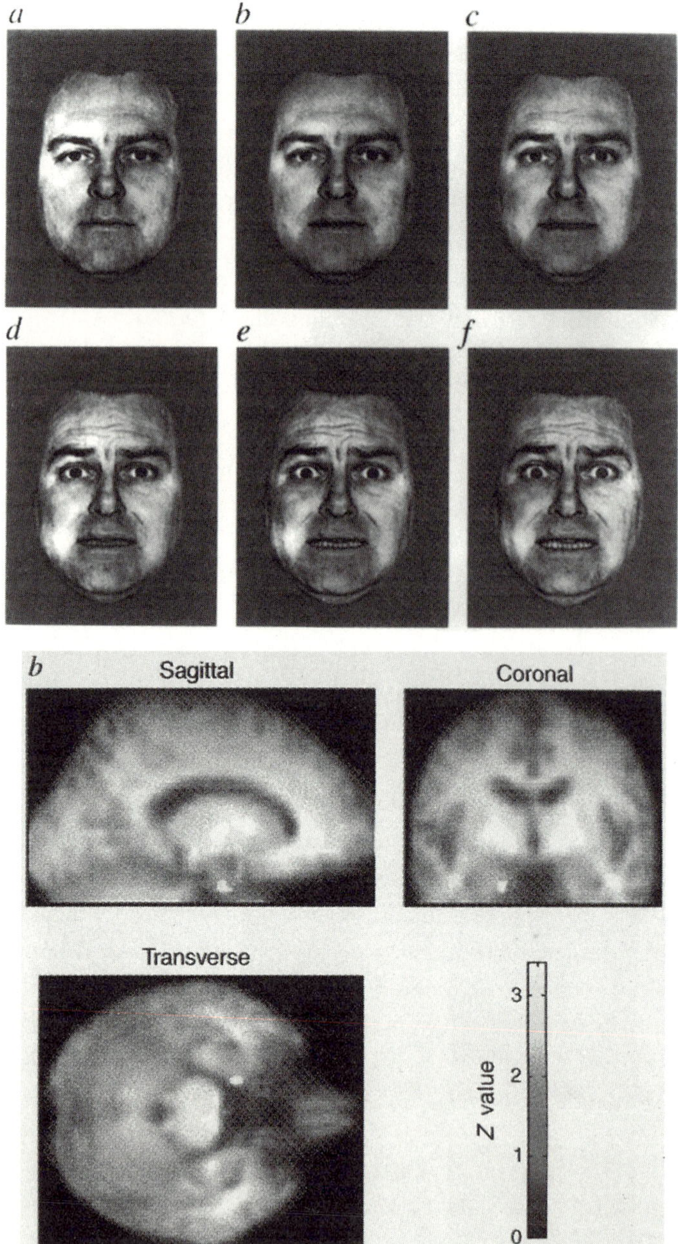

FIGURE 7.2.

vival. But it can also give rise to abandonment of the social group, to a loss of the sense of common cause. As a result, it is associated with the definition of evil.

Ricoeur: One can, I think, approach the problem of evil at three levels of analysis. First, at the level of description, considering the various configurations of evil, I see at least three distinct forms of violence: violence in language—slander, defamation, treason, perjury: in short, destruction of language through the rupture of pacts; violence in action—murder, attack on the physical and mental integrity of others; finally, institutional violence, which is to say destructiveness on the part of institutions whose function goes beyond the survival of individuals. Because the *polis* offers a much vaster temporal horizon than the life of an individual, institutional violence—which we may call "war," in the broad sense of *polemos*—proves to be particularly formidable. The level of description does not go beyond lament. We deplore evil and the many forms it assumes. At this first level, then, we remain within the multiplicity of evil.

Changeux: In the forms of evil.

Ricoeur: To my mind, there is already a certain rupture at this level with what I would call the biology of cruelty. The cru-

---

FIGURE 7.2. Brain imagery of fear.

Six faces that systematically vary the expression of fear (to the point of paroxysm at lower right) are presented to a subject. A very focused neural response develops in the left amygdala, whose intensity increases with the level of fear and decreases with the level of happiness. From J. S. Morris, C. D. Frith, D. I. Perrett, D. Rowland, A. W. Young, A. J. Colder, and R. J. Dolan, "A differential neural response in the human amygdala to fearful and happy facial expressions," *Nature* 383 (1996): 812–815.

elty of animals is part of their plan of life and survival, first by virtue of the food chain, but also by virtue of the predatory aspects of living creatures in their relations with each other. Here there is no morality: it simply is thus. But human beings are not violent in the way that animals are cruel. I believe this is the first point that needs to be made. Purposeful violence is peculiar to humans—at this point we find ourselves at the second level.

Changeux: I object to the term *cruelty* as applied to animals. You criticized de Waal for his sometimes anthropomorphic description of the behavior of the apes. Can foxes be said to be cruel if they contribute by their ferocity to the equilibrium of the rabbit population? Human beings, on the other hand, are conscious of their actions. They are capable of self-evaluation and possess a capacity for attribution that makes it possible for them to imagine the suffering that they can inflict upon others with cruelty.

Ricoeur: You are right: men alone are cruel, not animals. At most, animals are fierce—for the fabulist! One passes to the second level when one asks whether, behind the various forms of evil, there is something that might be called a structure or an origin of evil. With this question, we change registers and take the word *origin* in a very different sense than that of physical or organic causality; let us say instead that it is a question of a sort of negative legitimation, what Kant called the "universal maxim of evil." It is no longer a question, then, of lament but of admission or acceptance, and therefore of a highly reflective level. At the same time, we encounter an enigma—to the extent that each of us, taken individually or as members of a communal or political group, experiences evil as something that is already present. This aspect of heritage, together with that of responsibility, is, I think, at the root of the thought of sages in all cultures and religions, Judaism and Christianity among them—a reflection upon the antecedence of evil, upon the fact that it has forever preceded us. This, I believe, is the point at which one passes from the level of lament to that of admission: I recognize that I always come after evil has begun; that I belong to this line of descent.

But that is not the end of it. This is not the last stage of the meditation. There is still another heritage in addition to that of evil, another tradition—the tradition of goodness. The third level is thus that of a call for help, of trust in a fundamental rescue. The possibility of this recourse is related to the question of whether the radicality of evil is such that it affects what I would call creational radicality. The problem posed by the great myths is how to give a voice to this fundamental act of trust. However radical evil may be, says the myth of Genesis, goodness is still more radical. To put the matter in Kantian terms, if evil is radical, goodness is original (*ursprünglich*)—that is, inherent in man. I have never used the expression "original sin," which is due to a late, rationalizing interpretation, an anti-gnostic gloss. The harm done by this pseudo-concept cannot be emphasized enough. As for the basic conviction of Judeo-Christian thought that an original predisposition toward goodness and justice will prevail, I would say it is this tendency that governs attempts to improve the condition of the human species. It is this concern, to save the fundamental goodness of mankind, that I call religion.

Changeux: No: saving the fundamental goodness of mankind is our common concern as human beings. It has nothing to do with religion. I would even say that this purpose can be realized only by raising the debate from the level of the mosaic of particular moral communities, whether religious or philosophical, with their various contingent and constraining social conventions, to that of the body of moral sentiments peculiar to the human species as a whole. To my mind it is improper to rank sympathy and solidarity among the categories of religion. As a historical matter, it is obvious that religion has exploited these fundamental moral sentiments; but, contrary to the propaganda it puts out, it doesn't have a monopoly on them.

Ricoeur: I see religion as consisting in a fundamental approval that comes from somewhere farther away and higher than I am; in my courage to live and to make goodness prevail over the evil whose radicality I have both lamented and accepted. The fact that evil may always be with us does not make us a condemned species, because we are fundamentally approved and assisted in our courage to live. As the Protestant theologian Paul Tillich puts it, religion is "the courage to be."

Changeux: I find this definition of religion much too exclusive. This "courage to be" seems to me to be a general trait of the human species that allies motivation and reflective consciousness. It may possibly be reinforced by religion, but it is also reinforced by associative activities having nothing to do with religion. This courageous effort to be, this effort to conscientiously persevere, this *conatus*—we find it in the first place in our brain, without any need to appeal to a higher authority.

Ricoeur: But here, religions differ not only because they have a partial view of the fundamental and limited means of transmitting it, but also because they have different conceptual (and pseudo-conceptual) views to convey. The first of these views is the mythic, which tells fabulous stories and draws upon the imaginary to explore the inscrutable. In this respect myths of origin are quite remarkable. They proceed exactly as we do, working backward from the human condition as it is perceived by the culture of the period in the direction of fabulous beginnings. Take the biblical account of creation and the fall. It was read in terms of the prophetic message of the Second Isaiah announcing the return from exile. Since the Jewish God had not been annihilated by defeat, by exile, he was believed to reign over peoples and over the entire universe, such as it was then known. So one sorted through related myths and, working backward, constructed origins compatible with the election of Israel. And this story was told, as today paleobiologists tell theirs, from the beginning to the end, from the institution of the Sabbath in the most recent account of Genesis. We no longer read it as a "true" account, or even as a prescientific account. There was no first man. The function of myth is entirely different—it consists in coordinating the nature of the world with that of ethical commandment.

There is now fundamental agreement among scholars that the biblical story, which moreover is very similar to Egyptian and Mesopotamian accounts of creation, is a work of speculative imagination, a way of wrestling with enigma. How can it be, one wonders, that evil is radical and yet goodness is still more fundamental? The account that we read in Genesis is in reality a learned account. It is not a childlike account, but a product of wisdom—a narrativized wisdom, that tells a story: once there was a man who was good, but then he did something bizarre, abnormal, and he became bad. Goodness and malice are presented successively, whereas in fact they overlap. I would say that the radicality of evil is superimposed on the originality of good. The wisdom of the Egyptians, Hebrews, and Mesopotamians resides in precisely this, the telling of a story, for lack of anything better since they were not equipped to speculate in the manner of Kant, Hegel, or Nietzsche. But something fundamental is preserved by this art of storytelling: the predisposition to goodness is stronger, more profound than the propensity for evil. This is the reading Kant gave of the myth of Genesis in his "Essay on Radical Evil," the first part of *Religion within the Limits of Reason Alone*. Kant also used different words to describe good and evil: in the case of evil he referred to a propensity (*Anhang*), and in the case of good to a predisposition (*Anlage* or *Bestimmung*). If religion has a meaning it is to be found here, in the attestation of support, of help offered to what I would call poetic resources, to our capacity to liberate goodness, to deliver it from captivity. This symbolism is quite Lutheran, by the way—the captivity of Babylon, projected back to the origins of mankind.

Changeux: I am touched by the sincerity and poetic vigor of your remarks. My only fear is that this "narrativized wisdom," which I respect and whose aesthetic power I value, is limited to the community that internalizes its rules and symbolic details. It is not obvious to me what help is offered by a reading of Genesis to a Chinese Confucian or a Thai Buddhist. Now, as I said earlier, the major cause of violence in the world today, along with economic and political conflict, is cultural conflict—clashes of civilizations in which the incomprehension of rival symbolisms is a dominant, although not exclusive, factor. How can this difficulty, which becomes more threatening by the day, be overcome? To the extent that human beings perceive their own suffering, I think that they can also, with the help of the attribution system in their brain, imagine the suffering they produce in others, whether close by or far away. We are in complete agreement on this point.

As for what you call the level of admission, I think that it is necessary to distinguish a dual heritage. On the one hand, there is all that we have inherited from our biological ancestors, including patterns of neural organization that are quite prior to those that characterize the human brain. But with evolution there have developed, as I say, mechanisms of consciousness that may help us to control violent behavior. It is at this level of conscious, and perhaps even unconscious, space that memories of our cultural heritage intervene. Now the memory traces peculiar to a given culture are very largely tied to education, to the setting in which the child has grown up. They provide elements of comparison for self-evaluation, for moral judgment. Might it be said then that nature and culture "naturally" meet in the physical traces of cerebral memory? Our two heritages—biological and cultural—merge and mutually enrich each other in ways that at the level of human societies produce what are called civilizations.

You mentioned the heritage accumulated by human wisdom, which permits us to reflect, to elaborate doctrines, moralities, philosophies, conceptions of life and of individuals as members of a social group. Many forms of ethics are associated, moreover, with traditions that make no reference to a God. Confucianism and Buddhism, to cite two examples in the Eastern tradition, are materialist philosophies whose aim is essentially ethical. Buddhist doctrine is fundamentally agnostic, rejecting from the outset any notion of revealed truth. It is a strong, liberating wisdom composed of individual prohibitions but not of commandments. The principal moral philosophies of the Western tradition, for their part, are the work of secular philosophers. One thinks in this connection of Aristotle, Epicurus, Descartes, Hume, Diderot, and Nietzsche—not omitting Spinoza, who, it should not be forgotten, was excommunicated by the Jewish community of Amsterdam with the imposition of the *herem* (ban) in 1656.

This civilizational heritage is obviously very important. One cannot get rid of it. Besides, why would one want to get rid of it? We live in the cultural heritage of Western Judeo-Christian societies, with the new and added difficulty—but also a source of richness—of multiculturalism.

Ricoeur: I do not in any way object to your idea of a dual—biological and cultural—heritage. But we find ourselves today witnessing the ongoing transmission of the message, not its first sudden emergence. It is precisely at this stage of development that views diverge. In speaking of the "fundamental," I have tried to reserve as far as I could, within the Jewish and Christian traditions, the possibility of a discourse that does not name God—that names no god. The Mosaic avowal of the unutterable name, magnified by Schoenberg in his opera *Moses und Aron,* is a gesture of this sort: "Unrepresentable!" shouts Moses. Isn't naming itself a form of representation? This avowal carries us back to myth. Myths are fantastic combinations of elements that, at the time of their invention, manage to say something more important than other contemporary accounts are able to say; the Judeo-Christian myth of origins represented an alternative to those that were then available—one that dogmatic thinkers later unfortunately erected into a pseudo-scientific, pseudo-historical discourse in which the poetic, metaphorical dimension was lost. In the end one wound up with the trial of a Galileo or a Darwin, blown out of all proportion by fundamentalist upholders of a supposedly creationist doctrine. We need to recover the ludic element of myth, which is to say the element of intellectual curiosity and poetic inventiveness.

Changeux: Even if there isn't an infinite diversity of symbols, myths are eminently variable from one tradition to another, from one social group to another, from one historical moment to another. Their "ludic" element may well be pleasing, particularly when allied with an aesthetic and poetic force; but it cannot be forgotten that myths are very often vehicles for doctrines of exclusion and violent ideologies. Reference to some unnamed "fundamental" seems to me very dangerous. It is only a short step from the fundamental to fundamentalism.

Ricoeur: Once again one must go back to the moment when

myths are formed, a stage prior to that of transmission, when social conventions are dominant.

Changeux: But how can you say that Christian or Judeo-Christian myths are more "true" than the myths of the Incas or those of Buddhism? Being in principle unverifiable, they are all equally valuable! But they have in common an aesthetic, singularly human power that seems to me a potentially stronger force in contemporary societies the more completely they are stripped of dogmatism—the moral view of a majority of the members of a community, whether Catholic, Jewish, or Buddhist, imposed on a dissenting minority.

Ricoeur: First, there is no truth apart from a myth of origins. Its claim to truth is spelled out in the message of deliverance, of which it is the flip side. A new symbolism arises in connection with language, which is where I live and where I learn. Elsewhere perhaps I would have learned something different.

Changeux: We agree, then, that there exists a fundamental historical and cultural contingency in the expression of religion. Its purported message of deliverance, if any, can only be aesthetic. The beauty of a Bach cantata suffices to comfort us as well, without our having to assume the burden of believing in eternal life or the resurrection of bodies: a message of humanity reconciled suffices.

Ricoeur: Religion nowhere exists in a universal form. It is fragmented, because the exploration of the fundamental is too enormous a task. It exceeds our ability to measure; it consists in an excess of tale-telling. Thus Bergson, for example, in the *Two Sources of Morality and Religion,* speaks of this *fonction fabulatrice* as the source of myths. But such excessive invention yet preserves something essential. Radical evil, to use

Kant's language, exhibits a specifically traditional aspect that is poorly expressed in the biological language of a transmission of a heritage, first of all because there is no truth of acquired characters. The history of evil follows from itself in an inscrutable way, Kant argued, because in order for it to be discerned one has to join together, in a pseudo-conceptual discourse, two things that are dissociated in our ordinary everyday experience: the experience of a transmitted heredity and the experience of imputability, of being held accountable for one's acts. The idea of a transmissible moral responsibility is extremely difficult to conceive, which is why I call this the second level, the level of admission: I admit that there is a kind of inexhaustible—perhaps inscrutable and actually impenetrable—conjunction of apparent contraries in the idea of violence as something that is transmitted by birth (and in this sense is blameless) and yet at the same time is something for which each individual, judged separately, is held responsible.

Changeux: It seems to me in any case that the search for objective knowledge and the reasoned and critical debate that accompanies it may help us better to understand violence and its origins, and to arbitrate conflicts more effectively in the interest of peace. I don't see why this purpose should be denied science as a matter of principle. I don't see why we shouldn't try to construct, on the basis of such knowledge as well as past human experience, a view of the world that tends to eliminate conflict and to promote sympathetic relationships among individuals within society. Enterprises of this type have existed in the past, outside of any religious context or reference to some "fundamental." Léon Bourgeois, for example, developed a model of *solidarisme,* or fellow feeling, on the basis of the biological model of contagious disease that, together with Pasteur's results, "proved the profound interdependence that exists among all living creatures, among all beings. . . . In formulating the microbic doctrine, [Pasteur] showed how much each of us depends on the intelligence and morality of everyone else."[17] Thus, he wrote, "It is a duty to destroy these mortal germs, and to assure our own life, and to guarantee the life of everyone else."[18]

Relying on the work of Edmond Perrier on animal colonies, Bourgeois tried to connect science and morality by devising an "artificial order" of nature that would have the force of a biosociological law of unity among living things. On this view, human societies form "united groups" whose "equilibrium, preservation, [and] progress obey the general law of evolution."[19] Furthermore, "The conditions of existence of moral being that the members of a single group form among themselves are those that govern the life of the biological aggregate."[20] A duty of solidarity is thereby created, a duty of mutual responsibility. "Society is a contractual organism. It requires the consent of the beings of whom it is composed."[21] The purpose of this contract of solidarity is to promote justice, by substituting itself in human relations for the idea of competition and struggle: "Agreed, mutual, and united association among men, whose object is to assure to all, as fairly as possible, the advantages resulting from common funds and [a] guarantee, again as fairly as possible, against common risks."[22] Again, "Science and sentiment are associated in social work."[23] The "moral good is to will ourselves and to conceive ourselves as members of humanity," united against risk in order that "inequalities of social origin are not added to natural inequalities."[24]

This notion of fraternal duty—quite forgotten today—takes the form of a positive obligation, involves no higher metaphysics, and is capable of supporting a republican morality. It is in urgent need, I believe, of being revived.

Already with Darwin one finds the hope that the sympathy that manifests itself within a particular social group—within Western societies, for example—might be extended to humanity as a whole. The rights of man were a first manifestation of this sympathy, of a universal fraternity that refuses denominational or ideological hegemony. The celebrated biologist Rita Levi Montalcini and the Group of Trieste, to which I belong, have proposed a charter of human duties that would coordinate the principal obligations of humanity in the face of poverty, racial and sexual discrimination, war, and threats to the natural environment.[25] This sort of project seems to me indispensable.

One of the great handicaps such a project faces is a lack of unifying symbols. I know—you're going to say that I take back with one hand what I throw out with the other! The problem is how to associate an ethical discourse that involves objective facts and "civilizing" practical injunctions, whose consequences can be rationally assessed, with a symbolism that appeals to the imagination and creates a mutually reinforcing relationship between desire—including pleasure—and norms.

A universal secular morality that is open, tolerant, and benevolent nonetheless lacks a concrete common symbolism made up of real-life stories, authentic historical accounts that would make it possible to inculcate children with elementary rules of ethics (figure 7.3). I have in mind something like the "illustrious men" of ancient Greece who served as examples, models for living. Today, secular education is very inadequately covered in the media. If one takes into account the multicultural aspect of our society, in which coexist Catholics, Protestants, Muslims, Jews, Buddhists, and so on, all of whom have internalized different symbolic systems, it is reasonable to suppose that between 30 percent and 40 percent of the population is nonetheless made up of nonbelievers, who are left in the lurch at the moment, without any other symbols than those associated with maximizing profits and individual advantage.

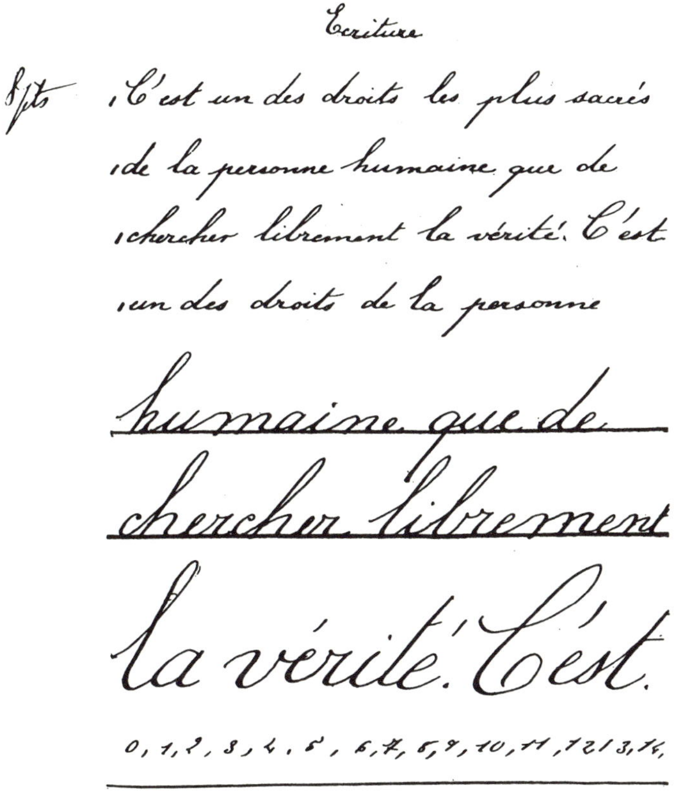

Ecriture

8 pts C'est un des droits les plus sacrés de la personne humaine que de chercher librement la vérité. C'est un des droits de la personne

humaine que de

chercher librement

la vérité. C'est.

0, 1, 2, 3, 4, 5, 6, 7, 8, 9, 10, 11, 12 13, 14,

FIGURE 7.3. Writing exercise of a public school pupil (13 February 1905). From Jean Baubérot, *La Morale laïque contre l'ordre moral* (Paris: Seuil, 1997). The text, repeated in letters of increasing size, reads: "To search freely for the truth is one of the most sacred rights of the human person."

Ricoeur: I entirely subscribe to the plan for arbitrating conflict that you formulate, following Léon Bourgeois and his theory of solidarity, with due allowance for its basis in a biological model. It is a program on which all those who have gauged the true extent of the influence of violence can agree. As a practical matter, the project of achieving peace among religions and Kant's "perpetual peace" are linked together in the contract of solidarity you mention. I observe only that this contract does not solely involve a biological model; instead, as the history of ideas (including the historical reception of Darwinism) confirms, a social model and a biological model are jointly constituted in it, with all the risks of ambiguity this implies. Perhaps we can discuss these later. In any case there is no question whatever, a priori, of refusing science the ability to draw from its own practice an ethics of veracity—a critical ethics—necessary to preserve the precarious balance between criticism and conviction. As for the lack of a unifying symbolism that you deplore in connection with your humanist and secular enterprise, why don't you draw upon the symbolic treasures of the great religions? You can always reinterpret them to suit your own style of belief. In this regard I would distinguish between the secularism of the state, which is the product only of abstention, and that of civil society, which is the product both of confrontation and collaboration. I am just as concerned as you are by what might be called a symbolic deficit affecting nonbelievers, who may actually make up more than 30–40 percent of urban youth.

Changeux: They may indeed. The problem is real. For all these youngsters, it becomes increasingly difficult to assimilate Judeo-Christian or Islamic mythologies, which so often run counter to common sense—and which explains why sometimes they seek refuge in sects of one sort or another. Can't a remedy be found for this lack of a common symbolism in Western societies?

Ricoeur: For my part, I think we must confront the dangerous tendency of the religious person to claim to have access to sources of truth that are denied to others. Not only would I correct this sentiment, I would educate believers to recognize and accept three things. First, the recognition I have already mentioned that religion is fragmented, that it is itself a pluralism. We have barely begun to have a dialogue among religions, which is very difficult because it amounts to upholding a paradox: through my religious culture I have access to symbolic resources and therefore ways of mobilizing my energy, my courage to live; but at the same time the limited character of mythic structures and rituals as well as grand dogmatic interpretations restrict the very access that is given me to these resources. I must therefore confess that religion not only goes beyond its own expressions but that it resides not merely in my world but elsewhere as well. Consequently I must be prepared to say that Buddhism, despite its atheism—and perhaps also Confucianism, although I remain somewhat reluctant to include it—has something that is profoundly religious.

This, then, is my first corrective: the religious sphere exists outside my religion. Secondly, I belong to a culture that has experienced the relationship between conviction and criticism. Judeo-Christian culture has always been confronted with its other, whether this has been Greek, Cartesian, Kantian, or rationalist thought or, today, scientific materialism. This is one of the peculiarities of our culture. Not only, therefore, is there the religion of other religions, but also—this is my second corrective—the non-religion of my contemporaries. Whence my third corrective: the need to conceive politics no longer as a theologico-political phenomenon but as a set of procedural rules for living together in a society where there are religious persons and non-religious persons. This assumes that religious beliefs—those that are left—and non-religious convictions are both considered, in this phase of Western history, as fundamental or co-foundational. You were saying a moment ago that nonbelievers are left stranded. I do not wish to leave others stranded, but neither do I wish to be left stranded myself.

We are no longer living in the Enlightenment, when Voltaire urged the elimination of superstition—*Écrasez l'infâme*—and the devout replied, "Burn the heretics." All that is over and done with on both sides.

Changeux: It is not over and done with. Religious fundamentalism threatens the planet every bit as much as any other fanaticism, whether political or economic.

Ricoeur: But in the West it is finished. We are done with wars of religion. We have passed from war to tolerance, and from tolerance to equal status—what I call co-foundation. Your national advisory committee on bioethics is an example of co-foundation. You accept that several spiritual families or traditions contribute to what may be called the common good[26]—a common good that no one can define from the perspective of his own family; it is a limiting perspective, a line of horizon.

Toward an Ethics of Deliberation: The Example of Advisory Committees on Bioethics

Changeux: Advisory committees on ethical issues are increasingly common in the world today. Even if their mission concerns only ethical problems raised by research in the health and life sciences, they can serve as a useful model in trying to promote the public good. These committees have no legislative power, no administrative authority. In France, the bioethics committee I chaired gives opinions and makes recommendations. The questions referred to it (or which it takes up on its own initiative) cover a wide range of topics, from medical assistance in procreation to the various new problems that have arisen with the development of molecular genetics, including trials of medicines on human beings, grafts, and so on. More generally, this type of committee can instruct us on the way in which ethical questions are managed in the sort of multicultural society that we live in today and that the majority of people in the world, under the influence of globalization, will soon find themselves living in as well. The committee on which I served is made up of persons from different philosophical and religious backgrounds as well as from a great variety of professional fields: scientists, physicians, teachers, lawyers, philosophers. It is a limited group, but a competent and representative one, that gives itself over to reasoned debate. (As chairman, of course, I did not permit myself to influence debate; my role was to observe and to comment without interfering.) Views are exchanged on specific, well-defined topics, for example the precautions needing to be taken during the general application of genetic discoveries. Spontaneously, debate evolves toward a reconciliation of rational judgment with sentiments having the most intimate relation to our sense of humanity. Compassion and respect for the person are at the heart of the committee's deliberations. The same concern for humanity is found in every one of its members, whether he or she is an agnostic, an atheist, or a believer, a scientist or non-scientist. Naturally debate is open, and sometimes quite heated.

Ricoeur: It must be admitted that discord is a fundamental structure of human relations. I am against the desire to escape the conditions of bodily existence, even in its rational form, which is more or less what the praise of consensus-without-disagreement that one finds in the ethics of debate advocated by Habermas amounts to.

Changeux: Experience shows that nothing is achieved where consensus is the aim. In fact there is often a third way. Innovation and creativity make it possible to find solutions that are not merely the least of several evils but that actually represent an advance. This was the experience of our committee, for example, in considering the question of drug addiction. Ethical debate turns out to have an evolutionary dimension! Encouraging innovation allows normative solutions to be imagined that have the power to bring together people whose opinions differ at the outset. In other words, instead of trying to devise a model that accounts for an object, a phenomenon, or a natural process, as the biologist tries to do in examining, for example, the laws of heredity or the state of activity of a nerve cell, ethical committees attempt through collective discussion to work out models that lead to improved living standards while respecting individual liberties and personal dignity.

Ricoeur: I see the philosophical interpretation of scientific research as operating on two levels: the explanatory level, which has to do with modeling and verification/refutation, and, on the other hand, the practical level, to which science belongs as a theoretical practice.

Changeux: Here it's a sort of practice.

Ricoeur: It's a practice that comes to be incorporated with other bodies of human practice under the head of theoretical practice. There are pragmatic practices, as it were, such as those of various technologies; also aesthetic practices, political practices, and so on. Our problem concerns the intersection between theoretical practice and moral and political practices.

Changeux: In this instance it's a question of moral normativity, of an ethics of deliberation in which each person participates. Pluralism is inherent in such an ethics, since diverse arguments must be exchanged—with no argument, whatever its level of generality, being ruled out in advance—in order to arrive at a conclusion that will command general assent. To the extent that different views and arguments are expressed, it is possible, as Habermas emphasizes, to convince others, to encourage the internal configurations of the participants' "cerebral spaces" to evolve in such a way that, in the aftermath of debate, one winds up with genuine *agreement* on a new view of the matter. At bottom, I look at the elaboration of ethical norms as a practical exercise—I see these norms as provisional and permanently subject to reexamination, just as Descartes urged—the result of informed debate that relies on no a priori assumptions.

One of the common features of the evolutionary doctrines that I have defended in our dialogue is the free rein given to variation, to randomness, which is to say to imagination, creativity, innovation—in neuropsychological terms, to the production of "prerepresentations." In democratic societies, the capacity for ethical innovation will manifest itself in the form of debates—deliberations open to the widest possible number. Such deliberations will be assisted, in a non-exclusive manner, by the conceptual resources accumulated in the course of the history of human thought. Thus it is that bioethical philosophies make appeal *simultaneously* to Hippocrates' doctrine of benevolence, the utilitarianism of Bentham and Mill, Kant's respect for the human person, Aristotle's conception of justice, and Bourgeois's notion of brotherhood.

It is not a question, in any case, of wishing to defend some form of philosophical or ethical relativism. The desire to avoid adopting a single dogmatic position, in the interest of encouraging open ethical reflection, means refusing to accept any philosophy whatever, any system of argumentation, any model of society. In our discussion we have borrowed certain types of argument from certain philosophies and other types from others. This constitutes, from my point of view, a significant advance in the way in which ethics is conceived. The combining of "thought modules," characteristic of a mode of cerebral function already hinted at by Comte, is completed in an evolutionary perspective by a constant and reciprocal interaction with the social and cultural environment. In this way a selective philosophical eclecticism enters into the framework of what is intended to be an ethical, naturalistic, open, and tolerant universalism.

In other words, the naturalization of ethical models, rather than being seen as dehumanizing, because detached from symbolic systems peculiar to particular cultures, opens the way instead to an understanding of what is authentically universal in ethical reflection.

Ricoeur: I don't know if you have noticed that there are three chapters in what I call "my little ethics," not two. There is an Aristotelian level, the level of wanting to live, of the good life; a Kantian level, involving norms of universal scope; and finally what I call the level of practical wisdom, at which deliberation and decision have to respond to new situations. It is at this third level that the discussions and opinions of your advisory committee make themselves felt.

Changeux: Once more our thinking converges, but this time by a quite different route. My interest is in expanding this model on a global scale, so that potential cultural conflicts may be converted into opportunities for peace. It is still necessary, and you yourself have insisted on this point, that *just institutions* exist to welcome such a project. They are being built. They will have to go on being built—initially, perhaps, through the universalization of law. As Mireille Delmas-Marty points out, the way is open but it is not mapped out in advance.[27] A considerable effort of good will and thought still needs to be brought to bear, followed by an educational program, which ought, I think, constitute one of the primary objectives of international institutions. Is this a utopian vision? From Lucien Sève I borrow this quotation from Heraclitus: "If you do not hope the unhoped for, you will not find."

Art as Peacemaker

Ricoeur: Allow me to take our discussion a step further: isn't it necessary to incorporate a specifically aesthetic dimension in this attempt to provide a co-foundation for humanity?

Changeux: This is my view. The aesthetic dimension offers a simple way to bring us together—*religare,* the Latin root of our word "religion"—without running the risks that dogmatic discourses involve. Children often confuse the beautiful and the good, which merge in a single process of intersubjective communication. From Poussin to Picasso, the picture transmits an ethical message: it guards against the errors of politicians; it reinforces the *exemplum* of the Stoic sage, Christian teaching, and the gesture of solidarity. The emotional power of forms, the capacity to surprise and to shock, the singular perception of coherence, rhythm, and novelty give art a force of communication that makes it an effective rival of religion.

When we contemplate a painting, for example, it may be supposed—hypothetically for the moment, but nonetheless plausibly—that the cerebral architectures of aesthetic pleasure initially engage the visual areas of the brain that analyze form, color, distribution in space, and possibly the simulation of movement. Moving upward in the cortical hierarchy, synthesis succeeds analysis as the brain reconstructs forms, colors, and figures in a coherent whole that occupies working memory. The apprehension of rhythm, which is to say the harmony of forms and colors, selectively activates the memories stored

FIGURE 7.4. *Self-Portrait as Laughing Democritus,* by Rembrandt van Rijn (1606–1669). Wallraf-Richartz-Museum, Cologne.

Few artists included themselves so often in their work as Rembrandt: more than thirty times in his paintings, twenty-six times in his etchings, and twelve times in his sketches. In this he carried on an ancient tradition by which the painter substitutes his own image for that of the person whom the picture is meant to depict. Rembrandt died a year or so after finishing this painting, on 4 October 1669. Here he does not refrain from showing the signs of aging that are visible in his face, but he interprets them in a positive way. In 1661 he had portrayed himself as the apostle Paul, whose teaching, adopted by the Lutheran reformation, ranked joy and mercy above the strict observance of the law. On the eve of his death he pictured himself at

in the long-term compartment and so gives meaning to the painting, or rather calls forth a multiplicity of sometimes contradictory meanings. A work of art draws upon the highest level of the hierarchy of cerebral functions, that of intentions and reason. It creates harmony between sensuality and reason without having to resort to explicit reasoning—free joy without deliberate expression! But art possesses an additional dimension, the faculty of stimulating the mind, the evocative power that makes images, memories, recollections, and gestures suddenly appear in the brain of the viewer or listener and, in so doing, provides food for thought and gives rise to dreams—to the shared dream of an authentically good life, with that freedom of speech and understanding of which only poetry is capable, but here without recourse to language. Indeed, it manages to do what neither law or morality, in their normative forms, nor science, with its language of rigorous objectivity, can: to develop the imagination, to inspire new plans for a shared and harmonious future. The image, by its evocative power, calls forth responsibility for others. *Ogni dipintore dipinge se*—every painter paints himself,[28] which is to say lets

---

his easel, laughing, while in the process of painting a figure with a doleful expression.

Democritus and Heraclitus have each been the subject of many paintings. Both are conventionally represented as being advanced in age, but Democritus is shown smiling while Heraclitus has a mournful demeanor. It is significant that Rembrandt chose to portray himself as Democritus rather than as Heraclitus. Democritus was, with Leucippus, the founder of the theory of atomism, whose materialist conception of the world was adopted by Epicurus and Lucretius and, later, by the skeptical thinkers of the seventeenth century led by Pierre Gassendi (1592–1655). Democritus's serene gaiety at having triumphed over immaterial fears and superstitions through knowledge of the things of nature, seen here in the person of Rembrandt, anticipated Spinoza's light-hearted irony and unrestrained joy.

the mask drop, eternalizes the person in eternalizing his own person and, and in a still more general way, himself as another (figure 7.4). All the arts tend to an intersubjective universal, to liberation from the constraints imposed by religions and political ideologies on the cultural identity of individuals and their freedom of thought and behavior.

One is often astonished by the creative power of the greatest artists—the "divine" Mozart, for example. One forgets the very early musical education by a demanding and authoritarian father, the child's appearances in all the great courts of Europe and his acquaintance with the greatest musical figures of the period; also how freely he borrowed from the works of his contemporaries, which he knew well. Mozart was particularly exceptional for his memory: legend has it that he wrote down, with hardly a single deletion, the entire score of *Don Giovanni*—which he must have worked out in his head beforehand. In general this is not the case for the majority of artists and writers, who hesitate, grope about, cross out parts of a work as it is being created. We still have little data concerning the neuropsychology of artistic creation. Nonetheless, one may venture a hypothesis—admittedly, a very speculative one—by analogy with the neuronal theory of knowledge developed earlier.

On this theory, creation proceeds according to an evolutionary process of trial and error, a strictly mental process at first, involving the recombination of mental objects, a tacit tinkering with forms and colors, and testing of their formal coherence and emotional power. It is no longer the rationality of the thought object that is selected, nor its fit with the objects of the real world, but its contribution to the evocative power of the work being created. Then a sort of evolutionary dialogue is set in motion, in the case of painting through the mediation of gesture, between the creator's brain and the work in progress, which involves the mutual adjustment of eye and

tion, with its attachment to icons, was perhaps the most receptive to imagery.

Changeux: Except that the icon didn't evolve. It was an art that remained totally fixed for centuries, while in the West both Catholicism and the Counter-Reformation experienced an explosion of pictorial creativity. Their churches became veritable temples of the image.

Ricoeur: I quite agree. Apart from theologians such as Urs von Balthasar, there was very little attention paid to beauty—even the beauty of the world, which the diversity of living things may once more help us appreciate. Let us therefore celebrate the beauty of the world!

Changeux: Agreed!

reason and leads to an equilibrium, not of ethical reasons, but of figures and colors in a coherent whole whose emotional force affects the creator as it will the viewer, and so becomes communicable in an intersubjective way. The artist follows the rules that his cultural milieu imposes upon him, but he also creates new ones. A sort of normativity develops, one that is variable from one artist to another and includes a sense of harmony or *consensus partium,* a feeling for novelty that excludes what has already been seen and heard while taking into account the subjective expectations of the public, even granting viewers or listeners the freedom to complete the creative process of the artist. Understanding a work in the way the artist intended demands the same cultural interpretation. But the multiplicity of meanings of a work of art, the absence of reference to linguistic formulas, opens up intersubjective communication to a public far larger than a particular cultural community. Art must therefore be included, it seems to me, in the co-foundation of a free and fraternal humanity.

Ricoeur: I thank you for this plea on behalf of art, in which I recognize the voice of an expert and a lover of painting and music. Like you, I grant that the aesthetic is an inexhaustible spring. This is what Malraux saw. Here we meet again with your desire for a symbolism appropriate to an ethical project of solidarity. What is needed is an imaginary museum.

Changeux: Yes, for such a museum has the power to bring together, to reunify—

Ricoeur: I am put in mind of Bergson's phrase: "To reach man it is necessary to aim for more than man."

Changeux: It suffices to aim for man, I think, for humanity as a whole. This by itself is asking a great deal. It is in aiming for more than man that serious dangers of fundamentalism and discrimination arise, threatening human life.

Ricoeur: But in "more than man" I include the aesthetic and the beauty of the world.

Changeux: I consider the aesthetic to be something strictly human.

Ricoeur: By "more than man" I also mean more than utilitarian man, who wishes simply to increase his advantage in the competition for material goods.

Changeux: Bourdieu's analysis of the economy or management of symbolism takes on an important dimension here. It goes without saying that the aesthetic brings a mode of pleasure, satisfaction, comfort that is quite distinct from any immediate utility. But it nonetheless possesses a positive power for humanity, allowing us to share the same emotion, to better understand each other.

Ricoeur: Medieval philosophers were quite right to link together in a vast system what they called the "transcendentals"—the true, the good, and the beautiful.

Changeux: One already finds this in Plato.

Ricoeur: Yes, for him the idea of the good was bound up with the idea of the beautiful. Indeed, there is only one word in Greek for the two ideas—a splendid thing! I readily grant too that the preponderantly Jewish component of Christianity led to the law and the commandments becoming predominant in relation to the aesthetic.

Changeux: But Protestantism ended up the same way, in the end becoming iconoclastic.

Ricoeur: That was not the case with Luther, at least not with regard to music. Bach was not excluded from Protestant churches.

Changeux: You're right. Why was music permitted but not painting? This is one of the paradoxes of cultural history.

Ricoeur: The paradox is not unjustified. If, along with the biblical Moses, one holds that the divine name is unutterable, a general prohibition of representation is apt to develop that affects all symbolisms to the extent that they tend to privilege images. This poses a real dilemma, which is magnificently expressed in Schoenberg's *Moses und Aron,* as I mentioned earlier. It isn't surprising that music should have been permitted, insofar as it does not represent or depict persons and things. And so music and song are magnified in the same Jewish tradition that proclaims the divine name unpronounceable. It was thought enough to read the beginning of certain psalms of David to the accompaniment of lutes.

Changeux: The image humanizes, reassures, reunites; whereas the abstract universe of the word that speaks the Truth, lacking human figures, is likelier to promote dogmatism and encourage discrimination. For my part, as an iconophile, I have always considered iconoclasm as a form of fundamentalism. I am struck, too, by the widespread prejudice against the smile of serenity and benevolence, so familiar in the Buddhist tradition but only very rarely encountered in Western iconography.

Ricoeur: No, there was a genuine debate in all the Christian denominations about the role of the image. The Orthodox tradi-

Fugue

A conversation about human nature—a sort of *vox humana,* or organ stop, that playfully mimics the timbre of the human voice, preserves the melody of its song, and sets us to dreaming without having to rely on words—will never exhaust discussion of the relation between science and ethics. It cannot close in upon itself. If it does no more than stimulate thought, it will have achieved its purpose. By comparison with the exceptionally rich history of philosophical thought, to say nothing of the vast treasures of literature, reflection upon human experience and wisdom that draws upon research in the neurosciences remains fragmentary. Even imperfect attempts to synthesize the constantly evolving knowledge they have so far yielded are few. If our dialogue succeeds only in helping arouse further reflection, in the context of a sincere exchange of views between the biological sciences and the humanities, it will have made a valuable contribution.

But our aim is not only to stimulate thought. We seek also to urge vigilance. The conflicts besetting the world today do not have any one single cause: economic rivalries, the balance of political power, subservience to markets that become more globalized by the day—these are all factors. But the collision of cultures, and the apparent incompatibility of so many different moral, philosophical, and religious doctrines, constantly call into question the possibility of bringing about, and then preserving, a just and stable society of free and equal citizens. Unless! Unless, rather than physically confront one another, all parties agree to take into account the teaching of the various branches of human wisdom in order to collaborate in a common endeavor, aimed at achieving peace and universal civilization—a universal civilization that will be free, just, and joyful.

Jean-Pierre Changeux

Paul Ricoeur

Notes

1 – A Necessary Encounter

1. J.-P. Changeux, *L'Homme Neuronal* (Paris: Fayard, 1983); available in English as *Neuronal Man: The Biology of Mind,* trans. Laurence Garey (Princeton: Princeton University Press, 1997).

2. See the accounts given in J. Monod, *Le Hasard et la nécessité* (Paris: Seuil, 1970), and F. Jacob, *Le Jeu des possibles: essai sur la diversité du vivant* (Paris: Fayard, 1981).

3. J. Monod, J. Wyman, and J.-P. Changeux, "On the nature of allosteric transitions: a plausible model," *J. Mol. Biol.* 12 (1965): 88–118.

4. J.-P. Changeux, "The acetylcholine receptor: an allosteric membrane protein," *Harvey Lectures* (1981): 85–254.

5. J.-P. Changeux, P. Courrège, and A. Danchin, "A theory of the epigenesis of neuronal networks by selective stabilization of synapses," *Proc. Nat. Acad. Sc. USA* 70 (1983): 2974–2978.

6. S. Dehaene and J.-P. Changeux, "Theoretical analysis and simulation of a reasoning task in a model neuronal network: the Wisconsin card sorting test," *Cerebral Cortex* 1 (1991): 62–69.

7. See Warren S. McCulloch, *Embodiments of Mind,* 2d ed. (Cambridge, Mass.: MIT Press, 1988); also A. Tête, "Le *mind-body problem:* Petite chronique d'une incarnation," in B. Feltz and D. Lambert, eds., *Entre le corps et l'esprit* (Liège: Mardaga, 1994).

8. B. Spinoza, *The Ethics and Selected Letters,* ed. Seymour Feldman and trans. Samuel Shirley (Indianapolis: Hackett, 1982), 104 [= Part III, Preface].

9. P. Ricoeur, *Oneself as Another,* trans. Kathleen Blamey (Chicago: University of Chicago Press, 1992).

10. See J. Jouanna, *Hippocrates,* trans. M. B. DeBevoise (Baltimore: Johns Hopkins University Press, 1999).

11. G. Canguilhem, *La Connaissance de la vie* (Paris: Vrin, 1965; 2d revised and expanded ed., 1969).

12. G. Bachelard, *La Formation de l'esprit scientifique* (Paris: Vrin, 1938).

13. K. Popper and J. Eccles, *The Self and Its Brain* (New York: Springer-Verlag, 1978).

14. A. Comte, *Catéchisme positiviste* (Paris, 1852).

15. P. F. Strawson, *Individuals: An Essay in Descriptive Metaphysics* (London: Methuen, 1959).

16. Kurt Goldstein, *Der Aufbau des Organismus: Einführung in die Biologie unter besonderer Beruchsichtigung der Erfahrungen am kranken Menschen* (The Hague: M. Nijhoff, 1934); published in English as *The Organism: A Holistic Approach to Biology Derived from Pathological Data in Man* (New York: Zone Books, 1995).

17. T. Nagel, *Equality and Partiality* (New York: Oxford University Press, 1991).

18. Lucretius, *The Way Things Are,* trans. Rolfe Humphries (Bloomington: Indiana University Press, 1968), 89 [=*De rerum natura* III, 92–96].

19. R. Misrahi, *Le Corps et l'esprit dans la philosophie de Spinoza* (Paris: Les Empêcheurs de Tourner en Rond/Synthélabo, 1992).

20. Spinoza, *The Ethics and Selected Letters,* 107 [=Part III, Proposition 2, Scholium].

21. C. Taylor, *Sources of the Self: The Making of the Modern Identity* (Cambridge, Mass.: Harvard University Press, 1989).

2 – Body and Mind: In Search of a Common Discourse

1. R. Descartes, *Treatise on Man,* in *The Philosophical Writings of Descartes,* trans. J. Cottingham, R. Stoothoff, and D. Murdoch, 3 vols. (Cambridge: Cambridge University Press, 1985), 1:99 [emphasis added]. Note that pages 99–108 of this volume contain substantial extracts of the 1664 edition but not the complete text.

2. Ibid., 1:107.

3. R. Descartes, Letter to Père Mersenne (April 1634), quoted in G. Minois, *L'Église et la science* (Paris: Fayard, 1990), 401–402; extracts of this letter can be found in English in *Descartes: Philosophical Letters,* ed. and trans. Anthony Kenny (Oxford: Oxford University Press, 1970.)

4. R. Descartes, *L'Homme* (Paris: Charles Angot, 1664). The manuscript left unfinished by Descartes at his death was called *Traité de l'homme,* hence the usual English title.

5. Ibid., in *Œuvres de Descartes,* ed. C. Adam and P. Tannery, 12 vols. plus supplement (Paris: Cerf, 1896–1913; reprint, Paris: Vrin/Centre National de la Recherche Scientifique, 1964–74) [hereafter abbreviated as *AT*], 11:165–166; see the discussion of the Cartesian model in S. Gaukroger, *Descartes: An Intellectual Biography* (Oxford: Clarendon Press, 1995), 279–281. Another excellent biography has recently appeared as well: G. Rodis-Lewis, *Descartes: His Life and*

Thought, trans. Jane Marie Todd (Ithaca, N.Y.: Cornell University Press, 1998).

6. Descartes, *Treatise on Man,* 108.

7. Lucilio Vanini (1584–1619) was put to death by the Inquisition for having questioned the immortality of the soul and for having proposed, for the first time, that man is descended from the apes.

8. F. Azouvi, "La formation de l'individu comme sujet corporel à partir de Descartes," in G. Cazzaniga and C. Zarka, eds., vol. 1, *L'Individu dans la pensée moderne, XVIIe-XVIIIe siècle* (Pisa: ETS, 1995).

9. See, for example, G. Rodis-Lewis, *L'Anthropologie cartésienne* (Paris: Presses Universitaires de France, 1990); B. Baertschi, *Les Rapports de l'âme et du corps* (Paris: Vrin, 1992); and D. D. Kambouchner, *L'Homme des passions* (Paris: Albin Michel, 1995).

10. R. Descartes, Letter to Père Mersenne (31 December 1640), in *AT,* 2:303; see also Kenny, ed. and trans., *Philosophical Letters,* 89.

11. R. Descartes, "Cogitationes privitae," *AT,* 10:213; see too Cottingham et al., *The Philosophical Writings of Descartes,* 1:2 ("So far, I have been a spectator in this theatre which is the world, but I am now about to mount the stage, and I come forward masked"). Note also Descartes's April 1634 letter to Mersenne in which, quoting Ovid (*Tristia* 3.4.24), he says his motto is "He lives well who is well hidden" (*Bene vixit, bene qui latuit*).

12. See P. M. Churchland, *Matter and Consciousness: A Contemporary Introduction to the Philosophy of Mind* (Cambridge, Mass.: MIT Press, 1984) and *A Neurocomputational Perspective: The Nature of Mind and the Structure of Science* (Cambridge, Mass.: MIT Press, 1989); also P. S. Churchland and T. J. Sejnowski, *The Computational Brain* (Cambridge, Mass.: MIT Press, 1992).

13. The view of the brain as a projective system is developed in A. Berthoz, *Le Sens du mouvement* (Paris: Odile Jacob, 1997).

14. J. Babinski, "Contribution à l'étude des troubles mentaux dans l'hémiplégie cérébrale (anosognosie)," *Rev. neurol.* 27 (1914): 845–847.

15. N. Geschwind, "Behavioral changes in temporal epilepsy," *Archives of Neurology* 34 (1977): 453.

16. D. Schacter, ed., *Memory Distortion: How Minds, Brains, and Societies Reconstruct the Past* (Cambridge, Mass.: Harvard University Press, 1995).

3 – The Neuronal Model and the Test of Experience

1. I. Meyerson, *Les Fonctions psychologiques et les œuvres* (Paris: Vrin, 1948).

2. See, for example, A. Clark, *Being There: Putting Brain, Body, and World Together Again* (Cambridge, Mass.: MIT Press, 1997).

3. See J.-P. Changeux, Rapport au ministre de la Recherche sur les sciences cognitives (1989).

4. M. Merleau-Ponty, *Phénoménologie de la perception* (Paris: Gallimard, 1945).

5. See the general introduction to J.-L. Petit, ed., *Les Neurosciences et la philosophie de l'action* (Paris: Vrin, 1997), 1–37.

6. J. Decéty, D. Perani, M. Jeannerod, V. Beltinardi, B. Tadary, R. Woods, J.-C. Mazziotta, and F. Fazio, "Mapping motor representations with positron emission tomography," *Nature* 371 (1994): 600–602. See also M. Jeannerod, *The Cognitive Neuroscience of Action* (Oxford: Blackwell, 1997) and J. Decéty, "The neurophysiological basis of motor imagery," *Behav. Brain Research* 77 (1997): 45–52.

7. J.-P. Changeux and A. Connes, *Conversations on Mind, Matter, and Mathematics,* trans. M. B. DeBevoise (Princeton: Princeton University Press, 1995), 11–40.

8. J.-P. Changeux and S. Dehaene, "Neural models of cognitive functions," *Cognition* 33 (1989): 63–109.

9. G. M. Edelman, *Neural Darwinism: The Theory of Neuronal Group Selection* (New York: Basic Books, 1987).

10. For a fuller discussion see Changeux, *Neuronal Man,* 126–169.

11. G. M. Edelman, *The Remembered Past: A Biological Theory of Consciousness* (New York: Basic Books, 1989).

12. F. Dretske, *Naturalizing the Mind* (Cambridge, Mass.: MIT Press, 1995).

13. J. Proust, *Comment l'esprit vient aux bêtes* (Paris: Gallimard, 1997).

14. Changeux et al., "A theory of the epigenesis of neuronal networks by selective stabilization of synapses."

15. E. Husserl, *Logical Investigations,* 2 vols., trans. J. N. Findlay (London: Routledge and Kegan Paul, 1970), vol. 1, part 1.

16. C. S. Peirce, *Peirce on Signs: Writings on Semiotics,* ed. J. Hoopes (Chapel Hill: University of North Carolina Press, 1991).

17. A. Young, "Functional organization of visual recognition," in L. Weiskrantz, ed., *Thought without Language* (Oxford: Clarendon Press, 1988), 78–107.

18. C. Lévi-Strauss, *Race and History* (Paris: UNESCO, 1952).

19. B. M. Mazoyer, N. Tzoruio, V. Frak, A. Syrota, N. Murayama, O. Levrier, G. Salomon, S. Dehaene, L. Cohen, and J. Mehler, "The cortical representation of speech," *J. Cognitive Neuroscience* 3 (1993): 467–479.

20. R. A. McCarthy and E. K. Warrington, "Evidence for modality-specific meaning systems in the brain," *Nature* 334 (1998): 428–430; H. Damasio, T. J. Grabowski, R. D. Hichwa, D. Tranel, and A. Damasio, "A neural basis for lexical retrieval," *Nature* 380 (1996): 499–505; and J. V. Haxby, A. Martin, L. G. Ungerleider, and C. L. Wiggs, "Neural correlates of category-specific knowledge," *Nature* 379 (1996): 1649–1652.

21. Louis Althusser (1918–1990), French Marxist philosopher who was committed to a psychiatric hospital after murdering his wife, Hélène Rytmann, in November 1980. Criminal charges against him were subsequently dismissed the following year on grounds of insanity.

22. Changeux, *Neuronal Man,* 139.

23. M. Hodders-Algra, E. Brogen, and H. Forssberg, "Ontogeny of postural adjustments during sitting in infancy: variation, selection, and modulation," *J. Physiol.* 493 (1996): 273–288.

24. J. Droulez and A. Berthoz, "A neural network model of sensoritopic maps with predictive short-term memory properties," *Proc. Nat. Acad. Sc. USA* 88 (1991): 9653–9657.

25. M. Hodders-Algra, E. Brogen, and H. Forssberg, "Training effects in the development of postural adjustments in sitting infants," *J. Physiol.* 493 (1996): 289–298.

26. S. Dehaene and J.-P. Changeux, "A simple model of prefrontal cortex function in delayed-response tasks," *J. Cognitive Neuroscience* 1 (1989): 244–261. See also G. Edelman and G. Tononi, "Selection and development: The brain as a complex system," in D. Magnusson, ed., *The Lifespan Development of Individuals* (Cambridge: Cambridge University Press, 1996), 179–204; and W. Schultz, P. Dayan, and P.-R. Montague, "A neural substrate of prediction and reward," *Science* 275 (1997): 1593–1599.

27. J.-D. Vincent, *La Chair et le diable* (Paris: Odile Jacob, 1996).

28. In what follows I use the term "memories" as a shorthand for *evoked memories,* a particular class of mental objects that arises from the actualization of the *traces* laid down by perceptual experience. The material expression of a trace may consist, for example, in a change in the number and/or efficacy of postsynaptic receptors, which would remain latent and persist until recall. Recall may be thought of as a mobilization of the neuronal network (together with its latent traces) by electrical and/or chemical activity that *reconstructs* a state of activity similar, but not necessarily identical, to the original percept that laid down a particular trace. The latent trace directly contributes to the "shape" of the recalled, or evoked, mem-

ory—for instance, by facilitating the firing of neuron A (rather than neuron B), which was initially excited within the pattern of the original percept, but not otherwise.

29. H. Jonas, *The Phenomenon of Life: Toward a Philosophical Biology* (Chicago: University of Chicago Press, 1966; 2d ed., 1982).

30. R. Wise, "Neurobiology of addiction," *Curr. Op. Neurobiol.* 6 (1996): 243–251.

31. T. Robbins and B. Everitt, "Neurobehavioral mechanisms of reward and motivation," *Curr. Op. Neurobiol.* 6 (1996): 228–236.

32. D. Janicaud, ed., *L'Intentionalité en question* (Paris: Vrin, 1995).

33. E. Pacherie, *Naturaliser l'intentionalité* (Paris: Presses Universitaires de France, 1993).

34. P. F. Strawson, *Individuals: An Essay in Descriptive Metaphysics* (London: Methuen, 1959).

35. J. Decéty, J. Grèzes, N. Costes, D. Perani, M. Jeannerod, E. Procyk, F. Grassi, and F. Fazio, "Brain activity during observation of actions: influence of action context and subject's strategy," *Brain* 120 (1997): 1763–1777.

36. F. de Saussure, *Cours de linguistique générale,* part I, chapter 1, §1 (Paris: Payot, 1980), 98.

37. É. Benveniste, *Problèmes de linguistique générale* (Paris: Gallimard, 1966).

38. D. Sperber and D. Wilson, *Relevance: Communication and Cognition* (Oxford: Blackwell, 1986).

4 – Consciousness of Oneself and of Others

1. Ricoeur, *Oneself as Another,* 170.

2. R. Wise, "Neurobiology of addiction," *Curr. Op. Neurobiol.* 6 (1996): 243–251.

3. W. Singer, "Neuronal Synchronization: A Solution to the Binding Problem?," in R. Llinás and P. S. Churchland, eds., *The Mind-Body Continuum* (Cambridge, Mass.: MIT Press, 1996), 101–130; C. von der Malsburg, "The Binding Problem of Neuronal Networks," in ibid., 131–146.

4. W. Schulz, P. Dayan, and R. Montague, "A neural substrate of prediction and reward," *Science* 275 (1997): 1593–1599.

5. S. Dehaene, M. Kerszberg, and J.-P. Changeux, "A neuronal model of a global workspace in effortful cognitive tasks," *Proc. Nat. Acad. Sc. USA* 95 (1998): 14529–14534.

6. W. James, *Psychology: Briefer Course* (Cambridge, Mass.: Harvard University Press, 1984), 251.

7. F. Lhermitte, J. Derouesné, and J.-L. Signoret, "Analyse neuropsychologique du syndrome frontal," *Revue neurologique* 127 (1972): 415–440.

8. J. Cohen, W. Perlstein, T. Braver, L. Nystrom, D. Noll, J. Jonides, and E. Smith, "Temporal dynamics of brain activation during a working memory task," *Nature* 386 (1997): 604–608; see also S. Courtney, L. Ungerleider, K. Keil, and J. Haxby, "Transient and sustained activity in a distributed neural system for human working memory," *Nature* 386 (1997): 608–611.

9. See B. de Boysson-Bardies, *How Language Comes to Children: From Birth to Two Years,* trans. M. B. DeBevoise (Cambridge, Mass.: MIT Press, 1999), 29–35, 71–80.

10. H. Bergson, *Matter and Memory,* trans. Nancy Margaret Paul and W. Scott Palmer (New York: Zone Books, 1988), 73.

11. Pierre Nora, ed., *Les Lieux de mémoire,* 7 vols. (Paris: Gallimard, 1984–1992). In Nora's use of the term, *lieux* refers to a vast range of events and ideas that go far beyond the literal sense of "places" or "sites." See his preface to the abridged English-language edition, *Realms of Memory,* 3 vols., trans. Arthur Goldhammer (New York: Columbia University Press, 1997).

12. H. Ebbinghaus, *Memory: A Contribution to Experimental Psychology,* trans. H. A. Ruger and C. E. Bussenius (New York: Teachers College, Columbia University, 1913).

13. F. C. Bartlett, *Remembering: A Study in Experimental and Social Psychology* (Cambridge: Cambridge University Press, 1932).

14. D. Schacter, ed., *Memory Distortion.*

15. E. Loftus, J. Feldam, and R. Daghiell, "The Reality of Illusory Memories," in ibid., 47–68.

16. J. F. Kihlstrom, mentioned in ibid.

17. E. Tulving, "Human Memory," in P. Andersen, O. Hvalby, O. Paulen, and B. Hökfelt, eds., *Memory Concepts: Basic and Clinical Aspects* (Amsterdam and New York: Excerpta Medica, 1993), 27–46.

18. D. Sperber, "Anthropology and psychology: toward an epidemiology of representations," *Man* 20 (1982): 73–89; see also R. Debray, "À propos de la 'contagion des idées' de M. Dan Sperber," *Travail médiologique* 1 (1996): 19–34.

19. D. Premack and G. Woodruff, "Does the chimpanzee have a theory of mind?," *The Behavioral and Brain Sciences* 1 (1978): 516–526.

20. D. Premack, "'Connaissance' morale chez le nourrisson," in J.P. Changeux, ed., *Fondements naturels de l'éthique* (Paris: Odile Jacob, 1995), 139–153.

21. U. Frith, *Autism: Explaining the Enigma* (Oxford: Blackwell, 1989).

22. M. Piatelli-Palmarini, ed., *Language and Learning: The Debate between Jean Piaget and Noam Chomsky* (Cambridge, Mass.: Harvard University Press, 1980).

23. P. Bourdieu, *The Logic of Practice,* trans. Richard Nice (Stanford: Stanford University Press, 1990).

24. P. Bourdieu, *Méditations pascaliennes* (Paris: Seuil, 1997), 163.

25. J. M. Harlow, "Recovery from the Passage of an Iron Bar through the Head," *Bulletin of the Massachusetts Medical Society* (1868): 2, 3–20. The case is described in detail in A. R. Damasio, *Descartes' Error: Emotion, Reason, and the Human Brain* (New York: G. P. Putnam, 1994), 3–33.

26. Quoted in Damasio, *Descartes' Error,* 8.

27. E. Husserl, *The Crisis of European Sciences and Transcendental Phenomenology: An Introduction to Phenomenological Philosophy,* trans. David Carr (Evanston, Ill.: Northwestern University Press, 1970).

28. See J. Decéty, "The neurophysiological basis of motor imagery," *Behav. Brain Research* 77 (1997): 45–52; M. Jeannerod, *The Cognitive Neuroscience of Action* (Oxford: Blackwell, 1997); and A. Berthoz, *Le Sens du mouvement* (Paris: Odile Jacob, 1997).

29. J. Proust, "Causalité, représentation et intentionalité," in D. Janicaud, ed., *L'intentionalité en question* (Paris: Vrin, 1995), 311.

30. Message of John Paul II to the Pontifical Academy of Sciences at the Vatican, 23 October 1996.

31. O. Bloch, *Le Matérialisme* (Paris: Presses Universitaires de France, 1985).

32. A. Berthoz, *Le Sens du mouvement.*

33. J.-P. Changeux, *Raison et plaisir* (Paris: Odile Jacob, 1992), and *Création et neuroscience: Bicentenaire de l'Institut* (Paris: Fayard, 1994).

5 – The Origins of Morality

1. See E. Mayr, *The Growth of Biological Thought* (Cambridge, Mass.: Harvard University Press, 1982).

2. S. J. Gould, *Full House: The Spread of Excellence from Plato to Darwin* (New York: Harmony Books, 1996).

3. See P. Ricoeur, *Time and Narrative,* 3 vols., trans. Kathleen McLaughlin and David Pellauer (Chicago: University of Chicago Press, 1984–88); also "Le scandale du mal," *Esprit* (July–August 1988), special issue devoted to Paul Ricoeur.

4. Ricoeur, *Oneself as Another,* 24.

5. Quoted in P. Debré, *Jacques Monod* (Paris: Flammarion, 1996), 222.

6. F. Jacob, *Of Flies, Mice, and Men,* trans. Giselle Weiss (Cambridge, Mass.: Harvard University Press, 1998).

7. P. Tobias, "Brain Evolution in the Hominoidea," in R. Tuttle, ed., *Primate Functional Morphology and Evolution* (Paris and The Hague: Mouton, 1975).

8. J.-P. Changeux and J. Chavaillon, eds., *Origins of the Human Brain* (Oxford: Clarendon Press, 1995).

9. See the discussion in Changeux, *Raison et plaisir.*

10. In this connection see P. Tort, *La pensée hiérarchique et l'évolution* (Paris: Aubier, 1985); C. Cela-Conde, *On Genes, Gods, and Tyrants* (Dordrecht: Reidel, 1986) and "The challenge of revolutionary ethics," *Biology and Philosophy* 1 (1986): 293–297.

11. C. Darwin, *The Descent of Man, and Selection in Relation to Sex,* 2d rev. and augmented edition (London, 1877), reprinted in P. H. Barrett and R. B. Freeman, eds., *The Works of Charles Darwin,* 29 vols. (London: William Pickering, 1986–89), 21:102.

12. Ibid., 126.

13. Ibid., 127.

14. Ibid., 129.

15. Ibid., 124–125.

16. E. O. Wilson, *Sociobiology: The New Synthesis* (Cambridge, Mass.: The Belknap Press of Harvard University Press, 1975).

17. R. Dawkins, *The Selfish Gene,* 2d ed. (New York: Oxford University Press, 1989).

18. See E. Sober and D. S. Wilson, "Reintroducing Group Selection to the Human Behavioral Sciences," *Behavioral and Brain Sciences* 17 (1994): 585–654, as well as their recent book, *Unto Others: The Evolution and Psychology of Unselfish Behavior* (Cambridge, Mass.: Harvard University Press, 1998).

19. C. Boehm, "Impact of the human egalitarian syndrome on Darwinian selection mechanics," in "Multilevel Selection," special issue edited by D. S. Wilson, *American Naturalist* 150, supplement (July 1997): 100–121.

20. F. de Waal, *Good Natured: The Origins of Right and Wrong in Humans and Other Animals* (Cambridge, Mass.: Harvard University Press, 1996).

21. J.-B. de Lamarck, *Système des animaux sans vertèbres* (Paris: Deterville, 1801).

22. See C. Renfrew and E. Zubrow, eds., *The Ancient Mind: Elements of Cognitive Archeology* (Cambridge: Cambridge University Press, 1994).

23. A. Espinas, *Des sociétés animales* (Paris: Ballière, 1877).

24. G. Romanes, *Animal Intelligence* (London: Kegan, 1882).

25. P. Kropotkin, *Mutual Aid: A Factor of Evolution* (New York: McClure Philips, 1902).

26. C. Bechara, H. Damasio, D. Tranel, and A. R. Damasio, "Deciding advantageously before knowing the advantageous strategy," *Science* 275 (1997): 1293–1295.

27. Spinoza, *The Ethics and Selected Letters,* 193 [=Part IV, Proposition 67].

28. Ibid., 196 [=Part IV, Proposition 73].

29. Ibid., 62 [=Part I, Appendix].

30. Ibid., 110 [=Part III, Proposition 9 scholium].

31. Ibid., 167–168 [=Part IV, Proposition 24].

32. Canguilhem, *La Connaissance de la vie,* 143.

33. Ibid., 145.

34. Ibid.

35. Ibid.

36. H. Jonas, *The Imperative of Responsibility: In Search of an Ethics for the Technological Age,* trans. Hans Jonas with the collaboration of David Herr (Chicago: University of Chicago Press, 1984), 70.

37. Ibid., 71.

38. Ibid., 73–74.

39. Ibid., 74–75.

40. Ibid., 86.

41. A. Fagot-Largeault, "Les problèmes du relativisme moral," in J.-P. Changeux, ed., *Une même éthique pour tous?* (Paris: Odile Jacob, 1997), 41–58.

42. Darwin, *The Descent of Man,* 21:94.

43. Ibid., 95.

44. Ibid.

45. W. von Humboldt, *Über die Verschiedenheit des menschlichen Sprachbaues: und ihren Einfluss auf die geistige Entwickelung des Menschengeschlechts* (Berlin, 1836); a new English version is available as *On Language: The Diversity of Human Language-Structure and Its Influence on the Mental Development of Mankind,* trans. D. Heath (Cambridge: Cambridge University Press, 1988).

6 – Desire and Norms

1. P. Gibert, *Bible, mythes et récits de commencement* (Paris: Seuil, 1986).

2. D. Lecourt, *L'Amérique entre la Bible et Darwin* (Paris: Presses Universitaires de France, 1992).

3. I. Kant, *Critique of Practical Reason,* trans. Lewis White Beck (New York: Macmillan, 1956).

4. I. Kant, *Anthropology From a Pragmatic Point of View,* trans. Victor Lyle Dowdell (Carbondale: Southern Illinois University Press, 1978).

5. R. Blair, "A cognitive developmental approach to morality: investigating the psychopath," *Cognition* 57 (1995): 1–29.

6. K. Lorenz, *On Aggression,* trans. Marjorie Kerr Wilson (New York: Harcourt, Brace, and World, 1966).

7. J. Mehler and E. Dupoux, *Naître humain* (Paris: Odile Jacob, 1990), published in English as *What Infants Know: The New Cognitive Science of Early Development,* trans. Patsy Southgate (Cambridge, Mass.: Blackwell, 1994); see also J. Mehler and F. Ramus, "La psychologie cognitive peut-elle contribuer à l'étude du raisonnement moral?," in Changeux, ed., *Une même éthique pour tous?,* 121–136.

8. I. Kant, *Zum ewigen Frieden: ein philosophischer Entwurf* (Königsberg, 1795); a translation by Lewis Beck was published in *Critique of Practical Reason and Other Writings in Moral Philosophy* (Chicago: University of Chicago Press, 1949) and, separately, as *Perpetual Peace* (New York: Liberal Arts Press, 1957).

9. F. Jacob, *The Logic of Life,* trans. Betty E. Spillmann (Princeton: Princeton University Press, 1993).

10. H. Atlan, "Les niveaux de l'éthique," in Changeux, ed., *Une même éthique pour tous?,* 88–106.

11. See J. Panskepp, "Towards a general psychobiological theory of emotions," *Behavioral and Brain Sciences* 5 (1982): 407–467 and, by the same author, *Affective Neuroscience: The Foundations of Human and Animal Emotions* (New York: Oxford University Press, 1998).

12. J.-D. Vincent, *The Biology of Emotions,* trans. John Hughes (Cambridge, Mass.: Blackwell, 1990).

13. Spinoza, *The Ethics and Selected Letters,* 167 [= Part IV, Proposition 22, Corollary].

14. Jonas, *The Imperative of Responsibility,* 43.

15. M. Mauss, *Sociologie et anthropologie* (Paris: Presses Universitaires de France, 1950).

16. C. Turnbull, *The Mountain People* (New York: Touchstone, 1972).

17. P. Levi, *If This Is a Man,* trans. Stuart Woolf (New York: Orion, 1959), 94.

18. Ibid., 98.

19. Ibid., 110.

20. See, for example, J.-P. Dupuy, "Les paradoxes de 'Théorie de

la justice': introduction à l'œuvre de John Rawls," *Esprit* 1 (January 1988): 72–84.

21. S. Zak, *L'Idée de vie dans la philosophie de Spinoza* (Paris: Presses Universitaires de France, 1963).

22. P. Kropotkin, *Mutual Aid: A Factor in Evolution,* ed. Paul Avrich (Harmondsworth: Penguin, 1972), 31–32. Kropotkin is quoting here the view of K. F. Kessler in *Memoirs of the St. Petersburg Society of Naturalists* 11 (1880) (passage slightly modified).

23. P. Kropotkin, *Ethics: Origin and Development,* trans. Louis S. Friedland and Joseph R. Piroshnikoff (New York: B. Blom, 1924), 52.

24. Ibid.

25. See ibid., chapter 2.

26. See also Darwin, *The Descent of Man;* J.-P. Changeux, "Point de vue d'un neurobiologiste sur les fondements de l'éthique," *Commentaire* 71 (1995): 539–549; and C. Cela-Conde, "Éthique, diversité et universalisme: l'héritage de Darwin," in Changeux, ed., *Une même éthique pour tous?*

27. E. Turiel, "Nature et fondements du raisonnement social dans l'enfance," in J.-P. Changeux, ed., *Fondements naturels de l'éthique* (Paris: Odile Jacob, 1993), 301–318.

28. J. Habermas, *Moral Consciousness and Communicative Action,* trans. C. Lenhardt and S. W. Nicholsen (Cambridge, Mass.: MIT Press, 1990), 63.

29. J. Rawls, *Political Liberalism* (New York: Columbia University Press, 1993), 53–54.

30. See Changeux, *Raison et plaisir* and *Bicentenaire de l'Institut.*

31. R. Carnap, *The Logical Structure of the World* (Berkeley: University of California Press, 1934).

32. A. Comte, *Discours sur l'esprit positif* (Paris: Carilian-Goeury et V. Dalmont, 1844), 128.

33. A. Comte, *Cours de philosophie positive,* 5th ed. (Paris: Schleicher, 1907), 3d lecture, 86; see also the entire second lecture.

34. E. Durkheim, *Règles de la méthode sociologique* (Paris: Alcan, 1895).

35. L. Sève, "S'entendre en éthique: actes de langage et langage des actes," in Changeux, ed., *Une même éthique pour tous?,* 197–210.

36. S. J. Gould and N. Eldredge, "Punctuated equilibria: the temporal mode of evolution reconsidered," *Paleobiology* 3 (1977): 115–151.

37. B. Russell, *Philosophical Essays,* 2d rev. ed. (London: George Allen & Unwin, 1966), 32.

38. P. N. Johnson-Laird, *Mental Models: Towards a Cognitive Science of Language, Inference, and Consciousness* (Cambridge: Cambridge University Press, 1983).

39. H. Atlan, "Projet et signification dans les réseaux d'automates: le rôle de la sophistication," in D. Janicaud, ed., *L'Intentionnalité en question* (Paris: Vrin, 1995), 261–288.

40. S. Dehaene, M. Kerszberg, and J.-P. Changeux, "A Neuronal Model of a Global Workspace in Effortful Cognitive Tasks."

41. C. Lévi-Strauss, *Race and History,* 39 (translation slightly modified).

42. Ibid., 41 (translation slightly modified).

43. Ibid., 21.

44. See A. Fagot-Largeault, "Les problèmes du relativisme moral."

7 – Ethical Universality and Cultural Conflict

1. S. Freud, *Moses and Monotheism,* trans. Katherine Jones (New York: Vintage, 1939), 21.

2. E. Durkheim, *Les Formes élémentaires de la vie religieuse,* 3d ed. (Paris: F. Alcan, 1937), 613.

3. E. Durkheim, *The Elementary Forms of Religious Life,* trans. Karen E. Fields (New York: Free Press, 1995), 477.

4. R. Rappaport, "The Sacred in Human Evolution," *Ann. Rev. of Ecology and Systematics* 2 (1971): 23–44.

5. Gibert, *Bible, mythes et récits de commencement,* 247.

6. R. Gibert, "Un thème meyersonien: les commencements dans l'histoire des religions," in F. Pacot, ed., *Pour une psychologie historique* (Paris: Presses Universitaires de France, 1996).

7. R. Girard, *Violence and the Sacred,* trans. Patrick Gregory (Baltimore: Johns Hopkins University Press, 1977).

8. H. Jonas, *Le Concept de Dieu après Auschwitz: Une voix juive,* trans. Philippe Ivernel (Paris: Payot/Rivages, 1994).

9. O. Flanagan, *Varieties of Moral Personality: Ethics and Psychological Realism* (Cambridge, Mass.: Harvard University Press, 1991).

10. C. Batson and J. Darley, "From Jerusalem to Jericho: a study of situational and dispositional variables in helping behavior," *J. Personality and Social Psychology* 27 (1973): 100–108.

11. O. Christin, *La paix de religion: L'autonomisation de la raison politique au XVIe siècle* (Paris: Seuil, 1997).

12. O. de Dinechin, "Quelle ouverture à une sagesse universelle dans les éthiques religieuses," in Changeux, ed., *Une même éthique pour tous?,* 58–73.

13. S. Freud, *Civilization and Its Discontents,* ed. and trans. James Strachey (New York: W. W. Norton, 1961), 69.

14. É. Weil, *Logique de la philosophie* (Paris: Vrin, 1950).

15. On Rawls's distinction between the rational and the reasonable, see Rawls, *Political Liberalism,* 48–54.

16. E. Drewerman, *Le Mal,* trans. Jean-Pierre Bagot, 3 vols. (Paris: Desclée de Brouwer, 1995–97).

17. L. Bourgeois, *La Politique de la prévoyance sociale,* 2 vols. (Paris: Bibliothèque Charpentier, 1914–1919), 1:57.

18. Ibid.

19. L. Bourgeois and Alfred Croiset, *Essai d'une philosophie de la Solidarité,* 2d ed. (Paris: F. Alcan, 1907), 6.

20. Ibid.

21. Ibid., 7.

22. Ibid., 46.

23. Ibid.

24. Ibid., 57.

25. *Trieste Declaration of Human Duties: A Code of Ethics of Shared Responsibilities* (Trieste: Trieste University Press, 1997).

26. M. Delmas-Marty, "Le droit est-il universalisable?," in Changeux, ed., *Une même éthique pour tous?*

27. Ibid., 153.

28. D. Arasse, *Le Sujet dans le tableau* (Paris: Flammarion, 1997).

Index